Death
and
Life

DEATH AND LIFE

by HELMUT THIELICKE

translated by EDWARD H. SCHROEDER

"The thing that more than anything else profoundly determines the way we feel about life is the way life is related to death."

Wilhelm Dilthey

FORTRESS PRESS

PHILADELPHIA

This book is a translation of *Tod und Leben. Studien zur christlichen Anthropologie* (Zweite Auflage; Tübingen: Verlag von J.C.B. Mohr [Paul Siebeck], 1946).

Library of Congress Catalog Card Number 75-117978

2430B70 Printed in U.S.A. 1-43

Table of Contents

Preface to the American Edition

The circumstances under which this book came into existence were marked by a certain amount of cloak-and-dagger adventure. In the early years of the Second World War I was removed by action of the state from my teaching position at the University of Heidelberg. Bishop Theophil Wurm of the territorial church in Württemberg, who played a significant role in the Confessing Church, accepted the outlaw and provided me with a pastorate in the little town of Ravensburg in the extreme south of Germany. There the secret police imposed an injunction which proscribed my traveling or speaking anywhere else in the country. Only in the town itself was I permitted to preach. I had long since been forbidden to publish.

In this enforced solitude I was thus enabled to pursue my studies undisturbed. I was seriously handicapped, however, by the fact that I did not have access to a library. Because of dislocations attendant upon the war even my own books were not at hand. But that too may have provided a certain stimulus for me to live for once entirely from the resources of reflection, with few books at hand either to assist or disturb.

It was under these extraordinary circumstances that this book came into existence. I actually wrote it only for myself, in order that I might come to some measure of clarity on fundamental questions of life and faith. At the time, I dared not even hope that the product of my enforced tranquillity would ever see the light of day. It is worth relating how that eventually came about.

One day several men from the World Council of Churches in Geneva came to visit me. They had heard of this manuscript, as well as of another I had written, and they wanted to take it along immediately in order to have it printed in Switzerland and made available elsewhere for use in theological study courses among German prisoners of war. In response to my surprised question how they intended to get it across the border, the manuscript of a man so hated by the regime, they said with a smile: We have a diplomat available whose luggage is immune to customs inspection.

And that is the way it finally happened. The manuscript went its way and I heard nothing more of it until quite a while after the war when I received a copy of the finished book. It had been published first in Switzerland and was subsequently to appear in several editions in Germany as well.

But the story does not stop there. One Sunday morning in Stuttgart, in one of the first postwar years, a man approached me in the sacristy after hearing me preach. He introduced himself as Reinhold Niebuhr. You can imagine what a pleasure it was for me to meet this great American theologian, even if I subsequently shuddered a bit at the thought that he had been among my hearers. He said he knew my *Tod und Leben* and thought my approach to the questions could help many readers come to some clarity on these issues. He was going to try to have the book translated into English. The translation did not materialize at that time, however. For American publishers it was evidently not a very attractive proposition to print the work of an unknown author.

Later it was I myself who decided not to let the book come out in translation. I was troubled by the fact that it had been written under such abnormally difficult circumstances and was not as polished and perfected as a book written in more comfortable times with the necessary literary aids available. In fact, I mentioned this concern to Professor Niebuhr in Stuttgart, but he thought that the very character of the book and the circumstances of its origin gave it a certain immediacy and vigor, for it is precisely in such situations that we apply ourselves directly to the real issues, to what is of overriding and basic importance.

Perhaps he was being too shortsighted—or too polite! I do not know. But since my friend and translator Edward Schroeder apparently shares his opinion, I am now willing to let this product of a time of deep darkness see the light of day once more. And I would extend a cordial greeting to my American readers, who for several years now have been echoing to me a response for which I am very grateful.

Hamburg, 1970 Helmut Thielicke

Preface to the German Edition

We are accustomed to thinking of death as the dividing line between the here and the beyond. If we assume that this notion is more or less correct, then a book which attempts to illumine the problem has two options. It may treat death in terms of its connection to the beyond, otherwise referred to as the other world, life after death, being swallowed up in nothingness. Or it may approach death in terms of its connection to the here, in which case it would proceed from the presupposition that the way we understand death has important consequences for our understanding of life, man, and the world, and that the effort to understand life as a Being-toward-death is indeed a meaningful enterprise, one that makes possible a productive use of the concept of death throughout the entire realm of anthropology.

The present treatise bypasses the former option altogether and is concerned exclusively with the latter, in the conviction that we are thereby very close to the biblical doctrine of man. For the orbit of biblical anthropology resembles, as it were, an ellipse, with sin and redemption—death and resurrection—as its twin foci.

At the same time we are convinced that by approaching the subject in this way we establish a promising point of departure for a fruitful dialogue with secularism. The fact is that this dialogue between the gospel and secularism, so essential for the life of both theology and the church, has almost come to a complete standstill. It is not our task here to inquire into the reasons for this, but I would cherish the hope that in thinking through the problem of death the reader might at least become aware of them, as I did.

It is not possible to get this dialogue going again by way of apologetics, which is like continuing to clap after the applause has ceased, in the manner of a Johnny-come-lately. It is not enough just to take a stand on questions discovered by others, not even if one does so in the self-conscious pathos reflected in such titles as "The Christian Answer to. . . ." But then neither can the dialogue be stimulated by undertaking to do dogmatics in monologue fashion, unconcerned about these questions. When dogmatics, all of its assurances to the contrary notwithstanding, still remains out of touch with the contemporary situation in which faith is proclaimed, it is also out of touch with the dialogue—and, we might as well add, with all missionary concern.

Indeed, the dialogue probably cannot be "stimulated" at all, because the ears which ought to hear are simply not ours to control. The Spirit of God blows where he wills. It is the Spirit and he alone who really has to create—or, more precisely, call—the participants to the discussion.

The present work does not purport to be a continuation of the interrupted dialogue. It is not a Socratic philosophical undertaking, posing questions in order to find out what men already know about the last things, and in that way perhaps exercising a measure of creativity. On the contrary, it is an avowedly theological work, which is to say it presupposes some acquaintance with the lost state of man's knowledge—and with the mystery of the Holy Spirit who is able to lead men into all truth, and who as a matter of fact is the only one who does so lead.

Despite all this, there are reasons for letting the book go forth in quest of dialogue. For one thing, there are certain problems and realities which, while they confront the completely secularized modern man as inescapable questions, at the same time constitute a central element of the church's proclamation. One of these is the mystery of human death. Church and world alike gaze spellbound on this third party, this common ground where willy-nilly their glances meet. And the greater the harvest of death in our blood-soaked world—the closer death strikes as each of us is compelled to traverse that harvest field and the louder the hoofbeats of the apocalyptic riders thunder over the earth—so much the more unflinchingly and intensively do church and world alike gaze upon this third party.

Ought we not to be driven into dialogue by the sheer fact of such gazing, that is, by the reality of the thing itself? Where God writes such a powerful musical accompaniment to his word about death and life should methodological gimmicks still be needed to open the conversation? The work itself will have to provide the answer to that question.

The initial impetus for its writing of course was not a concern for dialogue, but for the problem itself. However, now that the possibility of dialogue has arisen, as it were, *ex post facto,* it may be that the work can stimulate readers to pursue their own quest and pinpoint similar questions involving additional areas of common ground between church and world, thus fostering a dialogue based on the issues themselves. For it is only in the concern for the substantive issues that we can hope to find the fountainhead for that new shape of proclamation which all of us are seeking. The methods of proclamation will then take care of themselves, if we but hold fast to this fountainhead. We should not move to the question of method prematurely.

A final word concerning the structure of the work. In Part One we examine some of the proposals for overcoming death which have been advanced in the area of philosophical thought. The interesting thing about them, which the reader ought not to miss on account of the diversity of the viewpoints here so sketchily presented, is that they all have this in common: it is always man himself who stands behind the various interpretations of the world seeking to make them lasting objectifications of his own thoughts and attitudes. What is really expressed in and through the manifold interpretations is the mystery of the natural man, his self-understanding, that which in technical theological language we call natural theology. Part One is thus a critique of natural theology in terms of one specific issue, the problem of death.

In other words, in Part One our concern is not with what might be called the most important non-Christian ways of understanding death. If the reader were to contend that the particular interpretations here selected are not the most important in the history of thought I could only nod my agreement. Indeed, I would go on to add that even in respect of the thinkers and views which are here discussed I may not have attended to their most significant features. My intention, after all, is only to refer to them by way of making a point, and to utilize them as illustrative material in connection with Part Two.

One might argue that it would have been more appropriate to the subject under discussion if Part Two had preceded Part One. Such a judgment would be accurate to the extent that Part Two does disclose the vantage point from which the various concrete philosophies were in fact evaluated from the very outset. Despite this possible criticism, however, I have chosen the present sequence for methodological reasons. The discerning reader will soon see that even Part One is not intended as a philosophy of existence but as theology proper.

It ought not to go unmentioned that in face of the vast complexity of the problems involved, and the breadth of knowledge and of intellectual and human experience required, I am only too painfully aware of the provisional character of my endeavor. The work was begun in 1939 and interrupted time and time again, primarily by service in the armed forces but also by a far-reaching vocational shift occasioned by my enforced suspension as a university professor at Heidelberg. A Swiss edition of the book, first published in the summer of 1945 by the World Council of Churches in Geneva, preceded this German edition.

Letter to a Soldier about Death

Dear Hans:[1]

In your letter you referred to the many prewar prophesies which said that if the apocalyptic rider of war were once again to roar across our fatherland, it would produce a blazing storm of inner awakening. From all their various illusions, idolatries, and petty concerns people would once more have to wake up to the ultimate true realities: death and God.

And now while convalescing in the hospital you write that this expectation, reasonable as it was, has not come to pass as far as most men are concerned. Even genuinely apocalyptic encounters with death—with death in its grisliest forms and with the most sadistic revelations of man's nature—did not as a rule, all expectations to the contrary notwithstanding, serve to proclaim God's law and his visitation. Often it appeared that all of this only made the hardened hearts still harder. One may think that with the rousing reveille of God's alarm clock every man would now have to sit up and take notice, but the screaming force of events seems rather to

[1] The addressee of this letter, sent on Totensonntag (Sunday for the Commemoration of the Dead) in 1941, was killed shortly thereafter when his plane was shot down over the Mediterranean Sea. He was my beloved Heidelberg student Hans Felix Hedderich, whose doctoral dissertation *Die Gedanken der Romantik über Kirche und Staat* (Gütersloh, 1941) was banned at home while he was out fighting on the front as a soldier. This letter may serve as a simple token to his memory. His lively response to my lectures on death, reworked here in this book, was often a source of strength and encouragement to me.

have had the opposite effect. What most men experienced in all of this, consciously or unconsciously, was nothing but the disclosure of pure power conflicts, in which their only course was to stand fast and resolute like the "soldier of Pompeii," using their own thick hide as armor for their soul. "The play of forces and in the midst of it one's own personal fate—simply lies in the hands of fate." And with that the discussion as a rule came to a close.

What is this, Hans? What is the reason for it?

You write about the older generation in the trenches of the First World War: "Regardless of how dead their Christianity may have been, how conventional or falsified by liberalism. . . at least they had once learned a few hymns by heart, or knew a psalm or two, or a few Bible verses, which in the hour of their extreme personal peril actually began to resound for them in a marvelous way. The seed long hidden finally sprouted after all, once the sharp plowshare of war had torn open the hardened soil. But is there any such dormant seed left at all in our soil today? . . . Without this seed events remain incomprehensible, and the best way to get by is just to close one's ears, and with that part of one's soul which he can control just trust to luck and fate."

I think, my friend, that in these words you have really hit upon the heart of the matter, though this matter too lies concealed in the hands of God and refuses to relinquish its secrets.

After all, it was that way too in the divine history revealed to us in the Old Testament. It was not the events per se—the terrors, wars, natural catastrophes, and aroused populace—that opened the way to God. Not even the famous "march of God through history" was noisy enough to force people to listen. It took more than that. People finally began to listen and turn to God only when the prophets and patriarchs, empowered by the gift of God's Spirit, were there to "interpret" that march and those events. The promise was attached to the Word of God, not to God's march. At best, it accompanies the march only in such a way that God must speak if his march is to be distinguished from the logical progression of events and from the seeming miracles performed by his human instruments as they stride brazenly across the face of our planet.

The flapping of God's cloak, a corner of which we would like to snatch, can leave man quite unaffected unless God sends along with it the wind of his Spirit. Bismarck himself was well aware of that when he spoke these famous words about "God's cloak." He knew not only the cloak, but also the Spirit. Otherwise, it would have been sheer madness and presumption for him so to designate that scrap of cloth in his hand. Unless one recognizes that it is the same Lord who stands behind both the impoverished garments of the Crucified One and the rustling mantle of the second apocalyptic horseman, unless one recognizes this one Lord in such a way as to see that both of these garments are vestments of the divine majesty, his eyes remain blindfolded.

In saying this I have already in effect stated my conviction that we should be painting the impoverished garments of the Crucified One before the eyes of men only in such a way as to simultaneously "interpret" the rustling of God's cloak in our time. God not only speaks, he also marches. And why should we not dare to take the risk, indeed why should we not be obliged to take the risk of speaking now about that marching as well, once we have placed ourselves under the discipline of his Word? Everything depends on us and our comrades taking everything that God sends, and living and marching through it with that well-known "lamp unto our feet" which he has provided for our way. And perhaps you theologians out there, even more than the preachers in the pulpits, are today called to listen to the command of the hour and train yourselves to be the kind of Socratic theologian who walks through the markets and the dugouts, the lookouts and the lonely command posts, going from man to man, asking questions and answering them, often holding your peace while others speak, precisely in order to let this lamp shine into the ambiguity of events.

God's march through these events cries out in fact for just that sort of person, someone who will interpret it. Everyone—even the most obtuse—notices the footprints of something enormous passing by, but no one has any idea as to who it is: whether it is the men who are making history, or history which is making men, or perhaps fate—or indeed the Lord of history.

For one thing is surely clear, and here you will have to agree with me, namely, that everything which we experience, the elevating as well as the terrifying, and above all death, addresses its question to every man. Think for a moment of the way in which men see themselves called in question by the manifestations of our transitoriness, especially in war. You have only to think of New Year's Eve, and of how some men hold their ears and cry amidst the din, "Let us eat and drink for tomorrow we are dead," while others spend this same hour, this symbol of man's passing away, in prayer, viewing it in the light of eternity. Both of these responses make it clear that all men—the one kind as well as the other—hear in this moment the grass of time growing. All are aware of being confronted by the question: What road are you on and how near are you to its end? Only in the *answers* is there a difference. Both are asked the same question. Now I should think that we Socratic theologians whom God has sent to be among our comrades would have to take up that question of death which the present New Year's Eve—this hour of war—places before everyone.

I will try to show you what I mean.

The question of death veritably cries out at people, screams at them, and so many try to smother its screams with a gag in the mouth. They stifle the cry, whether it arises when their own life is in danger, or when a comrade falls at their side, or when they see the stiffened hordes of the enemy scattered across the battlefield. They have two cudgels at hand for jamming into the screaming throat of death.

One is to say that what is transpiring here is simply "a segment of nature." It is the rhythm of becoming and perishing which here expresses itself in the fact that we must die. That's all there is to it! However furious the tempo of war, it is nothing more than this natural rhythm.

I should like to tell you a little story, not just for the sake of reporting this particular incident, but because the same thing is happening everywhere at the moment and this story is therefore a powerful illustration. An eighteen-year-old tank gunner, a talented young man who intended to study at the university, wrote to me

—although we were not personally acquainted—to comment on something I had published that had made a deep impression on him. From his letter one could detect the storm and stress of his adolescent years. He was well-read and genuinely searching. Much of what I had written he had only half understood and much of what he wrote was speculative and lacking in balance, as is often the case with young boys whose intellectual hunger goes well beyond what their limited life experiences can assuage. I envisioned him as a young fellow who had, so to speak, shot up overnight and whose "inner sensibilities" had not yet caught up with the growth of his intellect. In answering his letter I first struck down the intellectual edifice he had constructed and then I suggested that he simply "do" the truth vis-à-vis his comrades, by serving them in the midst of danger; only in this way and not by way of abstract speculation would he come to know "whether this teaching is from God." In a brief response to my letter, he acknowledged the validity of what I had said and promised I would hear from him again after he had worked it through for himself in this way —praying, doing—and gotten farther along. He sensed that it was now a matter of getting started. The next thing I heard about him was that he had died in battle. Shortly afterwards, from the effects found in his pack, there came a half-finished letter addressed to me in which he had started to report on the first shaky steps he was making in the task to which he had set himself. Before he could finish his letter, he had fallen in battle.

Why do I write this to you, Hans? Because I was suddenly struck by the fact that it was certainly *not* the rhythm of life which had snatched away this half-fulfilled young man just as he was beginning to stand on his own feet. On the contrary, here was a case of this rhythm breaking off precipitously and shatteringly right in the middle of a letter. Ought we not to learn here, we as well as the many others who experience the same thing, that death is in fact an enemy, a contradiction, and that death ought not to be? Does it not sever and destroy the bonds of life and friendship? Does it not take away the best of our youth and shatter the lives of thousands of others? Is it not really an *un*natural *dis-*

order, as the Bible portrays it? I believe a good deal would already have been gained if we would stop trying to conceal this unnaturalness behind a facade of solemn phrases. Even the grandeur of the cause for which a sacrifice is rendered dare never deceive us about the fact that in death something unique must pass away with all its promise and all that God intended for it.

"Something unique"—that brings us to the second cudgel with which men try to choke the cry of death. Man always dies his death alone, no matter how embedded he may be in the particular fellowship which sustains him to the very end. How often have we sung:

> To die at home in one's own snug bed
> Is to enter alone the ranks of the dead;
> But great is the fellowship here, we say,
> In falling together like new-mown hay.

And yet this stanza deceives. Dying alone in the hospital perhaps reveals even more clearly than falling on the battlefield that death is like the platform gate at the depot. Only one at a time can pass through, and above it stand the words: "Your life is nontransferable. Now it is you alone who are on the spot; for you the end has come." Ever since I came to realize this, ever since as a soldier I perceived how singularly alone one is, even in the midst of his comrades, when he himself is marked for death, I look at every marching unit with different eyes. To be sure, there is power concentrated in the mass of marchers. To be sure, amidst the singing the individual seems to dissolve into the one common body of sound. One can experience that completely only when he is himself a part of it—only when the marching and singing comrades surround him on all sides and almost extinguish his private existence. Nevertheless I have often had to think that every single one of those marchers lives in a dimension in which he is irreplaceable, completely alone. Each one carries his own guilt, his own cares, his own death. And I think of the final moments of a young soldier whose death I had to witness in a hospital, who said at the very end, "In this place you die all alone." He said this in the presence of his closest buddies, who were gathered about him.

It is my conviction, Hans, that if we realize how death strikes each of us in this dimension where we are not only members of a group but also individual persons, where something real passes away and cords are cut which cannot be reknit, then most of the flowery decorations with which we conceal God's most profound messages are already removed. If we really make that clear to ourselves, then we suddenly understand why the thought-world of the Holy Scriptures treats death with such massive earnestness. Nietzsche could still think that it was by means of its "other-worldly nonsense" that Christianity fostered what he called a "mis-use of the hour of death." But we know better. The men of the Bible knew that we are called to a life of fellowship with God, and that death therefore is corporeal *dis*order; it is "the last enemy." They knew that in the decisive things of life man is irreplaceable and solitary—in his guilt, "in his suffering the most massive hammer blows"[2]—and thus they took no refuge in any collective dream world to escape that dimension in which my death strikes me, in which I stand alone before God and in which, despite all the love which cries for eternity, for "deep, deep eternity," the living cords are all severed.

But in spirit I already hear your counterquestion: Should one really make the severe things of life that severe? By simply not noticing that abyss, by doing instead precisely what is commonly done on New Year's Eve, are not the heroic despisers of death, the believers in fate, simply pursuing an easier path, perhaps the only possible path for the masses?

You are right, my friend. Despising death is the easier way for the same reason that in other respects too the way without God is often the easier way; it is less inhibited. It is for this very reason, however, that Luther—although in human terms he is very impressed by them—fights against those despisers, because in their contempt of death they are at the same time despising Him who allows death. In blind opposition the despisers elevate themselves above the message that death holds in its bony fingers: that here man, who is forever out of bounds, is finally put back

[2] The phrase comes from the German poetess Lulu von Strauss und Torney.

inside his limits, that here the wall separating man from God's eternity is being erected, that wall which the rebel in us does not want to acknowledge and which in frenetic titanic defiance we tear down again and again.

Nevertheless—and now I'm asking with you: What would your comrades say if you were to allow the earnestness of the truth—and especially the earnestness of the truth of death—simply to stand, for the sole reason that it is true? Should not truth be that which serves life, that alone? And does anything else really serve life except that which reveals its abysses and makes us as daring and heedless of the outcome as the person who, because he does not know the dangers, stands resolutely against them?

I recently spoke about this with a very young man who had already debated the matter at length with Communist soldiers. We talked about why the atheists died so easily, at least appeared to die so easily as to be envied for it, often letting the tanks run right over them rather than give up, still throwing hand grenades when they themselves were already cut to ribbons. Is that greatness, is it heroism, is it insanity, what is it? The young soldier interpreted the phenomenon with what seemed to me to be the instinctive certainty of youth: They die so easily because they have nothing to lose. That is all there is. What then do they lose if they only lose themselves? They do not know him who is the judge, who makes them individual, irreplaceable persons, riveting them fast to themselves forever. They do not know "the infinite value of the human soul," which they possess as a creature and child of God who has been bought with a price. What then do they lose? What do they think they are losing?

My friend, here we come up against the ultimate mysteries of our faith. Death becomes a much more serious matter the more we have to lose, that is, the more we are aware of the true destiny to which we have been called, the more we know of the dignity and uniqueness of our person, which death strikes down.

I trust, dear Hans, that it is not necessary to warn you against understanding this dignity in terms of something intrahuman, or in the sense of a vain individualism with its cult of the personality.

The only reason we speak of "the infinite value of the human soul," is that we are so infinitely loved; we were bought at so great a price. God does not love us because we were so worthy; on the contrary, we are so worthy because God loves us.

Because God's love rests upon us, because Jesus died for us, we have that golden chain about our neck and that crown upon our head of which Luther speaks in the Large Catechism. It is this crown that gives us royalty, not vice versa; we do not receive the crown because we cut such a royal figure. The reformers spoke of the alien righteousness which we receive through Jesus. In the same way we can speak of the alien dignity that is bestowed upon us. This and nothing else is what is meant by the infinite value of the human soul. And this, you see, is what makes it so unnatural that we, these royal people, should die. Death does not strike some neutral "it," a body, an individual representative of a species. It strikes the one who has been so loved, and who has this destiny. Never has man been so highly spoken of as in the Bible. And nowhere else is death—for this very reason—such a serious thing, a matter of supreme and unattenuated gravity.

I do not want to close this long letter, dear comrade and brother, without opening to you yet one last perspective. Luther says in similar situations that only he who inflicts the wounds and permits them is able also to heal them. No one else. Illusions about death cannot do this; neither can hushed silence on the subject. Even the atheistic method of easy dying effects no healing; it only teaches how to bleed to death without looking. It proclaims the demise of an impersonal collective entity, not the end of a human being who is wrenched from just such anonymity when he is called by his name to be God's possession. No, God alone can heal the wound because he is the one who has inflicted it. Only he can heal it whose love reveals to us—so painfully and yet with such joy and promise—"the infinite value of the human soul." For now we know for certain that what dies in me is not an "it" but an "I," an "I" for which there is no substitute among all the comrades who march over my grave. In death I am really and irretrievably and in actual fact at my end. But at the same time I am one whose history with God cannot stop, since I am called by my name and I am the friend of Jesus. The Resurrected One is victorious and I stand within his sphere of power. Once more it is his "alien" life with which I am in fellowship and which brings me through everything and receives me on the other side of the gloomy grave. It is not the intrinsic quality of my soul nor something supposedly immortal within me that brings me through. No, it is this Wanderer who marches at my side as Lord and Brother and who can no more abandon me on the other side than he could let me out of his hand here on this side of the grave.

You know, of course, Paul Gerhardt's resurrection hymn:

> Now I will cling forever,
> Christ's member, to my head;
> My Lord will leave me never,
> But leads me through the dread.
> He rends death's iron chain,
> He breaks through sin and pain,
> He shatters hell's dark thrall,
> I stay his friend through all.

Should we then not make bold to interpret God's march through the travail of history and through the carnage of war in just this way? Indeed, are we not in fact compelled thus to interpret and explain it?! May God grant us the grace not to withhold from our neighbor the message we owe him about that march!

Introduction

Human Death and the Argument from Science

The remarkable sentence of the Apostle Paul that "the wages of sin is death" (Rom. 6:23) compels us to see that man's mortality is rooted not in creation but in his fall from creation. Thus death is not of the created *order;* it is *dis*order.

This is the decisive point of controversy with the various philosophies, which see death as an inevitable biological or metaphysical process, as something natural, a part of the order of nature, a necessary component of life itself. Accordingly death becomes an expression of the transitory and perishable aspect of nature.

The Bible by contrast views death in conjunction with sin and thus with man's *fall* from order. But in considering this we must from the very outset avoid misunderstanding man's biological death as an effect of which sin is the cause. The Scriptures portray human dying as something that occurs via the medium of biological death, to be sure, but still must be distinguished from that medium. Man's death, therefore, is qualitatively different from the merely biological death of animals. The opposite of biological death is biological life. The opposite of human dying (which occurs via the medium of biological death) is life from God, the sort that "though we die, yet shall we live" (John 11:25 ff.).

It is erroneous to view natural science as the chief opponent to this biblical perspective which ties death to sin. The one piece of evidence that might support such a viewpoint is the fact that arguments against a tie between sin and death are couched primarily in natural science terms. The arguments can generally be reduced to a rhetorical question: Is it not true that death reigns also outside the human realm in animals and plants, therefore beyond the realm of good and evil? Does it not appear to be an inevitable and ethically neutral process of nature? This might lead, of course, to the cleverly naive variation: Adam and Eve very likely ate animals too, not just forbidden apples, and since animals cannot be eaten alive but must be slaughtered, the fields of Paradise must already have seen the shadow of death.[1]

Whatever response we might make to such arguments, whether clever or comical, one thing must be kept uppermost in mind: It is not natural science as such that is stating its case here, but *man* who is using its arguments for himself. There is undoubtedly one side of death that is connected to biological processes, which are the proper subject of natural science. Thus death itself, when studied exclusively via immanent research methods, can be conceived as a fully immanent autonomous phenomenon. But to do so would be to remove one more realm of existence from its explicitly religious foundation, that is, its relationship to God, and to explain it only by its relationship to this world. The transcendental tie between death and sin would then become untenable. Dying would be biologically conditioned, and biology lies beyond good and evil. In this case the argument from natural science first of all allows man to understand himself on the basis of his self-contained finitude. Thus despite its intended posture of unbiased neutrality, the argument does have a definite ideological cast. To this extent we must carefully distinguish once more between the means, which is the particular line of argument, and the purpose therein expressed, which is man's proclamation of his own autonomy.

If we are clear on this point it quickly becomes apparent that theology's controversy with philosophical understandings of death dare not be carried on within the framework of natural science,

1 See Wolfgang Stroothenke, *Erbpflege und Christentum* (Leipzig, 1940), pp. 104 ff.

although this is the very approach that has characterized Christian apologetics for quite some time. Such an approach has usually resulted in nothing but amateurish nonsense; it has proved a stumbling block to the faith. Theology must instead come immediately to grips with that ideological concern which has here cloaked itself in the garb of natural science, or even of biological myth. If theology wishes to dispute and yet to remain genuinely obedient to the Scriptures, it must ask: What precisely is man's understanding of himself when he verbalizes his arguments with such scientific exactitude and such apparent unconcern for religion? Thus the present dispute about death and perishability is but one episode in the ongoing conflict not with natural science, but with natural theology, that is, with man's attempt to understand himself on his own terms and thus to be his own god.

Keeping this in mind, we propose to pursue our interest here in two directions. On the one hand we are interested in methodology. We will try to demonstrate with a concrete example how all apologetics (which today are thriving so luxuriously) must, despite their theological pretensions, be surmounted biblically. Apologetics must learn that Christian proclamation is addressed not to an ideological house of cards with its scientific pillars, but to the human brother who sits in that house and who has a very specific reason for building himself such a habitation.[2]

Secondly, we are interested in substance. We are anxious to see that the biblical proclamation about death with its *memento mori* gets a hearing in the midst of the tortured vitalism of the modern world, and to see that proclamation shatter vitalism's metaphysical presuppositions.

[2] I have given a more detailed analysis of this false principle of current apologetics in my book *Jesus Christus am Scheidewege. Eine biblische Besinnung* (Berlin, 1938), pp. 46-51.

Part One

Man and Death in Philosophical Perspective

"The whole life of the philosopher is a preparation for death."

—Plato[1]

"The summons of death comes to us all, and no one can die for another. Everyone must fight his own battle with death by himself alone."

—Luther[2]

"Death ought to remain outside, an alien entity daily kept at bay."

—Rilke[3]

[1] A free rendering by Cicero in *Tusculan Disputations* 1. 30, 74, Loeb Classical Library (Cambridge, Mass. and London, 1950), p. 87, of a famous passage in Plato's *Phaedo* 81. Leading up to this epigrammatic sentence are the following words from Plato: "The truth rather is, that the soul which is pure at departing and draws after her no bodily taint, having never voluntarily during life had connection with the body, which she is ever avoiding, herself gathered into herself;—and making such abstraction her perpetual study—which means that she has been a true disciple of philosophy; and therefore has in fact been always engaged in the practice of dying." *Phaedo* 80-81 (*Great Books of the Western World,* ed. Robert M. Hutchins [Chicago: Encyclopedia Britannica, Inc., 1952], 7: 232).

[2] American Edition of *Luther's Works* (Philadelphia: Fortress; and St. Louis: Concordia, 1955–), vol. 51, p. 70. [Hereinafter cited as *LW*.]

[3] From his wartime letter of 8 November 1915: *"Über Gott"* (Leipzig, 1934), pp. 14-23.

1.

The Anthropological Character of the Question about Death

THE QUEST FOR THE MEANING OF LIFE

Every attempt to get at the meaning of life must inevitably face the question of death. It is necessarily so, if for no other reason than that death appears in every life. If anything in life is a certainty, it is death; it conditions every moment of this advance toward death that we call life. Just as our walking is actually a kind of falling, though with every step we check our fall, so life itself is a matter of dying, a dying that is repeatedly held in check.

In this we see one of death's characteristics: It does not come upon us unawares, as in a sudden surprise attack, but accompanies us all along while we are still walking in the light. And since we must perforce reckon with it while we yet live, death is surely an integral part of our life. As we pass cemeteries and life-destroying processes of all sorts on our life's way, we cannot avoid these warning signs of our own end. And as surely as we know about it—indeed, are compelled to know about it—death is already part and parcel of this life, its characteristic trademark. We are compelled to face up to the fact that death is the one thing which is 100 percent certain, and that at some particular hour it will block our path, after having been the companion in whose "embrace" (as Luther says) we and our fellow travelers have walked our whole life long.

Saying this, however, we have not solved the question of death by any means, but initially have only posed it. For the question then becomes very pointed: What is this "thing most certain"? Since death is obviously as much a part of life as birth is, since it belongs to life as obviously as the border belongs to a country (and no one need tell a German how fatefully a border shapes man's history), therefore the only way to inquire about death is obviously to inquire about life.

Implicit in every statement about our life is a statement about death. But the finding out what life is also necessitates finding out what the meaning of life is. For the question "What is life?" cannot be answered by saying (e.g., of a civil servant's life): It is growing, working, raising a family, retiring, getting hardening of the arteries, dying; or (of a soldier's life): It is fighting, conquering, falling. In saying all this we have only indicated that of which life consists in respect to its content, in terms of its component materials. But this I do not have to tell the man who asks me, "What is life?" For this he knows already. Indeed, it is the very fact that he experiences all this that forces upon him the question, "What *is* life?" that is, "What is the purpose of it all?" "What *telos* determines it?"

We need only consider the occasions when people raise that question in order to understand that it is in fact the real one. For example, the first time it arises is perhaps at puberty, probably because man's awakening sexual nature, suddenly appearing out of nowhere and pushing for domination, compels him to stand apart and view himself as another person. This is the opposite of the sort of experience a child goes through when he stops referring to himself in the third person (thus standing apart and viewing himself as another person) and begins to use the first person singular. In crossing this threshold for the first time the child performs the act of self-identification. But the boundary experience of puberty—whether in nations, cultures, or individuals—suddenly compels a person to view himself from the outside, to see his whole self (not just a segment, e.g., the particular bump he got when fighting with the gang) and to be startled, yes, even frightened by it. This is the fear that goes with puberty. It overtakes a person whose growth and development to that point has been almost vegetative and unconscious, and in a sudden flash it illuminates his image and he sees himself in his own reflexion—as a stranger. It is this fear which, if it occurs at all on the level of intellectual awareness, finds expression in the question: Who am I and where am I going?[1]

The same question, however, also arises (and for pastoral care it is probably more significant) in the humdrum routine of daily work, where the synchronized company clock rules supreme. There are moments when, time and time again, man imprisoned here glances at this clock and suddenly reads his fate from the glow of its demonically phosphorescent face. In this moment he is not simply an employee who rises in the morning, eats, works, smokes his pipe, and then lies down again. On the contrary, he suddenly sees in all this routine a procession of milestones on a road that seems endless, but that must be leading to some sort of inevitable goal. At such times, when he is conscious not merely of the minutes but of the entire illuminated face on which they appear, in whose glow he comes to see himself (or better, becomes aware of his "self"), he goes through the same experience that a person is said to have when drowning or falling to his death: in a single moment his entire life unfolds before his eyes.[2] Where is it going? To what end will it lead? The German folk rhyme captures the mood of the question:

> I live, but know not how long;
> I die, but know not when;
> I travel on, but know not where.
> 'Tis strange that I should be so happy.

These then are some of the possible existential forms in which this questioning process occurs, when a man asks about himself

[1] These thoughts are confirmed by the observation that anyone who speaks with even a modicum of openness to teenagers on topics such as "the meaning of life" can count on very attentive ears.

[2] See the discussion of this last moment recapitulation in Georges Barbarin, *Der Tod als Freund* (Stuttgart, 1938), pp. 89 ff., 126. Cf. the extended treatment of this work below, pp. 76–77.

and in pursuing the question of meaning tries to draw some specific conclusions about himself. This process of inquiry is theologically critical because it is at this point that natural theology can break in. We will take a moment longer now to examine the *form* which this process takes.

THE INFINITE VARIETY OF MEANINGS

The question of meaning described above can be and usually is answered with some this-worldly value. My family, my nation, my posterity, my life's work—these are the usual answers to a man's "why" and "wherefore." As soon as I have discovered that one of these is the *telos* transcending my own life, then for me the question of meaning is obviously solved. And if this deduction is valid, then the problem of death is simultaneously cleared up. For when I posit a superordinate transcendental value as the meaning of my life, death clearly is not "the end of me." Death cannot possibly annul all my achievements and relegate them to meaninglessness, but on the contrary, they must be transformed into other values and preserved there, as it were, according to the law of the conservation of energy. In such a view death is not the end, but merely a transition. If I regard myself as taken up into and supplanted by the goal for which I lived (e.g., my nation) I am immortal, even if I happen to be an unknown worker or the unknown soldier. Here for the first time we begin to see faintly that the doctrine of immortality is a necessary component of every natural theology.

Since that which gives meaning, however, is thus elevated from the realm of the immanent into the transcendental, we see something of that law in operation which Saint Paul expressed in another connection: "He who sows to his own flesh will reap from the flesh" (Gal. 6:8). Here the term flesh (*sarx*) is precisely this immanent sphere of what is immediately evident,[3] a self-contained and self-content finitude.

This is documented by the fact that the meaning derived from

[3] See Rudolf Bultmann's essay "Paul" in *Existence and Faith* (Cleveland and New York: World Publishing Co., 1960), pp. 132-34.

a this-worldly value supplies no more than a provisional security and that the quest for meaning therefore continues unabated, almost self-propelled. The meaning afforded by family, nation, or humanity is obviously spurious and provisional because these realities are not genuine transcendental entities, "eternal grounds" able to abate temporal finitude. They are incapable of granting any peace, but can give at best only a temporary truce.

Again, this is documented by the fact that the quest for meaning continues. The transcending value in any given case always points in turn beyond itself, showing that it too needs grounding in a higher context of meaning. What occurs here we might call the "Faustian experience," referring at this point merely to the existential form, not the theological content, of the process. Faust's life is but a quest for the absolute, the one thing that offers meaning. Hoping to find it manifested in the realities of this world, he immerses himself in scholarship, in philosophy, in jurisprudence, in theology, and finally in Gretchen. But he never finds rest, only that temporary truce which is soon ended by the trumpet call for him to move on.[4]

If we apply this to the nation as an example of a transcending value, this pursuit of meaning forces us also to ask about the meaning of the nation and its history. Is this meaning to be found in happy grandchildren, or a higher standard of living for those who come after us, or fame and glory? But then, again, why is all this of any value? Whoever drinks from the springs of these pseudoabsolutes is forced to move on from one fountain to the next (Jer. 2:13; John 4:13). And if we cast a glance at the history of these ideological consolations, we are reminded of the Faustian wanderer who tries to cross a raging mountain stream by hopping from one rock to the next. The problem of death—after all, it is the attempt to overcome death that makes men ask the ultimate questions of "why" and "wherefore"—the problem of death arises threateningly again in this hopscotch from stone to stone. For even our own nation, supposedly the token of immortality that gives tangible meaning to our lives, itself eventually

[4] We shall treat the Faust problem in greater detail below, pp. 38–56.

dies.[5] And what greater entity, what higher kind of immortality is left to absorb this death? Can "humanity" fulfill such a function?

TWO STOPGAP SOLUTIONS

It is a good thing to have clarified how the quest for meaning pursues its never-ending course. For we can see from the path it takes that men always search for one of two solutions to bring the constant wandering to a halt and to provide something more than an interim answer to the question of meaning.

On the one hand men may attempt to relieve the relentless pressure of the problem of death (which is also the problem of life) by positing one particular value as absolute and then, by a conscious act of the will, refusing to inquire whether there is any other reality which might still transcend it in meaning. Such an attempt is precisely what is involved in all the talk about "our nation" as something eternal and indestructible. Here the act of absolutizing is especially obvious. And then it is but a logical consequence when imperceptibly and by degrees the ultimate criterion of good and evil becomes simply whether or not something is useful and beneficial for the nation so understood.

On the other hand, men may attempt to see the meaning of life not in some single, supposedly absolute aspect which they have posited for themselves, but in the infinite parade of life's finite realities, each one regarded as a fragmentary parable for that totality of life which, though hidden in the background, is nevertheless symbolically present to determine the meaning of the whole procession. To fulfill the meaning of one's life, then, is to wander like Faust from one entity to the next, in a diligent and unending search, never coming to rest at any absolutized and supposedly achieved goal.

In either case a man's mortal life is absorbed into an overarching higher configuration of meaning. In the first case man thinks of this configuration of meaning statically as a particular, concretely posited *telos* (e.g., "nation" or "humanity"). In the

[5] Cf. the conversation of the Swiss citizenry about the distant death of their nation in Gottfried Keller's *Banner of the Upright Seven,* ed. W. A. Neilson (New York: P. F. Collier, 1917).

second he thinks of it in dynamic terms as that totality of the universe which discloses itself only as he struggles and wanders.

Either way, if he could succeed, he would demonstrate that death belongs integrally to life. Death would no longer be something alien, contradictory, or puzzling. As ultimate and terminal finality death would be rendered impotent, null, and trivial, just as God himself is rendered impotent, null, and trivial when he is accommodated to us, made to conform to our human notions of reality. Vis-à-vis both of these—death so conceived and God so conceived—man no longer dies completely; he remains essentially intact while undergoing transition into that manifestation of life which is indigenously authentic for him.

Thus to diminish death's potency has been an easy task for the myth of our day. It casts a spell upon death which changes it to "perishability," and the eternal rhythm of growth and demise, becoming and passing away, outlasts the dying that occurs within it. The species lives longer than the individual, the nation longer than the citizen.

It is no accident, then, that the most celebrated ideal for the shape of death today is "to go down fighting for a cause." In this concept death clearly becomes an absorption of the personal into the suprapersonal, a change of life's form, a mere "transformation." In this concept more than any other, perishability is proclaimed as a law of life, which in the case of man is raised to a level of high personal significance by the fact that he is incorporated into the cause for which he dies and thereby becomes immortal. Whoever really fulfills his life thus enters into eternity. It is only "the man who does not live his life to the fullest" who "dies with the cry of the beast."[6]

THE TRIUMPH OF ANXIETY

In thus tracing the contemporary contours of a segment of natural theology[7] and describing it empirically, we should not

[6] *Das Schwarze Korps,* 22 June 1939, series 25, p. 11. [*Das Schwarze Korps* was the newspaper of the SS elite during the Third Reich. It presented the depth philosophy of the movement while *Der Völkische Beobachter* presented the party line for popular consumption.—Trans.]

[7] On the concept of natural theology see my *Kritik der natürlichen Theologie,* 2nd ed. (Munich, 1938).

conclude without making one final observation: that there is hardly any present-day physician who dares to tell one of his patients that he is incurably ill and must die.[8] Theoretically, that is, in philosophical thought, death surely belongs to life. Practically, however, anxiety triumphs as a sign that death is a fracture and an abrupt unmasking of life's supposed security (Ps. 39). Practically, death makes a mockery of any consolation from biological or idealistic theory. Practically, no one experiences the end of life the same way as life itself, as if they were seamlessly joined. Death seems rather to be radically disconnected, absolutely alien to life. Thus we can maintain that as a practical matter anxiety about the end of life stands in real contradiction to any theoretical explanation of death as natural. Here it must be said that anxiety is still anxiety, even when it is suppressed behind clenched teeth or when it takes refuge in an ideological scheme of immortality. In any case we should not let the verbose adolescent character of such "theoretical" sallies prevent us from seeing the enormously perplexed *man* standing behind the facile exorcist formulas with which he seeks to ward off his anxiety about death.

It is evident that man's dying—regardless of the technical cause—is something qualitatively different from that perishableness which seems to reveal itself when individual specimens pass away but the essential species remains permanent. Evidently I am something more and something other than just a specimen that can perish while the species itself survives.

What if this fact about my life should express itself precisely

[8] A prominent clinical physician, who personally is not at all frivolous, confided to the author that he lies to his patients up to the very end. One of the ancient Greeks, he maintains, might have been able to endure such a disclosure of imminent death, but men of today are unable to bear it, nor do they want to. In this respect Martin Heidegger has a characteristic observation in *Being and Time*, trans. John Macquarrie and Edward Robinson (New York: Harper and Brothers, 1962), pp. 297-98: "The expression 'one dies' spreads abroad the opinion that what gets reached, as it were, by death, is the 'they.' In Dasein's public way of interpreting, it is said that 'one dies,' because everyone else and oneself can talk himself into saying that 'in no case is it I myself,' for this 'one' is the '*nobody.*' . . . This evasive concealment in the face of death dominates everydayness so stubbornly that, in Being with one another, the 'neighbours' often still keep talking the 'dying person' into the belief that he will escape death and soon return to the tranquillized everydayness of the world of his concern. . . . In this manner the 'they' provides a constant *tranquillization about death.*"

when this life *dies?* It is true in other respects as well that in suffering and death man is much closer to the secret of his life than he is in joy, or in the midst of a blinding fixation. Joy is essentially a momentary event while suffering carries us to the limits of our life's possibilities, thus confronting us with ourselves. In time of joy one can *forget* God because the moment is already "occupied"; but in suffering one can at the most doubt him: "Where is my God now?" This is why pastoral care is practiced in the wards of hospitals but not on the streets at mardi gras.

What would we say if, despite all contrary philosophical and biological theories, man still experiences anxiety in the face of death and even becomes enslaved to this anxiety precisely because his life is qualitatively different from that of all other creatures, and because the normality of the creature's death contrasts sharply with man's monstrously unnatural death?[9] What if man, when he dies, should stand isolated and alone amid the rhythmic patterns of becoming and perishing that surround him? Did not God's Christ conquer human death, yet allow this rhythm to continue? Did he not raise the dead—a brilliant spotlight on the unnaturalness of man's dying—yet set no limits to the perishing flowers and animals? For it was certainly not at this point that he directed our attention to the birds of the air and the lilies of the field.

THE PERSONAL CHARACTER OF DEATH

Though the data of biological science suggest by analogy that human death is a natural element of life, and that this life remains triumphant because it survives beyond the demise of its individual manifestations, the Christian theologian cannot make such an assertion. If I were to consider death an elemental component of life and consequently view man as merely an interchangeable sample of his species, I would be denying and ignoring that most profound mystery of death which surfaces in man's

[9] F. W. Weber in his work *Gott in der Natur* (Berlin, 1936), p. 39, speaks of the unnaturalness of dying even so far as the laws of conflict operative in nature are concerned: "That death should be something natural is hard to believe if one has ever observed the way wild animals of all sizes and types run for cover, or noticed the anxious caution of the birds and the hesitating timidity of the fish."

anxiety. This is the mystery that it is *I* who must die, I in my quality as an individual, as a person, as something laden with unique value, existing only once as the only exemplar of my kind. The indissoluble residue of death's mystery that persists here is nothing other than the mystery of my I. According to the rule of the causal nexus, all phenomena are taken up into the effects that follow causally from them and are thus preserved, given permanence, and—insofar as they are living—immortalized. The mystery of my I, however, is that I am person, and precisely as person I am an exception to this rule.

To understand human death one cannot ignore the fact that the being who dies is not simply one extant human who can be replaced by some other extant human. He is not an interchangeable specimen of a species as animals are. Thus by virtue of man's uniqueness, human existence has a twofold qualification.

On the one hand human existence is qualified by man's individuality. Every man, despite everything that ties him to the whole human race and to his fellow countrymen, is the focal point from which he views the world.[10] Thus he actually possesses a world of his own in which all of life is related specifically and uniquely to him.[11] When the historian views man as a creature having a spirit distinct from nature and existing in his own historicity, he is calling attention to this trademark of historical existence. It is for this reason that Rickert says the method appropriate to historical science is "individualizing," while that appropriate to the natural sciences is "generalizing."

The real root of man's uniqueness is a second quality, his quality as person. What we have labeled "individuality" is only a very

[10] See Jakob Baron Uexküll's biography, *Niegeschaute Welten, Die Umwelten meiner Freunde. Ein Erinnerungsbuch,* 8th ed. (Berlin, 1938), which builds on the insight that every man is the center from which he views his own world.

[11] "It is a curious drama that man, who knows the supreme and inescapable law about the cessation of every life all around him and of every life that has ever been lived, still finds it personally oppressive to yield to that law. The notion strikes him as unbearable that this fantastic subjective world that he carries within himself, and that exists in this particular shape but once in time, should simply be wiped out. It is unbearable simply to collapse at the side of the road while the others travel on, conversing as though nothing had happened. . . . The vividness of this feeling . . . makes mockery of all logic," says Alfred E. Hoche in *Jahresringe. Innenansicht eines Menschenlebens* (Munich, 1936).

unspecified manifestation of this deeper essence. Saying that human existence is "person" existence means that man has been given the responsible task of determining his own being. It means that he can succeed or fail in this offer of self-determination; it is for this purpose that his time has been allotted him, the time in which his unalterable decision is to be made. This decision cannot be altered, simply because the time line of man's life cannot be reversed; it is unidirectional. This temporal quality of human existence is the very thing that makes this mandatory and fundamental decision something unique and unalterable. Temporality is the most basic element of man's unique and irreplaceable nature, the nature of human personhood. In considering man's decision within the directional time line we need not focus exclusively on moral decisions in the narrower sense, but quite broadly on his decision to take hold of his own existence, in this very act either fulfilling it or failing in the attempt.

These remarks have merely scratched the surface in describing man's characteristic as person, and the manner, for example, in which the issue is handled in general philosophical language. The purpose has been to shed light on the problem raised by man's unique and irreplaceable character and consequently also by his death. For the moment this suffices. Actually the problem raised by the qualitative difference between man's death and an animal's demise also appears in secular discussions of the subject such as the ontology of Martin Heidegger, even though it may then be suppressed.[12]

[12] See below, chap. 5.

2.

The Division of the I into Intrinsic and Nonintrinsic Segments

The philosophical attempt to render death impotent operates with very specific anthropological media. That is to say, the understanding of death is always embedded in a comprehensive understanding of human existence, and conversely, the understanding of existence is decisively shaped by the way death is understood as the extreme limit of this existence. Indeed the two must be seen together. If we are to understand what is implied in the biblical conjunction of judgment and death, and its all-out attack on this supposed life without death, this supposed security of life, then we must focus on the entire structure in which man conceals himself.

Anthropologically, the philosophical attempt to render death impotent always follows the same course. It divides man into an intrinsic segment of the I, which as a kind of immortal substance survives death, and a nonintrinsic segment of the I, which as an insignificant vessel for that intrinsic substance perishes, in fact ought to perish and can safely do so.

THE EXAMPLE OF PLATO

With these formulations we believe we have put our finger on the fundamental principle of all natural anthropology. What this means practically is perhaps most easily seen in the Platonic idea of immortality. In Plato's classic formulation man is divided into an immortal soul which is set free by death, and a body that holds him prisoner. Nietzsche's principle of division is by comparison extremely complicated (for reasons we shall show later). Indeed, it is precisely because of this that we consider Plato and Nietzsche within the close proximity of this single chapter. The extreme contrast between their ideas of death points up all the more the similarities in their principle of division, and provides significant perspectives for the analysis of philosophical thought which is to follow.[1] We shall have to content ourselves here with only a brief look at Platonic anthropology.

In the first place, death according to Plato's *Phaedo* simply signifies the separation of soul and body. The soul is always separable from the body, and in death that separation actually occurs. The soul therefore has an independent existence.[2] Hence the boldly assumed certainty of the soul's preexistence and postexistence.

Birth and death do not involve creation and destruction but simply a change in the relationship of the soul to the bodily material. The soul either seeks a body or else dissolves its previous connection with a body.[3] Thus birth and death occur in a rhythm of becoming and perishing which is identical with the rhythm of association, dissociation, and reassociation between soul and body. The soul itself consequently does not become or die. It remains as the unchanging substrate of all the constantly changing associations with, and separations from, the body. The body as empirical sense-datum represents the transitoriness of the phe-

[1] Plato's doctrine of immortality constitutes only one line among the many which Greek thought has taken in its wrestling with the problem of death. See below our discussion of Greek religion in comparison with Germanic religion; and on the Greek tragedians see the following works, some of which are treated more extensively below: Kurt Langenbeck, *Wiedergeburt des Dramas aus dem Geiste der Zeit* (Munich, 1940); Josef Sellmair, *Der Mensch in der Tragik,* 2nd ed. (Munich-Crailing, 1941); Walter F. Otto, *Die Götter Griechenlands* (Frankfurt a.M., 1934); Werner Jaeger, *Paideia: The Ideals of Greek Culture,* trans. Gilbert Highet, 3 vols. (New York: Oxford, 1943-45). See also Helmut Thielicke, *Schuld and Schicksal. Gedanken eines Christen über das Tragische* (Berlin, 1936).

[2] Is death not "the separation of soul and body? And to be dead is the completion of this; when the soul exists in herself, and is released from the body. . . ." Plato *Phaedo* 64 (*op. cit.,* 7:223).

[3] See Plato *Phaedo* 77 (*op. cit.,* 7:230).

nomena; the soul on the other hand is the sum and substance of that which is constant.

It goes without saying that these acts of association and dissociation are never confined to the temporal moment in which they occur. They are by no means limited to such chronologically defined moments as birth and death. On the contrary, they actually determine the life that unfolds between these two limits—and not just quantitatively in the sense that life is thereby begun or ended, but also qualitatively in the sense that they shape its very content.

This becomes apparent as regards what one might call the philosophical content of life, a content which depends entirely on the attitude a man takes—or during his lifetime comes to take—toward his own death. To put it another way, the degree to which a man attains knowledge, and thereby achieves an essential relationship to the ground of his being, depends on his attitude toward death.

This can be illustrated as follows. The immortality of the soul for Platonic thought is intimately connected with the soul's relation to the essence of things. One might describe this relation as follows. The soul is the adequate reflector of the essence of things, while the body is the adequate reflector of the sense phenomena in which that essence manifests itself, that is, of the multiplicity of the sense-perceptible world. Both body and soul are therefore related to the respective realms of being from which they themselves derive.

Consequently one can draw the conclusion—as Plato makes Socrates do in carrying "childish"[4] anxiety about death to the point of absurdity—that the soul is no more in danger of dissolution or susceptible of annihilation than is the realm of reality to which it belongs (the essence, the ideas and concepts), that realm of essential being from which the soul itself takes its being. For these metaphysical essences too (e.g., the concepts of sphere, cylinder, etc.) do not succumb to dissolution. On the contrary, they always remain the same even if their concrete manifestations

[4] "Strictly speaking, they are not our fears, but there is a child within us to whom death is a sort of hobgoblin." Plato *Phaedo* 77 (*op. cit.*, 7:231).

perish. The invisible always remains constant; only the visible changes.

Related to this is the further thought that the soul—as such an invisible and essential reality—cannot perish. For by its very concept the soul is the life principle, the invisible essence of life, as it were.[5] Consequently, in terms of its own being, simply by definition, the soul is unable to admit of death. Whatever is unable to admit the quality of straightness, we call crooked; whatever cannot admit the quality of death we call deathless. Socrates argues: Just as snow cannot be warm, nor fire cold, so the soul which bears and brings life cannot be dead.[6]

From this vantage point we see what is involved in the dissolution which occurs at death, as the mortal body separates from the deathless soul that outlives it: the soul goes to its own kind. If the particular soul has previously dissociated itself from body and senses, then at death it hastens to the blessed life appropriate to it.[7] The soul, on the other hand, that has succumbed to the allurement of the senses and fallen prey to the body (and hence forfeited its very nature) must wander about until it has again associated itself with a body, which (depending on its previous disposition) may be that of a donkey, hawk, wolf, bee, or ant.[8]

Here we see to what extent death, in determining life, is taken up into life, becoming, as it were, something existential. For as surely as the union of soul and body gives particular shape to the soul, and thus affords it a kind of satisfaction, so surely does it also represent an encumbrance and a burden for the soul in that it interposes between the soul and its appropriate realm (namely, the essence of things) the disturbing and confusing world of the senses. For the soul, death means a reawakening to that which is of its very essence.

Inasmuch as the true philosopher already aspires to coming

[5] Plato *Phaedo* 105 (*op. cit.*, 7:245).

[6] Plato *Phaedo* 106 (*op. cit.*, 7:246).

[7] The soul departs to the world which is like herself invisible: "to the divine and immortal and rational." Plato *Phaedo* 81 (*op. cit.*, 7:232).

[8] Plato *Phaedo* 82 (*op. cit.*, 7:233).

nearer to the essence of things, and thereby penetrating the world of shadows with its mere appearances, this philosophical effort itself can at the same time be characterized as an aspiring for death, for release. In fact in the *Phaedo* Plato speaks of the philosopher's "desire of death,"[9] and of the philosophical life as "the practice of dying,"[10] a Being-toward-death.

Death is thereby given both a negative and a positive quality. Negatively, death means the annihilation of the peripheral, non-essential realm of existence: the body. Positively, however, it means the awakening of existence to its own intrinsic life.

Here we see clearly the principle of anthropological division of which we have been speaking. It is operative not just with reference to the act of dying itself (as a moment in time) but actually helps to determine what life is. Man is immortal, death-less, because it is only a certain something *in* him, only his body, that is mortal, subject to time, mutable.[11]

A similar anthropology, leading also to the idea of immortality, is that of Immanuel Kant. In his fundamental distinction between the intelligible and sensible I-segments, the intelligible achieves moral perfection only after an infinite progression stretching even beyond death. For Kant death is merely physico-sensible and consequently unimportant.[12]

By further developing and extending this Kantian thought, Schopenhauer maintains that death strikes only man's phenomenal self, but not the real center of what he considers the *"Ding an sich."* Death may "well bring an end to his life (i.e., the phe-

[9] Plato *Phaedo* 64 (*op. cit.*, 7:223).

[10] Plato *Phaedo* 67, 81 (*op. cit.*, 7:225, 232).

[11] In considering the division of man, a division which repeatedly recurs in philosophical thought, we have spoken here of Plato because his is the most graphic example of this method of overcoming death. We must nonetheless at least mention the fact that there are instances outside our Western and historically accessible realm of existence in which biological death is not regarded as the ultimate limit of existence. In his *Magie und Religion* (Gütersloh, 1947) Karl Heinz Ratschow demonstrates that physical death is discounted also in the realm of magical thought; however, this is an area of human experience which lies beyond the scope of our present inquiry.

[12] See in Kant's *Critique of Practical Reason,* trans. and ed. L. W. Beck (Chicago: University of Chicago Press, 1949), pp. 225 ff., the notion of "infinite progress" as a "postulate of pure practical reason."

nomenon), but surely not to his being (*Ding an sich*)."[13] What is destroyed is life, "the objective world together with its medium of presentation, the intellect"; yet that says nothing about the intrinsic I that continues to exist. This life is only a dream; hence death is nothing more than an awakening, when the ideas that have become attached to our I retreat and we retire to what was originally our own,[14] namely, to the independent will, free from all knowledge and liberated from all the physiologically conditioned (and therefore perishing) projections of consciousness.[15]

NIETZSCHE'S NOTION OF DEATH WITHOUT TRANSCENDENCE

The same anthropological artifice that divides the I and renders death impotent could be shown with any number of additional examples. The most modern attempt of this sort, the one that is closest to the biological anthropology of the Third Reich, is surely that of Nietzsche. At the same time his is the most radically different from Plato's. Nietzsche's anthropology is well worth outlining here, since he extended that principle of separation to its most extreme limits. His position was a prophetic anticipation of our age and the contemporary philosophies which now hold sway. Hence it interests us not merely as a theoretical position but also as an acutely relevant one. We must keep alert, however, to catch the separation. Nietzsche's consistent emphasis on immanence forbids any all-too-facile assumption of some durable quality in the I external to the immanent as an avenue for attaining immortality.[16]

Nietzsche's pronouncements on human death are always directed polemically against the Christian "distortion" of death's reality.

[13] Schopenhauer, *Werke,* ed. Julius Frauenstädt, vol. 6 (Leipzig: Brockhaus, 1919), p. 287.

[14] Ibid.

[15] Ibid., 6:290. See also the thematic investigation, "Über den Tod und sein Verhältnis zur Unzerstörbarkeit unseres Wesens an sich," ibid., 3:528.

[16] In what follows we will consider specifically those conceptual models in which such division of the I is harder to detect than in the usually acknowledged examples. At this very point the principle we have postulated should prove itself.

When he calls the fear of death the "European disease,"[17] then the catalytic agent for this disease is (in his view) Christian anxiety about the other world, "the pitiful and horrifying comedy that Christianity has produced about the hour of death."[18] It is an anxiety that something from some other world will befall this life in and after death.

In opposition to this, Nietzsche would have us view death as something that belongs to life and thus—entirely in accord with the idea of perishability presented above—not something that befalls it from the outside, but something implicit in life itself which life endures as its own end.

"Take care lest we say that death is opposed to life."[19] It cannot be, if for no other reason than that Nietzsche's concept of life is explicitly nontranscendental. Hence neither life nor the boundary that death sets for it can be interpreted from some other world; the interpretation must come solely from life itself. But since death is thus a segment of life, it is placed into man's hands just as his life is. It is left to man to give it meaning and to shape it, just as life itself is.

To put it another way, just as life does not happen in man, but man living as active creative subject consummates his own life, giving it meaning and shape, in the same fashion man functions as the executor of his own death. He is an active subject in relationship to it.[20] Freedom for life is thus identical with freedom for death, which I allow to befall me whenever *I* will it, so that it does not become an accident to which my life would then be enslaved. "May you be given my death, the free death, that befalls

[17] *Friedrich Nietzsches Werke* (Leipzig: Alfred Kröner, 1917 —), 14:127. For what follows below, see Karl Jaspers, *Nietzsche: An Introduction to the Understanding of His Philosophical Activity,* trans. Wallraff and Schmitz (Tucson: University of Arizona Press, 1965), pp. 231 ff., 323 ff.

[18] *Nietzsches Werke,* 8:144.

[19] Ibid., 5:149.

[20] Death in nature is "death under the most abominable conditions, a death without freedom, a death at the wrong time, a coward's death. Out of love for life man should wish death to be otherwise—free, conscious, not an accident, not being taken by surprise." Ibid., 9:144. "When one eliminates himself, he does the most praiseworthy thing there is: he almost deserves thereby to live. . . . He has set the others free from his view." Ibid., 8:144.

me when I will it,"[21] "free for death and in death."[22] "One must invert the ridiculous physiological fact (i.e., death as something that befalls us biologically) into a moral necessity."[23]

If a man is able to shape his own death and thus apprehend it in freedom, the question arises: When is the proper moment? Expressed more profoundly: Where is the norm by which I measure my time? In response to this Nietzsche can say, "One must stop letting himself be eaten when he tastes the best," when the summit and limit of a life full of value has been achieved. If only man would cease "saying his unctious 'no' to life when there is no more time for yes. That would make him an expert at living and dying."[24]

Since man has this kind of time, filled with value and concluded with voluntary death, Nietzsche necessarily arrives at a basic division in man. On the one hand, man is one who evaluates himself, critically measures himself, and consequently from some particular moment onward condemns himself to death. On the other hand, he is also the object of that judgment who from the moment his value has run out becomes a worthless being.

Thus it is not accidental that Nietzsche arrives at anthropological assertions that sound very Platonic, namely, the separation of a "kernel" from the "pitiful substance of the shell."[25] As death occurs in nature the body is "the stultifying, frequently ill, stupid prison keeper, the master who designates the point where his noble prisoner shall die. Such natural death is nature's own suicide, i.e., the annihilation of intelligent being by the unintelligent."[26]

[21] Ibid., 6:106.

[22] Ibid., 6:108. "The consummator dies his death victoriously, surrounded by those who hope and vow. . . . But hateful to the fighter as well as to the victor is your grinning death that sneaks up like a thief. . . . Let your spirit and your virtue shine forth even in your death like an evening glow on the earth, or your dying will have come off poorly." Cited by Jaspers, *op. cit.*, p. 325. See also the chapter on "Voluntary Death" in *Thus Spake Zarathustra* (New York: Modern Library, n.d.), pp. 85 ff.

[23] *Nietzsches Werke,* 16:315.

[24] See ibid., 6:106-8.

[25] Ibid., 3:294.

[26] Ibid. See the perceptive exegesis of this thought in Jaspers, *op. cit.*, p. 324.

Life adjudges itself therefore to be no longer worthy of living and yet is itself this judge. Thus for a moment it rises above itself, so to speak, disappearing for an instant in an assumed transcendence in order from this vantage point to "pass judgment." And yet that transcendence — that higher judicial I-zone — is nothing genuinely transcendent that might remain beyond the time of life, but something that is also swallowed up in the nothingness of death. Nor is the norm by which the end is determined anything that can transcend this time of life. For with Nietzsche the norms for the ground, goal, and meaning of life are themselves immanent to life. Only that which enhances life is good and true. Life itself, to put it bluntly, is in every case the *norma normans* and any norms, ethical or otherwise, are the secondary *normae normatae,* derivative from it. Thus the norms stand in service beneath life and not in authority above it.

The end result is that the norm which for a moment transcends, measures, and ends life is precisely still this life itself. It is both arrow and target, both wave and ocean. Consequently it has itself in such control that it even controls its own death.

Hereby we have crystallized the decisive element in this attempt to render death impotent. The attempt is not to posit an immortal segment of the I in contrast to which bodily death is reduced to insignificance. On the contrary, the attempt is to transform death from a power over man to an instrument in man's power, that is, the power of the noble man over his own ignoble and worthless self. But even in this view, unfavorable as it is to all notions of immortality and transcendence, the same basic dividing of the I has to take place as we have shown to be the case in all natural attempts to render death impotent. Unique here is only the extreme to which Nietzsche pushes it, an extreme which in the very next moment upsets the thought into absurdity. For the transcendence posited here by which the I judges itself contradicts diametrically the antitranscendent nothingness in which it is swallowed up at death. (This is probably also the reason why all of Nietzsche's assertions about death seem vacillating and indefinite, laden with paradox.) Yet it is at this very point that the boundless excess, the divinization of human life, comes to expression. Man controls himself both in life and in death; death is but a means in his hand, a symbolic means whereby he shows how he has taken over his own life, how he ends it, and in all of this how he has it at his disposal. His life is not something created, something presented to him to be received. It is not a life that stands under the authority of the divine norm and terminates before God. Life is rather its own creator, the author of its own norms; it is legislator, judge, and destroying angel all in one. All paths are from it and through it and to it. It is the most colossal and most vitalistic and consequently—although it borders on insanity—perhaps the most consistent tour de force ever attempted against death. Man is God—death, where now is your sting? Hubris and nihilism, self-divinization and insanity are here in frightful proximity to one another.[27]

[27] A similar conceptual model that transcends death is to be found in the notion of the "eternal return."

3.

Man as Individual and as Vehicle for the Universal

It is a fruitful task to trace in Germanic religion how this thought of dividing man's I becomes a decisive means for coming to terms with death. Though we cannot take up this additional task here, yet we can briefly sketch the operative principle. It is especially important to do so since this is the only way we can understand why it is at this point that the biblical proclamation about judgment and death actually begins. For the biblical message (almost in protest against such division) takes man as a whole, makes him into a person before God, and thus places him face to face with the inescapability of his dying. Not until man understands himself as such a whole being who cannot be divided as he might wish does he come to see that his entire being must die and not merely his exterior shell. It is his intrinsic life, his existence before God, that comes to an end and must perish. The reason why death is such a central biblical reality is that death takes possession of man at the center of his being. By contrast the place of death in secular philosophy is peripheral, since the artifice of an I-division constantly recurs, allowing death to strike man only at his own periphery.

GERMANIC RELIGION

Granted this premise, we see the same process at work in Germanic religion. If Grönbech is correct, we do not find among our

Germanic forefathers "any fear of the ending of life."[1] To be sure Grönbech's own reasons for this, expressed in such statements as "life was so strong in its reality that death simply could not count against it,"[2] are not convincing. It would be more feasible to envision the exact opposite, that the intensity of their feeling for life corresponded with an equally strong dread of the threat of death. For death surely does shatter life's vitality. Everyday affairs and a look into the structure of human experience teach us that those very men who live from the resources of their own vitality are threatened by anxiety about the end.

Walter F. Otto[3] correctly calls attention to the fact that in Greek religion it is by experiencing the divine as the absolute fullness of life that a man comes to understand death not as a built-in, natural, legitimate segment of this life, but rather as the absolute alien, the very opposite of nature. "It is the living creature who is the very one that experiences death as the most alien reality and is never able to believe that it could have its place in the meaning and plan of life itself."[4] It is fallacious to conclude that the spirit of Homeric religion "is so ardently devoted to the dazzling brilliance of life that it no longer can even see death,"[5] and conceptualizes it therefore as absolutely incomprehensible nothingness. On the contrary the concept of Hades as a new shadow-existence in contrast to life would seem to be a clear sign that death is not simply nonexistence, but degenerate existence. The gods of life surrender and stand powerless in the face of *Moira*'s fatal hand.[6] *Moira* is the great and finally triumphant contradiction, which holds even the gods and their divine life under its control.

Hölderlin too—one might say in the name of the very brilliance of Greek belief in life—finds personal death to be incomprehensible, contrary to life: "I cannot conceive the thought of perishing,

[1] Vilhelm Grönbech, *The Culture of the Teutons*, translated from the Danish by W. Worster, 3 vols. (London and Copenhagen, 1931), 1:317.

[2] Ibid.

[3] *Die Götter Griechenlands* (Frankfurt a.M., 1934).

[4] Ibid., p. 342.

[5] Ibid., p. 176.

[6] Ibid., pp. 340 ff.

when our heart, the best that is in us, the only thing worth the trouble to listen to, pleads for survival in the midst of all its pain. May the God to whom I prayed as a child forgive me! I cannot comprehend death in his world."[7]

From this Greek view of life, which at least at this point of its self-understanding seems somewhat parallel to the Germanic notion, we may see the confirmation of our thesis against Grönbech: As the emphasis on the vitality of life is intensified, the alien and unnatural character of death also increases.[8]

If the Germanic man of earlier days apparently sensed no anxiety about death in this respect, this appears to be related to another factor. Initially Germanic man was hardly aware of himself as an individual; he lived so exclusively in the context of the tribe, in its welfare, in its peace, in its glory, that today we can hardly comprehend it. Hence individual death plays an inconsequential role because the hero really does live on in the welfare and glory of the tribe—and not merely in the sense of an immortal name, an immortality in the memory of men.[9] So the heroes are completely satisfied to live their lives anew in some other man of their clan and the "question of their own identity simply cannot penetrate through the mass of the old premises."[10]

What constitutes man's intrinsic being is not his individual

[7] Hölderlin in a letter to Neuffer (upon the death of Neuffer's fiancée) (Jena, 8 May 1795). *Sämtliche Werke,* vol. 6 (Stuttgart: Kohlhammer, 1954), p. 171.

[8] For the Greek concept see the article on "death" in Gerhard Kittel, *Theological Dictionary of the New Testament,* trans. G. W. Bromiley (Grand Rapids, Mich.: Eerdmans, 1964 —), 3:7 ff.

[9] See the example adduced by Grönbech from the Vatsdoela-saga in which the young mortally-wounded hero Thorolf bids his brother to transmit his name to posterity: "My name has lived but a little hour, and thus I should be forgotten as soon as you are gone, but I see that you will increase the family and become a great man of luck. I wish you would let a son be called Thorolf, and all the lucky qualities which I have had, those will I give him; then I think my name shall live as long as men dwell in the world." When Thorstein, his brother, responds, "This I will gladly promise you, for I look that it shall be to our honour, and good luck shall go with your name as long as it is in the clan" (*op. cit.,* p. 312), it is clear that the issue is not simply the continuation of a name in our modern secularized sense, but that the name is only a symbol for the highest possible concrete form of continued living in the clan.

See also the description of the dead king who continues to rule via the medium of his clan: "He is king in death by virture of what he is, not of what he was. And what he is depends entirely on the activity of his kinsmen." Ibid , p. 322.

[10] Ibid., p. 313.

existence, but his living in and living on in the welfare and honor of the clan which represents him. Here too we find parallels in the Greek notion of "fame" which takes on a significance for conquering death remotely similar to that which "welfare and glory" have for the Teutonic clans. Bultmann means basically the same thing when he argues in the Kittel article that achieving fame gives man the "opportunity of bringing death as an act into life"[11] and thereby—in terms of our formulations—of divesting death of its character as absolute end. Since fame is most often achieved in fighting for one's homeland *{polis}*, and since this action is conceded to grant an even greater chance for achieving immortality, the parallel to welfare and glory in the Germanic clan is even more vivid.[12]

It is in this sense that the Germanic idea of immortality must be understood. In death the individual member of the clan retires and the clan (that power which already possessed welfare and glory through him) transfers these holy forces to be lived out in other clan members. "As long as life is inseparably bound up with a whole [namely, the whole of the clan], so that the individual cannot exist at all as individual, the sting which should set the thought of one's own incarnation in motion is lacking."[13]

Now it becomes completely apparent why death is considered insignificant, since death kills only the nonessential that is but slightly noticed if at all, namely, the individual bearer of the clan's powers, but it does not kill those powers themselves. Just as we cannot imagine an individual incarnation and immortality on the basis of these presuppositions, neither can we imagine any notion of individual death, since the individual in this sense is not yet there.

[11] Kittel, *op. cit.*, 3:9.

[12] Just in passing we might mention the remarkable fact that among both the Greeks and the Teutons the immortal continuation of individual life actually moves along two lines. On the one hand there is supraindividual continuation in the fame, or welfare and glory, of the overarching community. On the other hand there is Hades, or Valhalla. This represents, so to speak, a dotted line of the individual's continued existence, a shrunken, shadowy, floating, dreamy postmortem figure. This form of continuation may even be an indicator of the unresolved and dimly perceived problem of individuality and man's uniqueness which here retains an individual identity of sorts.

[13] Grönbech, *op. cit.*, p. 313.

THE BIBLICAL VIEW

Before beginning a dialogue on death with Germanic religion and its modern secularized adherents, it must be made clear that Scriptures view man in a manner completely different from the Germanic view in terms of the clan. In the Scriptures man is person, individual, irreplaceable. Not until man stands *coram Deo* does this unique irreplaceable quality become visible and audible. On the basis of his own presuppositions the Teuton could not possibly make sense out of the biblical message about death, that is, that death strikes man at the essential center of his being. Of course, neither can we on the basis of our own presuppositions make sense out of law and gospel; hence it is natural that law and gospel strike us as scandalous. For scandal simply means the collision of divine presuppositions with man's presuppositions and counterpositions. It cannot be eliminated until our presuppositions (our "eyes and ears," 1 Cor. 2:9) are transmitted by God's making us members of his new creation.

The Teuton cannot comprehend that death like a lightning bolt annihilates man himself and that the clan cannot serve as a lightning rod deflector until he learns that man exists as an irreplaceable self incapable of being exchanged with anybody else. Man also cannot substitute things, not even his riches, for himself; this is why Jesus says to him, "Go, sell what you have" (Mark 10:21). And the rich fool is compelled by death to abandon the protective barrier of the overstuffed barns he had erected all around himself in order to survive (Luke 12:20). Nor can man have his family take his place and absorb his life. This is why God says to Abraham, "Go from your country and your kindred and your father's house" (Gen. 12:1), and Jesus tells his disciples that they must be prepared to hate their father and their mother for his sake (Luke 14:26).

When Adam was called by God, he suddenly became aware that in his guilt he was unable to substitute "the woman whom thou gavest me" (Gen. 3:12). And the woman became aware that in her guilt she was unable to substitute the serpent who spoke to her with such guile.

Before God man is always pinned down to himself. There is a region of the I in which man is absolutely incapable of being vicariously represented by anyone or anything else, where he stands in infinite loneliness, all by himself. This is where God calls him by name, when God says to him: "Adam."[14]

In this region he has to die. And in this region death becomes a problem with no possible solution. For here is actual annihilation and no transformation.

The gravity of death is a problem identical with the gravity of the I, that is, the fact that I have no substitutes and am pinned down to myself, that I am in no position to take "the wings of the morning" (Ps. 139:9) in order to escape myself and become somebody else (a clan, an idea).

Unique individual existence is something other than a stage of pupation from which I awaken to a butterfly existence participating in supraindividual values. And we will yet see how the Bible quite indirectly teaches the gravity of death, by teaching in law and gospel the gravity of having an irreplaceable I when standing before God.

Is not anxiety about death, which remains despite all consolations and explanations, an anonymous witness that fundamentally we do sense something of that annihilation? Do we not sense that the I is to be destroyed and that at most an "it" remains? Our achievement or our name or the fellowship that surrounded us may continue, but *I* no longer exist. The mystery of death is nothing but the mystery of this I. The fact that biblical man experienced death as *the* enemy was based on his being compelled via the captivating Word of God in almost terrifying fashion to say "I" to himself: "I, wretched man that I am. . . ." It rested on

[14] In a totally secular book of our day there occurs a perceptible echo of this Christian insight: "I should like to believe, from the depths of my innermost isolation which even love no longer can share—neither your love, nor the love of my people, nor any other human being's love or affection. I should like to believe that there is still someone who with his love can penetrate this solitary isolation. . . . Here too in this utter solitude I need to be called and committed. Even there where humans and human demands are no longer able to penetrate. And I have the feeling that so long as we do not create this quiescent space within ourselves in order to hear this call to commitment, our innermost heart remains empty and we have no durable foundation." Walter Kessler, ed., *Und eines Tages öffnet sich die Tür. Briefe zweier Liebenden* (Berlin, 1940), pp. 224-25.

his knowing, "I alone, I—for whom there is no substitute—am the one who is meant when God pronounces judgment and calls to decision." In that moment he was stripped of everything, literally everything—his being a Jew (or a Greek), his father's house, his friendships, his money. In the moment of such divine calling all these things were revealed as means by which men attempted to lose their selfhood in order to make themselves secure and escape the divine threat. All these things became for biblical man a sign of that shrubbery behind which Adam sought to conceal himself.

It is therefore completely inaccurate to think that the Christian perspective on death's terrors (even excluding its corrupted form of "sizzling in hell") centers primarily on man's standing alone at death, having to leave everything behind, departing this world naked and empty-handed, just as he first entered it naked and empty-handed (1 Tim. 6:7). This negative fact of "having to leave it all behind" is not the point of the biblical statement. Instead the accent rests on the exposure of the self that occurs when possessions must be left behind. Here the self confronts death and can no longer crawl back to hide behind those possessions. *I* must surrender; *I* am the one being led to death, while the "it" with which I had bedecked myself continues on.

Not until man's irreplaceable selfhood, his solitary isolation before God, becomes clear, does death become fatal. Its fatal character is concealed if man considers himself personless, I-less, as did the Teutons of old. And the anthropological form of this personless, I-less perspective, as we have sought to trace it, always consists in a division of man into a "super," that is, a "non"-personal I-segment which is imperishable, and his individualistic qualities which do perish.

HEGEL'S PHILOSOPHICAL IDEALISM

Hegel's system of thought is obviously similar to Germanic religion in making it possible to ignore death. History as the self-realization of the spirit, according to Hegel, acknowledges the individual only as an insignificant vehicle, a mere transition stage.

As something "special" within that self-realization, the individual takes second place behind the species, which portrays the universal and to that extent is closer to the idea. One can even say that inasmuch as the species portraying the universal wants to keep itself going and allows this to be done in the flux of the generations, it must constantly relegate the individual to a merely transitional entity and to that extent kill it. The pairing of the individuals by virtue of which they seek to gain a place in the species consequently becomes the first step in their own self-dissolution, that is, in their death. The species preserves itself only via the destruction of individuals who in the pairing process fulfill their destiny, and since they have no higher one, they thereby move on toward death.[15] One can frankly say that the original inadequacy of the individual in relation to universality "is its original sickness and the congenital cause of death."[16]

Therefore death does not touch the sphere of the idea, which is life proper, but only individuality as life's im-proper transition stage. And even here one cannot really say that death is destruction, since on the contrary it is the creative self-liberation of the species or idea from its individual bondage and self-alienation. Corresponding to this conception of death, Hegel's notion of immortality is not an extension of the life of an individual nature, but that which realizes itself via this natural base and even in spite of it, namely, the reality of rational thinking as a universal entity existing for itself. For the subject of this thinking is the spirit which proceeds from the individual in nature—thus using it only as a means—whereby this individual transcends itself. What happens in this thinking process is nothing less than that the absolute spirit does its thinking within the individual spirit. Mortality exists only in the fact that the idea, the universal, is not adequate to itself but has surrendered to alien individuation and now in order to realize itself must constantly overcome the individuation. Therefore when the individual dies—if one can express

[15] G. W. F. Hegel, *Sämtliche Werke,* ed. Hermann Glockner (Stuttgart, 1955 —), 6 (*Enzyklopädie*): 217.

[16] Ibid., 6:224.

it this way—it is no radical death simply because individuality is no radical fact, only a transition. Indeed, when the individual dies the species gains a victory in breaking its universal self loose from the fetters of individualization. To that extent such dying is a victory of the spirit; it is self-realization of the idea. Thus death is no radical and consequently terrifying fact, for even though it does signify cessation and nonbeing, it does so only by striking individuality, an I-segment which actually participates in nonbeing right from the start and consequently cannot strictly speaking be terminated or killed. What is intrinsically proper to man, the spirit, is unscathed by death. Indeed, via death it comes into its own. Death does not contradict man's destiny. On the contrary, it enables him to achieve it. Death has become a meaningful law. As "perishability" it is the ladder to immortality. In fact it is actually the enabling instrument for immortality.

Thus when we confront Hegelian idealism we come again to see that the problem of death is only a modified form of the primary problem of man. Can man be divided into peripheral and central I-zones, into nature and spirit? Can man forsake the shape of his concretized I, become something other than himself, transcend himself and let the species replace him? Can he really succeed in keeping the fatal bullet from striking his individual shell until he has forsaken it and changed over into other forms, so that he can, as it were, observe this fatal shot from the outside and no longer feel himself struck down by it?[17]

[17] The notion that the species remains eternally present while the individual passes away and sinks into the past has perhaps nowhere been expressed more profoundly and with greater vision than in Schopenhauer's work, "Über den Tod und sein Verhältnis zur Unzerstörbarkeit unseres Wesens an sich" ["On death and its relationship to our indestructible essential being"]. He says: "Thus everything lasts but a moment and hastens toward death. A plant and an insect die at the end of summer; an animal and man after a few years; death reaps tirelessly. Nevertheless, as though completely oblivious to it, even as if it were not really true, everything seems always to exist in its proper place as if it were all imperishable. Plants are always sprouting and blooming, insects humming, man and beast standing in indestructible youthfulness, and the cherries that we have enjoyed a thousand times before confront us again each summer. The nations too exist as indestructible individuals, though at times their names may change. Even their actions, their drives, their sufferings are always the same, although history continually speaks of them as something new. For history resembles a kaleidoscope which presents a new configuration with each turning although we actually have the very same thing before our eyes. What therefore is more irre-

pressible than the thought that such coming and going does not touch the real essence of things, but that this remains unaffected by it and is consequently imperishable? Hence it follows that anything and everything which wills to exist really does exist continuously and without end. Consequently in every given moment all the species of animals from the gnat to the elephant are together in full force. They have already renewed themselves many thousands of times and in the process still remained the same. They know nothing of the others of their own kind who have lived before them or who will come after them. It is the species that is always living, and conscious of the imperishability of the species and of their identity with it the individual members exist in good cheer. The will to live is manifest in the endless present. Since this is the form of life of the species it never ages, but always remains young. Death is to the species what sleep is to the individual or what blinking is to the eye, the absence of which identifies the Indian gods when they appear in human form. Just as the world disappears when night comes, although it does not cease to exist for a moment, so man and beast seem to pass away via death while their true essence continues to exist undisturbed." *Werke,* ed. Julius Frauenstädt, vol. 3 (Leipzig: Brockhaus, 1919), pp. 547-48.

4.

Man as Transitional Form and Bearer of the Universal in Goethe's "Faust"

Although the division of the I in Plato, Kant, and Hegel—to cite the examples we have taken—was easy to recognize, it is detected in Goethe only on closer examination. Nietzsche's extremely antithetical anthropology, of course, has already prepared us for difficulties. With Goethe the difficulty lies primarily in the fact that the concept of action which gives meaning to life keeps that active life focused upon itself. Thus it deflects the man of action from taking any interest in some other I-center which might conceivably extend beyond the action of the moment, as though immune to that "e'er-aspiring struggle onward" which the present moment requires. Such interest could only be speculative, not active, and therefore would be sterile. In Goethe this thought is centered especially in his notion of entelechy, in the context of which the problem of immortality arises quite vividly. Here too the point of all his thinking is action, which keeps life focused on itself; speculation about a future life does not concern him. Some of Goethe's thought which seems to contradict this is nevertheless subordinate to this primary interest, as we will see below.

Since the life of action has such strong self-interest, concerned, as it were, with the immediate moment and not with continued existence, it is not surprising that Goethe's division of the I is by no means so apparent as it was in the other thinkers we have treated. All the more we are challenged to an analysis which here too will demonstrate the validity of our thesis that such separation renders death impotent. In addition Goethe's thought about death seems at many points to connect with the concerns of biologically-oriented philosophies current today.

LIFE'S FULFILLMENT IN ACTION AND STRIDING ON

In order to get at Goethe's formulation of the question we shall first analyze the scene of Faust's death, which by virtue of its immediate connection with his active life carries a minimum of speculative ballast and is almost pure proclamation. Then we shall incorporate Goethe's thoughts on entelechy and the monads into our interpretation.

None of the forms of being suffice to give Faust in his striving the realization of the unconditioned absolute that he seeks, neither theology, nor medicine, nor any other intellectual discipline, nor anything else. No solid form provides that ultimate which "holds the world together in its inmost folds."[1] From the signs in the book of magic he learns

> Into the whole how all things blend,
> Each in the other working, living!
> How heavenly powers ascend, descend,
> Each into each the golden vessels giving.
> (477 ff./17)

But this is only "pageantry" (454/17) and leaves him languishing even as he gazes upon the sign. The ultimate, which alone gives meaning, he finds in hastening from one form of being to the next, since individually—insofar as they become isolated and do not point beyond themselves to the fullness of all others—these forms are unable to grant any lasting contentment, any "eternity" (3193/96). Only

> Let him find pain and bliss as on he stride,
> He! Every moment still unsatisfied.
> (11451-52/336)

[1] J. Wolfgang von Goethe, *Faust,* trans. George Madison Priest (New York: Covici Friede Publishers, 1932), ll. 382-83, p. 15. (Subsequent citations from Faust will be made by line and page as above, e.g., 382-83/15.)

In this manner of striding on, guilt arises of necessity in the very moment when one of those infinitely manifold forms which Faust is compelled to storm through, to taste, and then to forsake (in order to grasp that center of life present in all of them), turns out to be a living human being in its uniqueness, that is, when Gretchen crosses his path. Here he must forsake a living human being who trusts him, since she too is no bearer or incarnation of life's substratum of meaning. If she were, she could bring to a halt his striding on. But even this human being is only one example of that "eternal womanly" which attracts him as an idea but not when it is concretized as an individual in Gretchen. So here too his path leads on from form to form and broadens out into an endless road. Faust must "stride on."

This then is clear: The meaning of his life, the unveiling of its innermost ligament, Faust cannot find in any single form, neither in philosophical truth which might give him peace, nor in any earthly entity. The individual forms are simply parables of the whole. They provide a glimpse of that innermost ligament only in the unending plenitude of man's encounters with them.[2]

If the meaning of the whole is not to be gained by setting up one of life's individual forms as the absolute, neither can it be found in an other-worldly existence separate from this life, as though life itself were devoid of all divinity and merely a dusty marching route to some terminal goal that transcended it. Even the aging Faust, who has "desired," "achieved," and yet again "yearned," who in the early stages of his earthly career has "stormed through life" (11437 ff./336) and now in wise circumspection as an old man has finished his journey—even this aged Faust rejects that emergency exit into the other world.

> The view beyond is barred to mortal ken;
> A fool! who thither turns his blinking eyes
> And dreams he'll find his like above the skies.
> (11442 ff./336)

[2] This is reminiscent of the young Schleiermacher who saw the universe mirrored in the microcosm of its individual forms and parabolically reflected in them. See his *On Religion: Speeches to its Cultured Despisers,* trans. John Oman (New York: Harper & Row, 1958), esp. the second speech, pp. 26 ff.

And with the same fervor of those early days whereby he made exorbitant demands on life, a fervor now laden with experience that has become the sum total of his life, he commits himself once more to the pain and bliss of striding on—almost to the action of striding on as a goal in itself rather than as a means for arriving at a goal. Thus he is completely thrown onto this life in which such striding occurs. It is the competitive path of this life that leads him past the plenitude of forms that line the way.

It is in connection with this immanent teleology of life, the macrocosmic law fully parallel to Goethe's notion of entelechy as the microcosmic law, that the problem of death now arises.

DEATH AS THE TERMINATION OF STRIDING ON

"Self-contained finitude" directs attention to itself for unlocking the content of its meaning. It does that so to speak in centripetal fashion—like an organism that structures itself from its own center outward. One might imagine that death would constitute a crisis for such centripetally-shaped meaning insofar as death puts an end to any individual participation in meaningful life. Death seems to remind us that the phenomenon of life is not only conditioned by the timeless eternal character of the centripetal motion, but that it also unfolds in connection with a linear time line, which at some point comes to an end. In any case Faust's earthly days had this dimension too. He was subordinate to time, which itself marches toward an end, laid out as it is in view of death. What does death look like when it is farewell to a wandering that as such desires to be eternal like the "e'er aspiring struggle," yet dismisses its servants when the hour has come? Does Faust have some place he can still go that would grant him additional life? "The view beyond is barred to mortal ken. . ." (11442/336).

> Time conquers—here the old man lies in sand.
> The clock stands still—
> Stands still! No sound is heard.
> The clock's hand falls.
>
> (11592 ff./340)

What meaning is there to the fact that in the midst of the circular movement the linear time line suddenly emerges, recognizable by its own termination? Does this not constitute a judgment upon a life of wandering and searching, if such a life has not included this terminal point in its calculations either as a disturbance, or as an alien body, or even as the terminal goal, and if regardless of how it is viewed death has never been brought up for discussion? Has not Faust rejected the prayer of the psalmist that God would teach him to reflect upon the fact that his life has a goal? Without this knowledge is not Faust merely a wanderer, almost the wanderer per se, who has no goal and does not even want to arrive anywhere? Is he not like one who searches for God without actually wanting to find him, because he finds in the *act* of searching his satisfaction? Is he not less a wanderer than an adventurer?

It is indeed true that Faust is overtaken by this thought and that the Menetekel warning of his life's time line laid out toward death appears on the boundary wall of that life itself. But this Menetekel does not have the glow of truth to dazzle and overpower him. It has rather the pale appearance of something ghostly and the whispering sound of a bad dream that cannot be real. For just such arguments appear in the mouths of the four ghostlike gray women, "Want," "Worry," "Guilt," and "Distress," those specters of the dream world by which the dark powers entangle Faust (11412 ff./335). Or they emerge from the mouth of Mephistopheles, who in contrast to them is surely a reality, but whose authority is broken by the time Faust's life is at an end. "Death as the end" is the thesis of ghosts or the slogan of the devil; that is all.

So the reminder of the end, the reminder of the linear time line now brutally breaking through rings out in the midst of life's circular motion as it rounds itself out:

> The clouds gather o'er us and blot out each star!
> Behind there! Behind! From afar, from afar
> There cometh our brother, there cometh he . . . Death.
> (11395 ff./335)

But this vision of the linear disintegrates in the face of the dying Faust's triumph when he is able to say to this very last moment, "Ah, linger on, thou art so fair" (11582/340). For him therefore this terminal is caught up and supplanted by an eternal present tense, a present tense in which the entire round of the course which he has fought through and of all life's future courses rests as in the depth of a mirror: "Everything real is purified, symbolically dissolving itself."[3] Thus simultaneously with this end point, this hour of Faust's death, there arises before his eyes, as a parable of life and action, the seawall against the ominous ocean, that wall which will compel the coastal residents, in daily battle against the hostile element, to conquer for themselves anew their freedom and life. This wall constitutes, as it were, the renewed incarnation of life's course of conflict from which Faust in this moment must retire. And in looking at this course which he has constructed he breaks forth in a song of triumph:

> The traces of mine earthly being,
> Though aeons pass, can perish ne'er.
> (11583-84/340)

Why can they never perish? Where does this triumph over death come from? Faust does not say that he will survive beyond death, but only that his traces will not be eradicated. How so?

We have already alluded to the decisive point in referring to the seawall and the newly won land that Faust's genius wrested from the sea. It is in his works that Faust continues to live in a very special sense, which to be sure we must still describe more precisely. He is immortal not in himself, but in his achievements which will bear witness to him. It is not he who lives on, but an "it" that owes its existence to him.

But that by itself will not suffice for an understanding of Faust's conquest of death, which has a still more profound point. For with reference to the works which are to praise him one could still raise basically the same objection, that the linear time line will someday terminate them too. Even works are someday subject

[3] [See the "Conversations with Eckermann," esp. those of the years 1827-30 wherein Goethe expounds at length on the content of "Faust II."—Trans.]

to the saying: Time is the master. "Eventually the day will come when clouds of smoke will rise even from the ruins of Troy."[4] Even the seawall, at least in the form in which it arose under Faust's creative hands, will someday perish, probably even quite soon, and have to be erected anew.

But with this observation we come a step closer to the decisive factor in the idea of immortality. It is precisely this fact that the wall is perishable, and that the protected land will always have to be conquered anew, which ensures Faust's immortality. For here the wall serves as illustration for that life which is passing away and must be won again in conflict. Perishability and immortality are the beats which set the rhythm of life. What is genuinely imperishable therefore is the dynamic act of conquest and not the small patch of new territory that results from this act. Hence such newly-won territory, insofar as it is a static result, is no more a final goal in itself than is philosophy or Gretchen. On the contrary, what counts is only the *act* of conquest:

> Of freedom and of life he only is deserving
> Who every day must conquer them anew.
> (11575-76/340)

At this point in our analysis we begin to realize how Faust copes with death. There are two reasons why his "traces" cannot perish. One is because the battle, the searching and wandering of his life constitute a parable of life itself as it will always continue. Secondly, they will not perish since Faust's work itself, as something constantly to be conquered anew, possesses the same parabolic character and therefore is not to be understood as a precipitate that can be separated and dissociated from his personality. His work is a new reflection of his personality, just as his personality for its part was a reflection of life. All of these are but variations of the same primeval phenomenon, in which they have their being, for which they are parabolic, and in which (in a Hegelian sense) their individuality is caught up and transcended.

[4] The line is from Goethe's "Achilleis," *Goethes Sämtliche Werke. Jubiläums Ausgabe,* vol. 6 (Stuttgart and Berlin, 1902), p. 235.

Wherever this primeval phenomenon seeks to manifest itself, wherever life exists as struggle, as searching, as ever-striving aspiration, as action, there Faust the eternal wanderer will be living. Life itself is the immortal monument of the earthly days through which Faust has wrestled as a paradigm and parable of all of life. In this life he will continue to have his being and keep on living. In more than just the Hegelian sense he is caught up in life.

And when the blessed spirits bear Faust's immortal self away at the end, this does not mean that now the portal is being thrown open, to a transcendence which from Goethe's perspective does not even exist. On the contrary, this is a symbolic gesture which confirms the validity, the "caught-up-ness," of such a Faustian life. An impressive hint of this immanent rounding out of the Faust drama is the fact that in place of "immortality" Goethe had initially spoken of Faust's "entelechy" which is carried away by the angels.[5] This entelechy (*En-telos-echeia*: that which has its ground, goal, and meaning within itself[6]) is nothing but the immanent teleology of life itself possessed in the immortality of an organism that lives from its own immanence. Faust's entelechy is thus only the microcosmic parable of macrocosmic life itself, a parable not simply in the sense of valid timeless parallelism, but in the sense of that magic substantive participation described in Goethe's *Orphische Urworte.* This work sets forth the connection between the teleology of individual life (complete in itself and unable to escape itself) and the law-abiding macrocosm of the course of the sun and the planets.

And even the chorus of the penitent women (the great sinner, the Samaritan woman, and Mary of Egypt) at the very end of the Faust drama does not beg mercy for him, which would constitute authoritative forgiveness via an other-worldly agency. On the

[5] Max Heynacher, *Goethes Philosophie aus seinen Werken* (Leipzig, 1905), p. 79. See also Th. Vogel, *Goethes Selbstzeugnisse über seine Stellung zur Religion,* 3rd ed. (Leipzig, 1903), pp. 134-35, and Karl Justus Obenauer, *Goethe in seinem Verhältnis zur Religion* (Jena, 1921), pp. 13 and esp. 106-7.

[6] See Erich Przywara, *Religionsphilosophie katholischer Theologie* (Munich and Berlin, 1927), pp. 22 ff.

contrary, they request a mercy which would confirm the validity of Faust's life even though, and especially because, his life had to become guilty, because in his pact with Mephistopheles he fought and suffered through the dualism of good and evil which actually constitutes the creative dynamic of life. This confirmation, this almost analytic judgment of God, constitutes the interior meaning of the forgiveness requested. It is not some forgiving acceptance of Faust into an other-worldly sphere which would be immune to such dualism and would contain an eschatological good with no contradictions. When the "angels soaring in the higher atmosphere, bearing Faust's immortal part" confess "Lo! rescued is this noble one from evil machination" (11934-35/350), it can only mean in this context that such evil was unable to hold Faust. For Mephistopheles' role in Faust's life possesses only teleological significance and necessarily becomes for him a means for eros to press toward completion.[7] Mephistopheles does not deflect him from his "primal source" (324/11) but is only able to urge him on to the fulfillment of his own self. The more other-worldly the conclusion of the Faust drama sounds (if only because of the scenery and the transfigured characters), the more this-worldly it actually is, and all the more monumental is its testimony to the immanent teleology of life's course coming full circle and repeating itself again and again in brand new orbits.

THE LAW OF SEPARATION

This then is Faust's immortality. He lives on in life per se of which he in his person and work was a parable. It is only for this reason that death is "the highest moment" (11586/340) into which the meaning of life is compressed, for death is fulfillment and transition. His individual shell falls, to be sure, but for him this shell was only a point in transit, just as one generation is only transitional in the unending chain of the species as it con-

[7] Mankind's activity can languish all too easily,
A man soon loves unhampered rest;
Hence, gladly I give him a comrade such as you,
Who stirs and works and must, as devil do.
(340 ff./12)

tinues to live on by means of these individual generations and their individual bearers.

Thus we encounter once more the artifice of dividing the I. To grasp this accurately is our main purpose. Here the division is between a nonintrinsic I-segment which is Faust as an individual man, and another I-segment which constitutes Faust's immortal part, his entelechy, that is, Faust as representative of life per se. Only by making his individuality a matter of indifference is Faust able to achieve immortality. In his uniqueness, in the singularity of his I, Faust is not significant enough that his destruction would make any difference. What counts is only his representing the event of life. For Faust it is cyclical time with its eternal return that reigns over all, the time in which life evolves by dying and rising, knowing nothing of death in any ultimate sense. By contrast, the perspective that takes man's personhood seriously does indeed know of this death, since it perceives time as the linear and limited line marked by the milestones of guilt. And one cannot expunge this guilt by backtracking on the time line since he cannot repeat his performance again; the immutable past remains eternally present before the eyes of God.

For Faust there is no eternity in which any kind of god could make inquiry into his unique existence and the unique encumbrances on his time line once it has been irretraceably traversed. Such a unique Faust does not exist, nor can his guilt be fixed uniquely or immutably. On the contrary, guilt is but one beat in the rhythm of life that he represents and thus does not belong to Faust but is to be charged to the account of this rhythm itself. There is no eternity at all on whose shores Faust's unique time line would eventually have to run aground. Instead eternity is but fluctuating time in which such eternal striving occurs. Forgiveness bestowed from the eternal is therefore not any gracious "nevertheless" from God addressed to man's advancing guilt-laden time line. Instead forgiveness consists in "penitential benefits" which are "raised to eternal dimensions" (12063-64/354),[8] and thus it confirms the endless striving.

8 [Translator's rendering.]

In spite of all the biblical images used here it is apparent at this point that Goethe departs completely from what the Bible calls eternity. Biblical eternity does not mean that everything continues forever, but that at some time the end comes (the termination of the time line!) and eternity comes to meet us. Eternity comes to meet us as judgment whereby God finds our self, for he has called us by name and now we cannot get lost or hide, either from him or from ourselves, in all eternity. Viewed from this angle, Faust represents a fantastic attempt at concealment. He conceals his self by dissolving it in the rhythm of life, by setting up a cycle to annihilate the dangerous approaching entanglements of eternity. Eternity is transmuted into an immanent "in-terminability,"[9] like the perimeter of a circle. It is life's eternal return into itself in dying and rising, in "enjoying" and "languishing for desires," in the drive toward "the lofty ancestral fields" and in bondage to things inferior, in alliance with Mephistopheles and in the maturation which even that affords. This is the only way Faust achieves his immortality, by "abducting" his self, or (expressed otherwise) by reinterpreting his self as the transition point, as the microcosmic reflection of the law of life.

Faust becomes immortal by becoming personless. His intrinsic being does not reside in his individual personhood; thus its death makes no significant difference. Instead the intrinsic Faust resides in his participation in the macrocosmic mystery of the competitive law of life, of which Faust's life, his individual entelechy, was but a microcosmic reflection. So once more immortality is possible only by dividing the I into essential and nonessential I-segments, wherein what dies is viewed as the nonintrinsic segment, in this case individuality.

This division is carried through so consistently that one can

[9] See the more poetic presentation of the same notion of interminable infinity in Goethe's "Sprüche (über) Gott, Gemüt, und Welt," which can easily be transposed from the spatial picture into the time-eternity scheme:

> If in the infinite you would stand,
> Enter the finite on every hand;
> If from the whole your strength receive,
> The whole in the part you must perceive.
>
> *Sämtliche Werke,* 4:4.

clearly deduce which concept of time is appropriate to which. Time viewed as a line, as nonintrinsic and finally invalid, is swallowed up by time conceived as cycle. It is this cyclical time that is the core content of Goethe's "eternity" (un-endingness, interminability) which concludes the drama.[10]

MEPHISTOPHELES' KNOWLEDGE OF DEATH

Gruesomely enough, according to Goethe it is only the devil who perceives that in spite of everything Faust is mortal and perishing. As elsewhere, here too we have the juxtaposition of the two structures. Reflected in them is the same reality, but in each case it looks completely different because each mirror is different. It is a difference like that between concave and convex reflectors. In Mephistopheles we can clearly follow both images of time, the cyclical and the linear, which we also had to distinguish in Faust. But their ranking is reversed and their meaning altered.

In the first place Faust's death according to Mephistopheles is unconditionally the end, the termination point of a linear and irreversible time line.

> Time conquers—here the old man lies in sand.
> The clock stands still—
>
> (11592-93/340)

But now there arises for Mephistopheles too the question, or more accurately the fragment of a question, whether somehow this end, this "'tis past," cannot be caught up into the continuing law of life's struggle, of which Faust's existence has been a microcosmic embodiment. Actually even for Mephistopheles this is not unthinkable. However, for him it is not the path to immortality,

[10] Goethe's division of the I is more difficult to detect than that of others, since it is not a two-story affair as, e.g., is Plato's anthropology with its higher and lower I-segments (soul and body). Goethe sees man as an indivisible unity, an entelechy. The division comes to the surface only where we can view this unified man from two different perspectives. On the one hand in his quality as the individual transitional point with his perishable and nonessential uniqueness, and on the other hand in his quality as vehicle for the macrocosmic law of life. From whichever perspective he may be viewed, however, he is always the same man. Accordingly, death and immortality are also merely "perspectives" from which we look at man.

but to a cynical parody on immortality. This being caught up is a plunge into the "everlasting void," into the eternal whirling gyrations of nothingness. For what sense can there be—this is the tenor of Mephistopheles' question—in "e'er aspiring, struggling on," if it never gets beyond the act of struggling, if the goals finally achieved are only transitions to new phases of conflict. Conflict for conflict's sake is senseless. It is the cycle of the everlasting void.

> Past and pure Naught, sheer Uniformity!
> What good for us, perpetual creation?
> Created swept off to annihilation!
> Then it is past! You see what that must mean?
> It is the same as if it never had been,
> And yet whirls on as if it were not destroyed.
> I'd choose instead the everlasting Void.
> (11597 ff./340-41)

Thus cyclical time, time spinning like a top, produces nothing eternal. It is a void. There could be something lasting only if within that time line something eternal were created; but then "the clock's hand falls" and it is all over. This is the alternative, the Mephistophelian view of human reality that accompanies Faust's path to the very end. Death as the end or "deep, deep eternity" as the conquest of death are alternate forms in which we can view human reality, in which we *must* view it depending on whether we are Faust or Mephistopheles. We are less likely to view them as metaphysical realities than functionally as the contents of the decisions whereby we live out the existence assigned to us. The Mephistophelian view persists as a baiting temptation right to the very end. Liberation from Mephistopheles, the heavenly chorus's redemptive doxology about Faust's completed perfection, begins only beyond this terminus, beyond the point where "the clock's hand falls."

The latter is Goethe's own position, a way to surmount and transcend a dualism that here on earth is insoluble. This act of transcending takes on the form of a *Deus ex machina* which poets have conjured up in order by pure will and faith to establish a decision that is not granted in the form of knowledge to man as he exists this side of death. Mephistopheles is Faust's persistent temptation and even those who witness the concluding transfiguration are left with the question which of the two have the more profound intimations of eternity. Is it Faust who claims to see it in the cyclical immortality of his suprapersonal self? Or is it Mephistopheles who recognizes at least the shadow of an eternity when the clock's hand falls and he sees the nothingness of finite existence that turns like a top back into itself—even if he is devil enough not to see the cause of that nothingness and consequently even here at the moment of his most lofty truth is forced to remain "the spirit that denies," the spirit of "bare negation" (338/11)?

What Mephistopheles senses here with a shudder shows a spark of biblical knowledge about eternity. For according to the biblical view, as we have already said, eternity does not mean a constant "going on and on"; it means that time comes to an end and eternity comes toward us. Eternity presents itself as judgment. It is judgment upon time which inescapably and irretraceably comes to an end, even macrocosmic time viewed as the receptacle for suprapersonal powers by which I hope to overcome death. For sun and moon will lose their light and the stars will fall from heaven, and the end of the world will be the world's grave in which the world is finished (Matt. 24).

The only light that shines at this point is the light of resurrection, the light from beyond the grave, the light from the other side of that end. The demolition of human existence is something the devil Mephistopheles knows better than Faust—and he "shudders" (Jas. 2:19).

GOETHE'S NOTION OF ENTELECHY[11]

In order to round out our treatment of the idea of immortality in Goethe we must still give some attention to his doctrine of the entelechy. We have already referred to this doctrine above where we noted that in the concluding scene of *Faust* Goethe had orig-

[11] The following expanded treatment of the idea of immortality in *Faust* is especially relevant to contemporary biological world views.

inally referred to Faust's "immortality" with the term "entelechy." To be sure, the sparse references by Goethe to an immortality related to entelechy are to be used with maximum caution. These references certainly make up no "dogma" of immortality. On the contrary, they are extremely tentative and very occasional efforts. And when they do occur they are limited almost exclusively to a *via negationis* type of argument, for example, when Goethe on 19 October 1823 responds to Chancellor Von Mueller that it "is completely impossible for a thinking being to imagine itself a nonbeing, ceasing to think and to live."[12] However, in the same conversation he immediately appends the warning by no means to try to establish dogmatic grounds for this certainty nor in philistine fashion to flesh it out. In a very similar vein in his conversations with Eckermann he makes the ironic statement, "Ideas of immortality are something to occupy the upper classes and especially women who have nothing to do,"[13] while a competent man involved in active striving has enough to do in this world.

Just how then does this cautiously-introduced idea of immortality relate to the concept of entelechy? If we may take the classic conversation of Goethe with Falk on 25 January 1813, the day of Wieland's funeral, for our starting point, the answer is that initially he posits an "orderly ranking of the basic primeval component parts" of personality, the innermost of which contains the germ, the monadlike nuclear-I, which therefore might be thought of in analogy to Goethe's "primeval phenomenon." This nuclear-I possesses the character of being teleologically exclusive and self-contained in the sense of the Aristotelian entelechy. It thus constitutes the indestructible element of the I.[14] In view of the anthropology developed in *Faust* this immortal monad takes on significance in several respects.

1) It constitutes a durable element in the I which Goethe runs into again and again on account of that I-division which we have seen to be at the base of all doctrines of immortality: the division

[12] *Goethes Gespräche, Gesamtausgabe,* ed. F. Frh. v. Biedermann, vol. 3 (Leipzig, 1909), p. 26.

[13] 25 February 1824. Ibid., 3:77.

[14] Ibid., 2:170.

into an essential entelechic nucleus of a person, which is immortal, and the nonessential peripheral areas which perish. This becomes clear precisely in the face of Wieland's death when Goethe states very explicitly, "How much or how little of this personality finally deserves to continue existing is a question and a point that we must leave to God."[15] Within the personality there are stages of value with differing rank.

2) The immortal I-segment, the monad or entelechy, is in its teleological structure a microcosmic copy of total life. This is reminiscent of the parabolic structure of the Faustian life which we traced above in connection with the fundamental laws of struggle characteristic of suprapersonal universal life. The entelechy is, as it were, the cosmic I-segment whose immortality is identical with the immortality of the enduring and eternally self-renewing cosmos. In this sense Goethe says in the same conversation, "Creation's coming into being is entrusted to them [namely, the monads]. Whether called or uncalled they come by themselves on every path, from every mountain, out of every sea, from every star. Who can restrain them?"[16] It is surely in terms of this eternal participation in the cosmos, this eternal identity with oneself, that we must also understand the notion of eternal return with which Goethe concludes this conversation: "I am certain that, as you see me here, I have already been here a thousand times and I hope still to return a thousand times more."[17]

This notion of return appears earlier in an entry on his Italian journey[18] and surely stands in the background of his statement to Eckermann: "Every entelechy is a piece of eternity and the few years that it is bound to an earthly body do not make it old."[19] What dies therefore is only the individual receptacle of that cosmic content, the entelechy, which itself remains intact in its eternal identity even though involved in eternal metamorphosis.

3) These words as much as say that what is at stake here is

15 Ibid.
16 Ibid., 2:174.
17 Ibid.
18 Venice, 12 October 1786. *Sämtliche Werke,* 26:111.
19 11 March 1828. *Goethes Gespräche,* 3:495.

not continued personal existence, preservation of the person in its individual and contingent uniqueness.[20] The impersonal character is clearly evident—beyond all that we have already mentioned—in the images of metamorphosis which Goethe occasionally sketches, for example, when he seriously envisions the possibility of meeting again "some day this Wieland as a star of the first magnitude after thousands of years have passed" and then "being a witness of how he with his loving light would refresh and enliven everything that even came close to him."[21] These are the kinds of thoughts which, following Leibniz and Spinoza, can be found also in Lessing.[22] At the same time words such as these clearly emphasize that the entelechy is the cosmic component in man.

In any case no connection at all between immortality and the notion of a moral personhood seems evident. Even the concept of "activity," which can only be considered unlimited and surviving beyond death[23] and which as such constitutes an essential root of Goethe's notion of immortality, is not activity in the sense of moral effort. The moral could at most be considered only one of the possible forms in which that activity occurs. Activity itself however is metaethical. It is a primeval expression of life itself, which Goethe most graphically renders as the "orbiting movement of the monad around itself knowing neither rest nor repose."[24]

[20] The words of Panthalis in the Helena scene of *Faust* II, "Not merit alone, Faithfulness too preserves our personality" (9983-84/293), hardly constitute contrary evidence in view of the inherent norm governing the mythical picture language as well as the actual focus on the lines of "merit and faithfulness." The word "personality" [*Person*] is not at all emphasized or specified. The lines must be interpreted in terms of an analogous statement of Goethe to Knebel (3 September 1781) which is nonfigurative and therefore clearer: "It is an article of my faith that only by perseverence and faithfulness in the present situation are we qualified for a higher level in the subsequent one and capable of entering it, whether it be here in time or there in eternity." In addition there is the famous word to Eckermann concerning unceasing faithful endeavor which obligates nature to continue such an existence beyond death (4 February 1829). Ibid., 4:62.

[21] Conversation with Falk. Ibid., 2:174.

[22] See the thoughts on reincarnation at the conclusion of Lessing's "Erziehung des Menschengeschlechts" and in his "Jakobi-Gespräch." For an interpretation of both see my book, *Vernunft und Offenbarung. Eine Studie über die Religionsphilosophie Lessings* (Gütersloh, 1936), 3rd ed., rev. and enl., 1957.

[23] See the conversation with Eckermann, 4 February 1829. *Goethes Gespräche*, 4:62.

In the same sense Faust's love, which "participates in him from above" as presented in the final scenes of *Faust* II, is the love which makes the lover a participant in perfection (e.g., 11751-52/345). This love is indeed a segment of that teleological eros of the entelechy, which the physician Eryximachus in Plato's *Symposium* characterizes as the fundamental force of the cosmos that "holds the innermost world together"—as Goethe himself would also say.

Right at this point the "nonpersonal" (in the biblical sense, but in other senses as well) character of this continuing existence becomes apparent. For it lacks that unique and irreplaceable character—that identity with itself—that arises in the one case under God's judgment, which puts its finger on "me" and isolates me from all things and all people on whom I might palm off my guilt or with whom I might try to switch places; and in the other case under grace, which also puts the finger on "me" and gives me the name by which it calls me. The soul's "lofty power" in Goethe's sense, the entelechy, is a suprapersonal cosmic element that changes its forms. It is this which the angels at Faust's death carry away in order to grant it another form of the parable, wherein the mystery of life's struggling and striving and orbiting will be reflected anew in a different and yet inevitably the same fashion. The intrinsic quality of man is not his self in its contingent uniqueness, but the self's transparency through which we see life's meaningful struggle—just as the intrinsic quality of an individual plant lies in its transparency through which we see the primeval plant.

Apart from the thought complex focused on the entelechy, which seems to be the prime factor in Goethe's discussion of death, he touches on the subject of death again in various other contexts. Thus, in his "Prometheus fragment" he proclaims the identity between death and life. In the most extreme feeling of joy and of pain, in our feeling of vitality as it is contained and released in the very experience of love, death announces itself as that moment which fulfills everything that we have longed for, dreamed for, hoped for, and feared. Death and the extremities of life lie side

[24] Sprüche in Prosa, *Sämtliche Werke,* 38:250.

by side. And after death, what then? Death is only the blissful sleep in which everything dissolves, in order then to come to life rejuvenated, to fear, to hope, to desire anew.

His Diwan poem, "Selige Sehnsucht" celebrates this proximity of death to the mystery of love and life in the symbol of the butterfly burning in the flame. It is that alien feeling that overtakes us and gives us a premonition that behind the act of reproduction, as an act of mystical unfolding of life, there is a yet higher secret of life which is simultaneously the secret of death. This is the mystery of dying and becoming, the mystery of transformation through flaming death. Here the perishing of which the "Prometheus fragment" speaks is raised to a higher level. To "die and become" transforms man from being merely a dismal guest upon an equally dreary earth.

However, in conversation—above all with Eckermann—it is always the notion of entelechy which appears as the grounds for the indestructibility of life and the conquest of death. Several concluding examples can document this more fully. "The thought of death leaves me in complete peace. For I have the solid conviction that our spirit is a reality of a completely indestructible nature. It is constantly operative from eternity to eternity. It resembles the sun which only seems to set according to our earthly eyes, although actually it never does, but shines forth unceasingly."[25] "But not all of us are immortal in the same way; in order to manifest oneself as something in the future, one also has to be something now."[26] "Those who hope for no other life are also dead to this present one. Yet such incomprehensible things as this lie too far away to become the object of daily observation and thought-destroying speculation. . . . A worthy man, one who sets out to be something decent and therefore has to strive and fight and achieve every day, lets the future world take care of itself while he is active and useful in this present one."[27]

[25] From the conversation of 2 May 1824. *Goethes Gespräche,* 3:104-5.

[26] 1 September 1829. Ibid., 4:163.

[27] Conversation of 25 February 1824. Ibid., 3:76-77. See the discussion above of Goethe's concept of action.

5.

Death Repressed and Privatized in Contemporary Secular Religion

We cannot conclude our treatment of the various types of non-Christian conceptions of death without evaluating secularized man and seeking to understand the way he comprehends the horizon of his existence. Our interest is conditioned less by the contemporary nature of the situation we are here treating than by the posture that secularized man assumes within the various types we have found.

Secularized man is characterized by two circumstances which we must clearly explicate. One is that here man's autonomous self-understanding has arrived at its ultimate possibility, namely, at the boundary of nihilism. And the other is that the movement toward this boundary is shaped by constant interplay with the message of Christ: either by an unconscious historical web that binds it to Christianity or by a conscious polemic whereby man seeks to secure his own indigenous life by rejecting what is presumed to be alien. Nihilism is the most extreme consequence of secularization, and precisely because of its tie with secularization it is nihilism *post Christum.* By virtue of his contact with Christianity the autonomous man of the Western world has in hand a most ultimate standard by means of which he can measure the interior truth about himself to a terrifying degree. Perhaps it is a curse imposed by Christ on those who desert him, that they have come to knowledge because of him without yet having the comfort that sustains them in this knowledge. No one can finally endure such knowledge without comfort. The law, as the genetic source of such knowledge, kills. Knowledge that cannot be endured leads to repression which expresses itself either in glorifying an illusion while ignoring ostrichlike the dangerous facts, or else in heroic defiance or frenzied attempts to forget. We shall have to keep this unconscious tendency in mind as we try to specify the secular interpretation of death. For death is the most dangerous of those dangerous facts; thus in secular man we see death variously glorified, ignored, or held in contempt.

HOW SECULAR RELIGION RANKS DEATH AND LIFE

The relationship between death and life as drawn by secular religion shows its antithesis to the Christian relationship between the two powers all the way down the line. But from the very outset we must once more keep in mind that this antithesis dare not be understood as a goal for its own sake, as though secular religion were only rooted in negativism. Even though this does apply to certain forms of Nazism's "Germanic faith," whose negative attitude has condemned it to sterility, it cannot be applied to secular religion per se. The anti-Christian aspect of secular religion signifies rather its desire to remove all alien religious veneer in order to present its own real essence in authentically pure form.[1]

Secular religion's designated goal is self-liberation of life, whereby life is understood on the basis of its own resources, as represented in the sustaining biological energies of existence (folk, race, etc.). This life receives its structural norms not from the outside but from its own interior resources, thus making the norms, as it were, an ideological superstructure originating from physical life itself.[2] Hence the pragmatic character of these norms, since

1 See the penetrating exposition by Theodor Litt on the impossibility of eliminating historical encounter with Christianity in his *Der deutsche Geist und das Christentum. Vom Wesen geschichtlicher Begegnung* (Leipzig, 1939).

2 See at this point Alfred Rosenberg, *Der Mythus des 20. Jahrhunderts* (Munich, 1930), with his thesis that race, so to speak, is the soul viewed from the outside and the soul is race viewed from the inside. The same applies to Hans Heyse, *Idee und Existenz* (Hamburg, 1935) who correlates *logos* and *bios* in similar fashion. See my debate with the notion in *Theologische Blaettern* 16, no.

life is not responsible to them as a subordinate is to a superior authority, but on the contrary the norms are subordinate to life, inasmuch as they must benefit, promote, and sustain it.[3] Such an inversion of authorities is expressed explicitly in the Nazi thesis, "Good is what benefits the *Volk*."

The process whereby life is liberated to become an autonomous authority cannot, of course, occur apart from constant reference to the "bondage" imposed upon life by Christianity. For it is from this bondage that life is liberated. What this means can be clarified by examining the way that life and death are related in both camps. Here we are once more back at our central theme.

If we were to attempt a crass contrast between the two it might be stated like this: From the perspective of the Christian faith, life is conditioned both forwards and backwards by a totality that encompasses it entirely. This is the horizon line of human existence which is visible in the events of birth and death. These terms themselves are but ciphers for much more complex events. Birth is a cipher for God's bestowing my life to me: "I believe that God made me." Death is a cipher for God's extermination of a life that is at odds with him and has not remained faithful in its creatureliness. (We will treat this in more detail below.) Death so understood casts a retroactive shadow upon birth—or, expressed without ciphers, the fatal end characterizes also the created beginning of the course of human existence so that one can no longer speak of creation without at the same time speaking of the fall and man's vulnerability to nothingness and to the end. Equally certain is the fact that death puts its distinctive stamp upon the horizon of

5/6 (May/June 1937). See also Kaethe Nadler, "Theologische und politische Existenz (Thielicke und Heyse)" in *Der Idee,* 1936, pp. 344 ff.

[3] See Nietzsche's remarks about truth as a force that either promotes or strangles life. He ranks truth not by the degree of its truthfulness, but according to the degree that it does such promoting or strangling. Truth is not something that "exists and is to be found or to be uncovered. Instead it is something that must be created. It is the name for a process which per se is without end, a process of grappling with truth and, in the fray, actively determining it. It is not a process of becoming conscious of something already established and determined" (*Friedrich Nietzsches Werke* [Leipzig: Alfred Kröner, 1917 —], 16:56). "Unconditional knowledge is a madness of the period of virtue; with it life would be demolished. We must sanctify the lie, the insanity of faith, the act of unrighteousness" (ibid., 13:124).

human existence. The adage *memento mori* is a legitimate reminder of the precipice that death injects into human life, how completely life stands in death's shadow and is conditioned by it. From this basis the New Testament even goes further to view death triumphing masterfully over life as the last enemy (1 Cor. 15:26), maintaining its dominion to the very end (Rom. 1:17, 21; 8:38; 1 Cor. 15:55).

While the biblical proclamation sees life as qualified by death and conditioned by death's horizon, secular religion reverses this and views death as receiving its distinctive trademark from life. It cannot be otherwise when life is elevated to the judge's bench as authority, when it becomes the supreme power of being, not only producing all values from itself (instead of receiving them from above) but also having to incorporate within itself as its own most basic content the process of becoming and perishing. Although in the Christian message birth and death constitute the horizon line which encompasses life, in secular religion life encompasses even the powers of being represented by birth and death, or in secular religion's more appropriate labels, the powers of being represented by becoming and perishing. Becoming and perishing are but variations of this life that is constantly in process and constantly self-renewing.[4]

To contrast these two positions very emphatically and one-sidedly we might say: Christian thought interprets life from death, and secular thought interprets death from life.

THE VALUE-FILLED LIFE[5]

What does such an interpretation of death from life look like?

[4] Compare the notion of death as metamorphosis, especially in the more popular secular literature on death. Typical of the group, particularly in its bald and boisterous expression, is Wulf Sörensen, *Freund Hein. Eine Dichtung* (Magdeburg: Norland-Verlag, n.d.). This thought permeates the entire breadth of the secular religion, including its genre of funeral orations.

[5] Since secular thought has not yet produced a classic spokesman who is universally acknowledged as such, I am forced to pinpoint the crucial theses on my own. Even if we build our argument on the rather narrow foundation of the newspaper article cited below, our interpretation does not represent an exaggeration inasmuch as we have constantly in view the whole intellectual milieu out of which these statements about death arise.

It unfolds in rather schizoid form from a basic notion of value. We shall take the liberty of citing a series of newspaper articles symptomatic of this thinking. They can serve in a special way as a seismograph for specific secular ideological eruptions and thus their views on death carry a definite symptomatic weight.[6]

The basic thesis is as follows: "The value of human life, yes, the very measure of achieved human perfection, is expressed in the individual's relation to death." This takes place when he is face to face with eternity (this word remains very ambiguous), when the value of that existence now terminating is decided. A person who has filled his life with value, whose life has been decent and hence perfect, is able at the time of its conclusion to enter "the peace of eternal sleep virtuously . . . worthily, and serenely," while one who has not lived his life to the full, hence imperfectly, has to die "with the cry of the beast."

The conquest of death envisioned here is not so much focused on some durable immortal quality of man from which only his individual shell is taken away. On the contrary, what is durable and immortal is the timeless value in a perfected form (actually in the sense of the Greek concept of *morphe* as a concretization of the reality in the world of ideas), a form that has made itself authentic. Death in consequence is rendered impotent not by being the transition to another form of existence, but by being simply the period placed at the end of a timelessly valid and thereby perfect sentence.

Although this view also understands that a man is unique, granted only once the chance to fill his life with value or fail to do so, still at the moment of death it allows time hardly any role at all. Certainly time has nothing to do with overtaking and extinguishing this unique phenomenon that has arisen within it. No, time can only carry on the work of perfection; at the moment of death time can only "promote the developmental success of the form." Whatever else is there dies with the cry of the beast.

Of course that immediately raises the question: Where is the

[6] See the article already cited above on p. 13 in *Das Schwarze Korps*, 22 June 1939.

judge who can measure and determine the worthiness of a given life, who can decide nothing less than whether death is condemnation or perfection?

In view of the ideology that underlies these thoughts one thing here is clear. This way of thinking must measure the value of a particular being exclusively on the basis of a predetermined idea of "life." Either it fulfills this idea or does not fulfill it, either it becomes the *morphe* of life or else it fails to do so. Such a life, however, is placed within the plenitude and processes of historical life, of which it constitutes one individual representation. Value-fulfillment, then, is not conceived in the sense of Goethe's entelechy, which realizes itself in an individual phenomenon as that individual portrays life. On the contrary, the underlying idea here is an organic totality as it exists, for example, in the supraindividual entity of race. Perfection of life consequently can only mean a pure expression of the race. However, since this race does not exist in the abstract, but drives toward historical expression and historical realization, perfection necessarily also entails meaningful involvement in this process of realization. But being meaningful signifies nothing else than being a serviceable means to the end which the supraindividual reality has itself.

It is obvious that these underlying factors for determining the value of a man's life, that is, its rooting in the transsubjective realities already mentioned, do not always have to be explicit in his consciousness. His existential experience of value generally can and will more likely occur in apparent existential isolation. Either a man looks at his life and rejoices to see the evidence of his value, for example, his accomplishments, or in the face of the evidence of his valuelessness he despairs with the cry of the beast. It is not impossible, however, but necessary, that when these values are brought into consciousness, for example, when he gives account for his performance or when he reflects on his life, he also sees the supraindividual framework within which the values are sketched.

At this point we see that the microcosmic existence of the individual is closely aligned to the macrocosm of the encompassing power, race. And thus the victory over death receives yet another accent. It is not only the perfection of a value-filled existence, but also incorporation into the historical process whereby the encompassing power comes to realization. Thereby perfection is no longer merely the end of a life that has fulfilled its meaning and destiny, not merely a falling away into dreamless sleep. For how could something be labeled perfection if it were at the same time annihilation? Instead perfection means being caught up and supplanted by the value that fills life. This value, however, is not to be understood in analogy to a timelessly valid Platonic idea; after all, it is only an expression of, and a higher moment of elevation for, life itself. Victory over death does not occur in some abstract timelessness as though existence were caught up into some timelessly sound values (e.g., a universal idea of the good) and were translated from temporal annihilation into another world beyond time. If this were true, one could and would have to envision an eternal eye before whose timeless view would stand every being that ever existed and was yet to exist, who had ever exhibited the eternal value in himself. On the contrary, death in this view is conquered when a being realizes those values which express and enhance life and thereby enters into the realm of this very life process. Time, which sets the punctuating period behind a completed existence and thus asserts its dominion, is the time of the race or, in other words, the time of the *Volk*. In any case it is a macrocosmic temporal reality in the framework of which an individual being arises and then again declines. Hence time is not the hostile executioner of perishability, but time is a friend. It does not destroy, but it perfects by accepting the gift of a value-filled life.

For this reason whatever else is present in the I can drift into oblivion without qualms if only the real task has been fulfilled. It is clear enough that when we follow the fragmentary basic thoughts of this extraordinarily contemporary proposition to the very end, we encounter the division of the I. It is not the sleep of death which constitutes perfection, but death itself as culmination of a value-filled life. This culmination simultaneously means a translation of the value-filled life into that stream of history which never ceases to flow. Whatever is translated into the "sleep" is merely what was nonintrinsic. This is the immortality offered by secular religion when orientated toward the idea of life.

SUPPRESSING THE ANXIETY ABOUT DEATH

In rather strange contrast to this ideological program stands the concrete fact of anxiety in the face of death; anxiety is undeniably there, even though it is given short shrift by the author of the article. In fact his basic thoughts are intended to be nothing but a fortifying answer to irrational anxiety about the specters of death's night. It is no wonder that the author is unable to explain this anxiety on the basis of his value ideas, and therefore must try to explain it historically. The specters of anxiety, in his view, have gained entrance into that dreamless sleep via Christian ideas of hell and similar alien apparitions. Thus they owe their existence to what Nietzsche called the nonsense Christianity has promoted about the hour of death. This factually present anxiety cannot be explained by any sinking into dreamless sleep, into nothingness, as it were, and still less by the idea that one's value-filled life is translated into history's realm of value. For with this idea that what is essential in one's life does not fall prey to annihilation but is translated (in the Hegelian sense), death could really come only as *"Freund Hein"*[7] and not as the power of destruction that drives me to despair.[8] In the face of this one cannot deny the irritating fact that de facto anxiety about death is present not only in spite of that experience of value but is in fact based on the experience of value, albeit value of another kind.

In his study of French secularism and its concept of death,

[7] *"Freund Hein"* is a designation for death in the poetry of Matthias Claudius.

[8] It is in this sense that Paul Krannhals is logically consistent when he measures the value of an individual according to his achievements for the supraindividual entities (state, *Volk,* cultural community, "soul" of the species, idea of god). Thereby he deduces that in view of a man's placement within the supraindividual realities his individual death is meaningless. See especially his *Das organische Weltbild. Grundlage einer neu entstehenden Kultur,* 2 vols. (Munich, 1928). In addition *Religion als Sinnerfüllung des Lebens* (Leipzig, 1933); *Revolution des Geistes* (Leipzig, 1935). See also the extensive appropriation and approbation of Krannhals in Otto Dietrich, *Die philosophischen Grundlagen des Nationalsozialismus* (Munich, 1935).

Bernhard Groethuysen arrives at the entirely correct conclusion that in every instance where "the last moment" is accorded special significance it receives this significance not by being a farewell from a basically valueless life. On the contrary, death receives its significance from "the value that is ascribed to life."[9] On such grounds one could say that anxiety about death is actually rooted in a man's consciousness of value, in that his life as person (the I) ceases to exist; the unique fades away. In the face of death's darkness the "cry of the beast" grows silent since an animal possesses no such value-filled life; a much more terrifying, though perhaps suppressed and sublimated, cry comes from man who sees his own self, his distinctive I, exterminated. Speaking of this cry, then, who is really doing the crying: man or beast? Is it a life that is value-filled or a life where value is not involved?

But precisely when we realize that such supraindividual value which is to be translated into history provides no explanation for such a cry, we are directed to that other stratum of value from which the anxiety does arise, namely, the value of the self as a person, an irreplaceable entity now coming to an end and in mortal isolation actually moving toward this end. Speaking in another context, Heidegger very forcefully portrays how human "talk" about death as "its reality is publicly interpreted" follows the line not that "I" die, but that "one" dies[10] and that it is anxiety that represses the thought of "I" dying and transposes it upon "one" as something exterior to me.[11] On this level, anxiety about death and consciousness of value are interrelated. By pushing the element of value onto a suprapersonal level, the level of that which

[9] *Die Entstehung der bürgerlichen Weltanschauung in Frankreich*, vol. 1, *Das Bürgertum und die katholische Weltanschauung* (Halle, 1927), p. 83.

[10] Martin Heidegger, *Being and Time*, trans. John Macquarrie and Edward Robinson (New York: Harper and Brothers, 1962), p. 297.

[11] See the words of Peter Ivanovich in Leo Tolstoi, *The Death of Ivan Ilych and Other Stories* (New York: New American Library, 1960), p. 102, as he views the dead Ivan: " 'Three days of frightful suffering and then death! Why, that might suddenly happen to me,' he thought and for a moment felt terrified. But—he did not himself know how—the customary reflection at once occurred to him that this had happened to Ivan Ilych and not to him, and that it should not and could not happen to him. . . . After which reflection Peter Ivanovich felt reassured . . . as though death was an accident natural to Ivan Ilych but certainly not to himself."

endures, therefore pulling it away from any anxiety about perishing, man only represses that more profound anxiety about the personal value of his uniqueness, his I, sinking into oblivion.

It is expressive of such anxiety repression that the paradigm for death is a far-off sacrificial death for a cause, especially a hero's death, in comparison with which normal dying in a deathbed seems strangely unreal. Such emphasis on sacrificial death, considering the ideological backdrop already presented, is entirely logical and consistent. For sacrificial death is the most explicit mode of filling life with value, inasmuch as a supraindividual value, for example, the nation that I am dying for, is certainly incorporated into my life as I die. Inversely, my life is also delivered up to the higher power where it is translated in a twofold sense. On the one hand this suprapersonal power is granted continued life by virtue of my sacrifice and thereby, so to speak, assumes the role of representing my departed life and maintaining its value; secondly, the memory of my sacrifice is kept alive. The cult of the dead hero is the primeval expression for this.[12]

REPRESSION AND STYLE OF LIFE

One cannot speak of these episodes of repressing anxiety about death and projecting the death-event to another level without calling to mind the style of life which secular man assumes and in which such reinterpretation of dying comes to expression.

In public secular life death plays practically no role at all except perhaps in terms of dying for a cause. Death is banned from secular life in such a remarkable way that one might ask whether its banishment from public view is the cause or the result of that conspicuous conspiracy of avoiding everything connected with death.

[12] Heidegger rightly calls attention to the fact that when one dies for another, despite the vicarious sense, the conclusion dare never be drawn that the other is relieved of dying. "No one can take the Other's dying away from him. Of course someone can 'go to his death for another'. But that always means to sacrifice oneself for the Other 'in some definite affair'. Such 'dying for' can never signify that the Other has thus had his death taken away in even the slightest degree. . . . By its very essence, death is in every case mine, in so far as it 'is' at all. . . .In dying, it is shown that mineness and existence are ontologically constitutive for death." *Op. cit.*, p. 284.

The following are some aspects of this banishment:[13]

1) All events which hint of the boundaries of human life are purged—whether consciously or unconsciously, whether arising from the will or the confusion of human beings—from public life.

Sickness as the symptom of perishability is largely banished to the hospitals. This applies especially to the gruesome borderline cases of mental illness. They are isolated and removed from public view. Movies and the theater of prewar Germany simply mirror the healthy life to such an exclusive extent that they thereby not only engrave the ideal image of a healthy person upon the spectator's heart, but at the same time nurture the illusion that this picture of health is life *in toto.* As a consequence of this illusory repression it then becomes possible to play off something like the idealized figure of a Kolbe[14] sculpture as the one symbol of life against the unnerving sculpture in the Bamberg cathedral of Bishop Friedrich von Hohenlohe (d. 1351), whose emaciated figure not only testifies to physical pain but also to the torment brought on by an overpowering knowledge of truth that has grown via suffering.

Related to this is the cult of youth, which is not part of the conscious intention of the public either, but results more as a consequence from the cult of good health.

The same repression is apparent in the events of birth and death. Only in rural areas might one still hear the cry of a mother giving birth. In the city the sound most often dies away behind the walls of the maternity ward. In any case the general consciousness is much more deprived of the glorious dreadfulness of this event than it was in earlier times. It is all the more so since the birth-event usually comes to public attention only in terms of population explosion, biological energy, and life's own joyous self-renewal. Birth is hardly ever considered in terms of the one's own personal perilous hour, an hour whose peril resides not merely in the physi-

[13] This section is closely related to several lines of thought in my work on cultural criticism, *Fragen des Christentums an die moderne Welt* (Tübingen, 1948).

[14] [Georg Kolbe, 1877-1947, a German sculptor whose statues and national memorials reflected the Greek ideal of physical beauty, was for a time highly favored by the Nazi regime.—Trans.]

cal suffering, but in risking one's life and in the thrilling horror of exposing one's own life as well as that of the newly born to the grand and ominous mysteries of human existence. Birth as a boundary situation of life is privatized and removed from the public eye.

The same applies to death, with which birth and illness are essentially related. Symbolic of this is the fact that in our cities, our genuinely public places, no longer do funeral processions pass ominously through the streets, at least not the major streets, the expressways. Instead these are reserved only for the ghetto of the cemeteries. This banishment is not intentional but results from considerations of transportation, hygiene, and economics. Still it is a remarkably crafty product of the dominant idea: indirectly and yet explicitly showing that death is ignored, and simultaneously helping create the conditions which allow for its being ignored.[15]

How are these facts to be understood? Are they the expression of life's genuine triumph that no longer knows death? Or are they the expression of a catatonic attitude that no longer wants to accept death as true because it cannot come to terms with it, because it can no longer generate the "courage to confront the anxiety about death"[16] and therefore in despair grasps at such systematic repression?

2) To this must be added that secular man intentionally avoids the existential situation into which death places a man, namely, the situation of solitude. For solitude throws him back onto the primeval roots of his personhood and strips him of the illusion that he is simply a piece of something called the crowd. The more a man becomes conscious of the vacuity and lostness in his personhood, the more he flees from it into the anonymity of being part of the crowd, into the frenzied activity of overwork and orgies, into the constant companionship of amplified noise that drowns out all the voices of emptiness. "The man caught up in the tempo of the times can find a vacation with relaxation and recreation only

[15] For a brilliant description of this depletion of content in public life see Paul Schütz, *Warum ich noch ein Christ bin* (Berlin, 1933).

[16] Heidegger, *op. cit.*, p. 298.

if he does not feel the stress of solitude."[17] In his *horror vacui* he is comforted by the voice of the portable record player even out in his canoe, while normally the cafe, the movies, and the lights of the city are able to take possession of his empty I-region. "All the unhappiness of men arises from one single fact, that they cannot stay quietly in their own chamber."[18]

In terms of the attitude toward death this style of life is significant because it eliminates any situation of personal solitude—Heidegger would say that quality of my life and death which makes it "mine and mine alone"—in which one would have to reckon with death. Thus it deceives man about the factual presence of his own indelible character as a person, even an inevitably mortal person. This style of life is also significant for the attitude toward death simply by brutally and physically disallowing the least space for the thought of *memento mori* to arise. Death does not exist; it is not supposed to exist for the man of secular religion.

The most significant illustration of this can perhaps be found in the mass dying of the Bolsheviks in the great offensives of the Second World War. Some ultimate aversion restrains Western man, who has at least a Christian tradition behind him, to speak here simply of "sacrifice" (i.e., of individual self-oblation) and of "heroism" (i.e., of a position consciously assumed in the face of personal death), since for him something decisive is missing for both terms. Such collective death of collective man renders it almost impossible to surrender one's spirit or to breathe out one's soul since both are dissipated into the collective nonexistence of the self. There no longer exists any self who encounters death as "his and his alone." All that is involved anymore is the elimination of a number. Death has taken a somewhat biological, animal cast. It has here become an extreme, but nevertheless especially clear, paradigm of secularized death per se, namely, death within the realm of anonymous man, a "crowd" death, whereby death has ceased to be "my" death because I have ceased to be "my self."

Rilke succeeded in expressing anonymous man's elimination

[17] From an advertisement for radios.

[18] Blaise Pascal, *Pensées,* Modern Library Edition (New York: Random House, 1941), p. 48 (#139).

of authentic human death in terms that pierce beneath the surface. He calls such collective death "little death" in contrast to grand, "mature," "authentic" death, giving the following eerie picture: "Now they are dying there in 559 beds. Factory-like, of course. Where production is so enormous an individual death is not so nicely carried out; but then that doesn't matter. It is quantity that counts. Who cares anything today for a finely-finished death? . . . the wish to have a death of one's own is growing ever rarer. A while yet, and it will be just as rare as a life of one's own. Heavens, it's all there. One arrives, one finds a life, ready made, one has only to put it on. . . . One dies just as it comes; one dies the death that belongs to the disease one has (for since one has come to know all diseases, one knows, too, that the different lethal terminations belong to the diseases and not to the people; and the sick person has so to speak nothing to do)."[19]

Within the collective, therefore, man is forced into a kind of death that is alien and impersonal to him and only characterized by the sickness that leads to it. Thus Rilke can say in his *Stundenbuch,* "For this is what makes death alien and hard, that it is not *our* death; it is one that finally takes us simply because we do not mature our own; therefore the storm proceeds to wipe us all out."[20] For this reason he pleads for a death that is personally his own, which makes a man solely a man and protects him from an animal's demise. "Oh Lord, give each one his own death. The dying that proceeds from such life, wherein he had his own love, meaning and troubles."[21]

[19] Rainer Maria Rilke, *The Notebooks of Malte Laurids Brigge,* trans. M. D. Herter Norton (New York, W. W. Norton & Co., 1964), pp. 17-18.

[20] Rainer Maria Rilke, *Das Stundenbuch* (Leipzig: Insel-Verlag, 1931), p. 87.

[21] Ibid., p. 86. Rilke is here propounding the thought that each one should bring his own death to maturity. Death has the significance of a fruit, which a man should let grow in his own life and which then belongs to him as his very own, grown to his own specifications. Bullnow's article "Existenzphilosophie" in *Systematische Philosophie,* ed. N. Hartmann (Stuttgart and Berlin, 1942), p. 391, calls attention to the fact that "in the final analysis the notion of death as a fruit to be nourished is still an evasion of the full force and sinister character of death." It approaches "once more certain conceptions already occasionally expressed in Romanticism." In Rilke's later works, especially in the "Sonetten an Orpheus," this changes completely and he understands death as failure and fragility, yet simultaneously something that enables "other men to perceive the meaning of being human at all" precisely in its own qualities of transformation and destruction.

But now back to our description of the secular style of life with its depersonalization via artificial maneuvers to avoid every encounter with one's own solitude. To express the secular style of life in a strict formula that would do justice theologically to the idea of flight from oneself and thus flight from death, one might say: the directional movement in the life of man when he is bonded to God is one of centripetal gathering, whereby he reflects on the basics and unifies them for restoration and growth. Thus he "girds up his mind" (1 Pet. 1:13; see Eph. 6:14; 1 Thess. 5:8) and is protected against losing himself centrifugally to the outside.

In complete contrast to this gathering movement secular man finds his recovery in dissipation,[22] that is, in losing himself. It is basically man's inability any longer to confront himself and his own emptiness face to face. A synonym for this dissipation is "diversion," which is not so much a sidestepping of some discomforting, worrisome thing as it is a sidestepping of one's own I, entangled as the I is in this worry, vulnerable to it with no counterforce of its own, and thrashing aimlessly as it confronts its own emptiness.[23] Secular man as a rule does not seek to confront the reality of suffering by standing fast (that would be a movement of centripetal gathering), by placing it within some larger meaning or by conquering it with a frontal attack. But by diversion and by looking the other way, he nourishes the fascinating dream that such tactics might make the fear and the reality that caused it disappear. A monstrous, even if unconscious, self-irony resides thus in the illusion that he might thereby successfully disdain the reality that generates the fear, as for example, death. The contempt which perhaps does arise is the contempt of concern, of refusing to acknowledge the reality. It is contempt assisted by an act of repression. But is that really contempt or is it not rather a terrifying, even if unconsciously attentive, fascination with death? Is this not precisely to be spellbound by it?

The dissipation which avoids death is thereby unconsciously an

[22] It goes without saying that we are here contrasting types which in praxis are not present in pure form, although on the whole they can clearly be recognized as types.

[23] Pascal, *op. cit.*, the section on diversion, pp. 48 ff.

important existential interpretation of death. In consideration of what we have already said about it we can specify its characteristics in several respects.

1) On the one hand dissipation shows that the one doing it is unable to withstand the objects of his anxiety, but turns away from them and to that extent represses them.

2) The frightening thing in this situation is not the object to be avoided, but the frightened man himself who is threatened with exposure in his lostness, his inability to master the problem.

3) The existential cause of dissipation is thus one's own emptiness. In other words, no counterforce is present to achieve mastery of the problem, neither the counterforce of intellect which might take the spellbinding object of terror and draw it into the light of some meaningful totality, nor the counterforce of power which could defy the specters.[24]

4) The existential cause of dissipation therefore is one's own vacuity which drives one to flee in the face of nothingness. When such cases arise we are accustomed to say that a man is bored, or when several are together, that they are bored with each other.

5) Dissipation is therefore simultaneously an expression of, a consequence of, and an actual occurrence of this vacuity. It is an expression of vacuity inasmuch as it proclaims anxiety vis-à-vis a nothingness that is becoming all the more obvious.

It is a consequence of vacuity inasmuch as the dissipating man can no longer be alone and no longer has any singularity, any self; this situation of having nothing anymore reminds him in terror that he ought to have it, that he has lost himself and that it is his own fault. Finally, dissipation is the occurrence of vacuity inasmuch as it drives a man to surrender ever more completely and to lose himself ever more totally. Man can still endure the vacuity only by ever more frantic attempts to have something external occupy his empty I-region, the vacated temple of God, for

[24] Ibid., pp. 79-80. There exist individual clear-eyed spirits such as Ernst Jünger who do not look away, but look the specters in the eye. Actually the situation of adventure into which they plunge is a higher way of avoiding the view. The chief characteristic of their fundamental stance is not standing ground in the face of the terror, but rejoicing in one's own fortitude and daring—a remarkable sort of therapy by inverting the view!

this zone is never unoccupied long. The more he reels, the more furiously he plunges into the frenzy. He seeks release from the impressions madly storming in upon him and taking possession of him, but he seeks it only through even stronger impressions, through the centrifugal tendency of an even more frenzied dissipation for which modern technology willingly supplies all sorts of auxiliary media. Of dissipation it is quite true: He who has nothing (and thus in dissipating seeks to forget and be secure), even what he has is taken from him by this very dissipation. Though dissipation may appear to be the pursuit of happiness, it is born of unhappiness. "If man were happy, he would be the more so, the less he was diverted, like the saints and god."[25]

6) Dissipation—always understood as the expression of an existentially conditioned style of life—must in the first place be understood as a direct diversion from death. Secondly, it is also an indirect one, that is, a diversion from the solitary I of human personhood, which in dying has no vicarious substitute and which hopes somehow via diversion and via "self-extinction by losing itself in" something to save itself from death. (A characteristic symptom for both forms of diversion can be found in the fact that secular man craves intoxication precisely at those stations of life which most clearly reflect his transitoriness: on the eve of battle and on New Year's Eve.)

7) Dissipation therefore is flight from nothingness and from the annihilation which man still sees approaching. Both of these —flight from nothingness and from annihilation—are inextricably interwoven. This becomes apparent if one considers that nothingness—as Heidegger labels it, "Being-toward-death"—is the looming shadow of annihilation coming to exterminate an existence that already knows itself to be null and void. Heidegger is right in connecting anxiety about death with anxiety about "Being-in-the-world" itself,[26] since death conditions such Being-in-the-world and belongs to it. Anxiety, or as we said, flight from death, is characterized by the knowledge that we are at the end of our rope

[25] Ibid., p. 60.

[26] Heidegger, *op. cit.*, p. 295.

just as surely as we will be someday when our actual death takes place; for it will be only confirmation of the public secret that we were already at the end of our rope. "Every man is a mere breath" no matter how securely he lives, or how much repression he practices (Ps. 39:11). Biblically interpreted, security might be labeled repressed anxiety. Conquered anxiety, however, when one is pulled free by the saving hand of God, is called "peace."[27] If Christ be not raised, that is, if there exists no real conquest of the power of death, liberating our self from subjection to death, then we are of all men most miserable (1 Cor. 15:14-19). This misery signifies that both the internal and external security of our life was no realistic peace, but repression of the paramount reality. It signifies that our self in its attempts at security by dissipation is exposed as one lost in nothingness. And our self in a dreadful involution of its nothingness—by means of dissipation and repression—has even lost that which it did possess. Is it not obvious to everyone, legible right from the faces of people today,[28]

[27] "Peace" according to the biblical use of language is not a psychological phenomenon. If one were to isolate peace psychologically, the psychologist's perception of it would probably be similar to the psychically isolated phenomenon of "security." Nevertheless the phenomena are objectively different. For peace initially takes place outside of man, in the objective peace with God by virtue of the reconciliation in Christ. This reconciliation, however, entails man's appropriating it from the posture of repentance. And repentance in turn means willingly turning away from the spellbinding powers of existence, from sin and its causes and consequences, in such a way as to face these powers realistically, consciously letting oneself be placed under judgment. Peace therefore is granted to man standing under the law; it comes even while man realistically shoulders his burden of slavery to sin and death, a slavery exposed by the law in all its realism. If one were crassly to juxtapose the two phenomena, peace and security, one might say: Security lives on the resources of untruth inasmuch as the true realities are repressed and an "as if not" illusion is the source of the self-securing existence. Peace, on the contrary, lives from the truth. Peace is bestowed in face-to-face confrontation with death's hideous strength and its yawning abyss.

[28] See Ernst Jünger, *Das abenteuerliche Herz,* 1st ed. (Hamburg, 1929), pp. 91 ff. "One can see that the face of the modern urbanite carries a twofold trademark: that of anxiety and that of the dream, the one more obvious in his movement, the other in his repose. . . . It is for this reason that street corners and bridges in the metropolis are so infinitely sad and depressing. Whoever has looked into the faces of fishermen in a southern harbor, who surely haven't a penny in their ragged pockets, knows for certain that it cannot be money which is able to bring out these half-sullen, half-harried beings. In a crisis such as this, in the midst of highest insecurity, no peaceful satisfaction is possible. There is but one thing that can be set against it: Bravery. . . .

"It is just as remarkable to observe the completely ossified, automated, and almost narcotic behavior of modern man in circumstances of repose, for example, that by repressing the ultimate concerns, especially that horizon which threatens our life, we do not by any means confine nothingness and emptiness to the position they have won but render them ever more vacuous and accelerate the loss of substance as though by some law of arithmetical progression? Does not man's flight into a state of lost personhood where death can no longer find a vulnerable spot (because death finds no prey extant and its victim has evaporated into the collective) simultaneously induce and promote that loss of personhood? Is it not true that man really cannot eradicate himself, that he always retains just enough personhood to despair over his loss of self and be compelled to repress the loss and seek escape from himself?

It is precisely this latter perspective that makes one thing clear: Neither the ideological repression of death by transfering value to supraindividual powers nor the ignoring of death by means of one's style of life can occur without some remnant of the subconscious knowledge that one must die,[29] even if funeral processions no longer pass through the main thoroughfares proclaiming their *memento mori.* As men hasten through these emptied streets with glances that manage to ignore everything eternal, they are of course expressing their alleged security in the face of threatening nothingness and annihilation. But do not these glances and this haste along such death-free streets simultaneously express a kind of spatial phobia about these emptied streets? Does not man still have a presentiment of some grim disaster and therefore flee from whatever nocturnal visions might confront him? Here, too, dying is still the gruesome mask, and despite attempts to aestheticize, repress, or avoid it, behind it all the grim token of death's anxiety remains:

while traveling on public transportation. One would hardly find such a degree of inversion and lostness present on these masks even in a Chinese opium den. The uncommonly similar and typical character of this expression betrays the decisive fact that the occurrences are inescapable and universal. . . . Wake up and be brave—that's what ought to be on our banner."

[29] One might only recall that according to Rom. 1:18 ff. despite man's idolatry and despite his repression of the true Creator he still retains some knowledge of him, a knowledge strong enough to make man responsible. For an age that knows so much about the unconscious, these thoughts ought not to be all too alien.

. . . unresolved the riddle of eternal night,
the earnest token of an alien might.[30]

The only ethos that man can still produce in this crisis of his own lost personhood is the aristocratic ethos of bravely holding out in the face of nothingness. In the words of Saint Paul this is the power with which the "miserable man" of 1 Cor. 15 looks nothingness and annihilation in the eye. "In a crisis such as this, in the midst of highest insecurity, no peaceful satisfaction is possible. There is but one thing that can be set against it: Bravery."[31]

DEATH REINTERPRETED AT THE LAST MOMENT

It might be helpful in this connection to consider the interpretation of death presented by the French physician Barbarin in the guise of psychological statistics.[32] Up to this point we have always examined secular religion's attitude toward death in two ways: first under the rubric of reinterpreting death by an ideological repression (cf. our line of thought on value-experience in the face of death), and then under the rubric of removing death from the public domain (cf. the thoughts on flight into personlessness and into dissipation). In both instances, however, death as a brute biological act—beyond all the problems about personhood that it causes—remains unavoidable. At least it remains unavoidable in the sense that every man in answer to the question whether he must die says yes, and even the man who has lost his personhood still has at least his *biological* end before his eyes (even though as a future reality it is not *constantly* before his eyes).

Barbarin now addresses himself to the task of clearing away even this remnant of death on the soil of secular existence. He does this with the aid of a wealth of material obtained from people condemned to death, from survivors of plane crashes, from people rescued from drowning at the last moment, etc. He shows statistically that the last moments before death are actually exhilarating

[30] Novalis, the fifth of his *Hymnen an die Nacht* in *Novalis' Werke,* ed. J. Dohmke (Leipzig and Vienna: Bibliographisches Institut, n.d.), p. 14.

[31] Jünger, *op. cit.,* p. 92. Note the overtones of, yet opposition to, the peace described above.

[32] Georges Barbarin, *Der Tod als Freund* (Stuttgart, 1938).

and liberating. It is only the pathway up to death's border that is characterized by suffering and shock, by anxiety and terror, whereas death itself comes as a friend and liberator, always accompanied by a state of euphoria.

For our consideration the factual content of these observations is immaterial. If we wish to focus consideration on man's understanding of himself, it is immaterial whether the process of dying is subjectively painful or not. What is important, however, is the viewpoint about the essence of dying which invisibly stands behind this statistical investigation with all its intended precision. This viewpoint, which is very instructive for the self-understanding of human existence at its base, is characterized by the fact that in its own way it too isolates, banishes, and represses the event of death. It isolates death both from life, over which death thus as yet casts no shadow and for which death is no companion, and also from eternity, to which it leads. Death is a point built into the life process at random which very casually, almost accidentally, constitutes the terminal point without in any way being characteristic of the life process itself. Life expires in a fade-out that is only of psychological, but not of ontological, interest. Death is considered the last moment, but no longer the last enemy. It is a last moment which still belongs to the sum of life's moments as the euphoric termination of them all, but death is no longer viewed as one of life's own constitutive features.[33] What an impoverished banishment of death this is, with nothingness itself as its trademark, and yet a banishment which often enough constitutes the only means for a physician to practice "Seelsorge" at the deathbed!

[33] In contrast to Barbarin see the profound statement by Maurice Maeterlinck, *The Treasure of the Humble,* trans. Alfred Sutro (New York: Dodd, Mead and Co., n.d.), p. 68: "Our death is the mould into which our life flows: it is death that has shaped our features."

6.

Secular Realism in Heidegger's View of Death

Martin Heidegger's interpretation of death stands as a monumentally singular phenomenon amidst these forms of secular religion.[1] It is the philosophy of an unrepressed knowledge of death, a knowledge that has been opened up in a very specific way.

The complex of questions related to death arises for Heidegger in one instance as he traces the phenomenon of "care" which he characterizes as "Dasein's basic state."[2] In addition death comes into focus as he investigates to what extent "Being-a-whole" is possible for Dasein, since the very phenomenon of care makes wholeness problematic. For "the structure of care tells us unambiguously that in Dasein there is always something still outstanding," that part and parcel of Dasein's basic structure is the fact that "there is constantly something still to be settled."[3] To this extent Dasein in its totality appears in principle to be beyond experience, because "when Dasein reaches its wholeness in death, it simultaneously loses the Being of its 'there,' "[4] and thus the very subject of the experiencing act ceases to be. Even experiencing the

[1] Here too our concern is not to present all of Heidegger's thoughts on the subject, but instead to highlight that aspect that is turned toward our present considerations.

[2] Martin Heidegger, *Being and Time,* trans. John Macquarrie and Edward Robinson (New York: Harper and Brothers, 1962), p. 293.

[3] Ibid., p. 279.

[4] Ibid., p. 281.

death of others is no help at this point because no vicarious representation in the act of death is possible.[5]

However, death is by no means simply to be understood as the terminal point in the course of life, as if it could really be compressed into that one spot in the manner in which Barbarin views it. Death's characteristic as the final point may at most reflect the biological fact that a life dies down the way an engine dies down when out of gas. Yet this dying down always represents only one side of death. In a unique way, however, death belongs to life itself. The end of life as something still outstanding, something that is "not yet," is not simply a future reality separated from my present, but as such it already belongs to my Dasein now. Even those aspects of Dasein which are yet to come are still Dasein; they belong to it. One might express the way the end belongs to Dasein as follows: "The 'ending' which we have in view when we speak of death, does not signify Dasein's Being-at-an-end [*Zu-Ende-Sein*], but a *Being-towards-the-end {Sein Zum Ende}* of this entity. Death is a way to be, which Dasein takes over as soon as it is."[6] "Death, in the widest sense, is a phenomenon of life,"[7] which Heidegger designates "dying" *{Sterben}* in contrast to the act of "demise" *{Ableben}*.[8] To this extent dying as a characteristic of life belongs to life itself. Every man is constitutionally thrust toward his death. He appropriates it and relates himself to it in every moment of life.

[5] Ibid., p. 284.

[6] Ibid., p. 289. Cf. Rilke, *Briefe*, 5:90-91 (cited by Hans Urs von Balthasar, *Apokalypse der deutschen Seele. Studie zu einer Lehre von den letzten Haltungen* [Salzburg and Leipzig, n.d.], 3:212) who sees this characteristic of death (as belonging to life immanently and not merely at the end of life) also operative in nature: "But nature knows nothing of any possibly successful repression [namely, of death—in this case Rilke means repression into the realm of ideas]. If a tree blossoms, then death blossoms in it as well as life; and the grain field is full of death which sends forth from its prostrate countenance a rich expression of life; and the animals move indulgently from one to the other. . . . Lovers do not live from the resources of the ones who have been taken from them; as if no separation had ever taken place, they dip into the overwhelming assets of their own hearts. Of them it can be said that God becomes real and death does them no harm; they are full of death by virtue of the fact that they are full of life."

[7] *Being and Time*, p. 290.

[8] Ibid., p. 291.

When compared with the secular repression of the knowledge of death as we depicted it above, Heidegger's restoration of this knowledge might be summarized as follows. First of all, death is an existential phenomenon.[9] As such it is characterized by the fact that when I have appropriated it, that is, in my dying, I cannot be vicariously represented. "No one can take the Other's dying away from him."[10] At this point human dying is distinguished in three ways[11] from the death of an animal, the death of one of a species, which Heidegger designates "perishing."[12]

1) One aspect is death's quality of being "mine and mine alone" in which no one can vicariously represent me. This "mine and mine alone" refers primarily to the fact that death strikes me personally, which fact I gladly conceal by letting an anonymous "they" come to my aid: "they" die, but not "I" die.[13] "The 'they' does not permit us the courage for anxiety in the face of death."[14]

2) Human dying is further distinguished in that dying also touches my existence. Existence is "that kind of Being towards which my Dasein comports itself"[15] It is entrusted to me only once as a task to be fulfilled during the time that my Dasein moves toward death. Since the particular course of my Dasein is unique, within which I either achieve or fail my existence, my "dying" is also unique in contrast with the "perishing" of animals.

At this point it becomes apparent that Heidegger's characterizations of death are very close to our previous tentative terminology on the uniqueness, the irreplaceable character, and the personal dimension of human dying. The irreplaceable aspect constitutes an analogy to Heidegger's concept of "mine and mine alone"; the personal dimension has a certain (even if only formal) connection

9 Ibid., p. 284.

10 Ibid.

11 Heidegger himself does not isolate these three aspects directly. They appear only indirectly. Nevertheless they are so close to his own line of thought that we are convinced we are not importing our opinions into his thinking.

12 *Being and Time,* p. 291.

13 Ibid., pp. 297-98.

14 Ibid., p. 298.

15 Ibid., p. 32.

to his concept of existence, inasmuch as both person and existence are constituted by the uniqueness in which they are carried out. It is in this unique "carrying out" of my existence, that I either hit or miss the mark of myself, that is, that unique disposition of my Dasein. Expressed with more precision: the way I carry out my existence characterizes my life's time as a time of decision and I move through this time only once with no possibility for revision. (The concept of person as we use it will be filled with more positive and more precise content in Part Two.)

In all of this Heidegger expresses the solitary isolation of human dying, the Being-toward-death of personified Dasein. This dying is in a qualitatively different realm from that of biological death.

3) Heidegger's concept of death is qualified by the fact that dying is a characteristic of Dasein itself from its very beginning, and consequently cannot be confined to a chronologically terminal point, that is, compressed into the act of perishing and thereby repressed from Dasein itself. This is implicit already in what was said in point one above. Dasein as totality is Being-toward-death and inasmuch as Dasein is cognitive of itself, it entails the appropriation of this death. Here too human dying is characterized by its distinctiveness. Since there is no doubt that a human being's existence as Dasein is distinguished from the kind of existence animals have (even though this distinction itself in essence stems from man's being qualified by dying), by the same token human dying is qualitatively and infinitely different from biological termination. Human dying appears gruesome and yet sublimely singular as it looms up out of the realm of the biological. It interrupts the rhythm of procreation and perishing with a precipitous silence reminiscent of the sudden quiet that greets a strange guest when he enters a circle of close friends. In the face of this alien event Dasein is called upon to forego all illusion and repression, and, in the anxiety that arises when he does so, willingly to admit anxiety and to appropriate death in freedom.[16] Not dissimilar to this thought is Karl Jasper's speaking of "being ready for death."[17]

[16] Ibid., pp. 310-11.

[17] This being ready for death is an attitude in which "life is overcome without despising it. The pain of death must always be experienced anew; existential

If we compare these qualities of existence as Heidegger sees them in human Dasein and human dying (mine and mine alone, irreplaceable, Dasein as Being-toward-death, the mania for repression) with the other secular ideological types which we introduced as paradigms of natural man's interpretation of existence, we notice a uniqueness about his thought that cannot be incorporated with them.[18] For, as a typical quality of natural man's interpretation we detected the drive toward immortality everywhere, for example, in such things as the tendency toward depersonalizing, the proclamation of suprapersonal entities, the idea of substitutionary representation, etc. Inextricably bound together with all that, we saw the trend toward repression which penetrated even the most sublime ideological forms.

Now in Heidegger we see all this removed. We detect everywhere in his world of thought a realism about dying known otherwise only in the biblical message about death. This is because it proclaims the uniqueness of human personhood, the irreversible character of the course of time (time of decision, the notion of *kairos*) and the impossibility of having other persons, things, or powers, replace anyone in his life and death.

Where does the singular stance of this secular philosophy come from? In Heidegger's philosophizing we find ourselves suddenly transplanted into a landscape set off by a post-Christian picture frame. Since it is in the frame of a secularized existence, his philosophy simultaneously makes clear that it is not proposing a pure paganism, but is still holding out in its shattering clash with Christianity. In the midst of its collapse it can move neither back to a pre-Christian naive ignorance nor forward to an a-Christian neutral understanding of human existence, where the Christian elements are simply eliminated.[19]

certainty can always be attained anew. Life becomes more profound, existence more certain in the face of death; but life remains in danger of losing itself in anxiety before the emptiness in which existence shrouds itself." Karl Jaspers, *Philosophie*, vol. 2 (Berlin, Göttingen, and Heidelberg, 1932), p. 227.

18 This distinctive quality is applicable to Jaspers too, although not to the same extent. It is less applicable, as we shall yet see, because of his greater independence of Christian categories.

19 Contra Rudolf Bultmann: "Die Geschichtlichkeit des Daseins und der

It is a report on the human situation based on a nonillusionary realism, but—to use an illustration—it is the kind of realism found in the reports of a foreign correspondent who indeed sees men dying, indeed sees their worries and even the manifest evidences of their anxiety, yet does not penetrate the inner connections and the subsurface aspects of the events. Heidegger sees, as it were, the consequences of a judicial verdict—man thrust toward death, incarcerated in his cell of temporality—but not the verdict itself that created this situation.

To move away from the illustration, this means that the knowledge that Dasein is subject to death, even the many details of that knowledge, arises from the nonillusionary way in which God's law, especially in its Pauline formulation, exposes the existence of fallen man.[20] Missing here, however, is the category which first unlocks the mystery of that fallen situation: sin. (The same is true of the constitutive elements of Dasein labeled "care," "anxiety," etc.) The question of Dasein's wholeness to be sure makes itself heard. But this wholeness is not here viewed in terms of the power that creates this Dasein, grants its destiny, limits it, and "surrounds it on all sides" (Ps. 139). Instead its wholeness is viewed from the point of death, so that "death as a structuring power is brought into the Dasein."[21] As a result death, which is only an instrument of limitation in the hand of God, is elevated to being an end in itself. The symptom of Dasein's situation (namely, that before God for very specific reasons we are at an end) is made into a genuine cause. It is the sign of that "revolt of the means" which sets in wherever man's bond with God has

Glaube," *Zeitschrift für Theologie and Kirche* 11 (1930): 339 ff., esp. 340; see also "Das Problem der natürlichen Theologie," *Glaube und Verstehen* (Tübingen, 1933), pp. 295 ff., esp. 305 ff.

[20] In terms of Heidegger's philosophical borrowing from Christian theology, see K. Löwith, "Grundzüge der Entwicklung der Phänomenologie zur Philosophie und ihr Verhältnis zur protestantischen Theologie," *Theologische Rundschau* (1930), pp. 26 ff. See also his "Phänomenologische Ontologie und protestantische Theologie," *Zeitschrift für Theologie und Kirche* 11 (1930): 365 ff. and F. Traub, "Heidegger und die Theologie," *Zeitschrift für Systematische Theologie* 9 (1931): 686.

[21] This apt phrase is from Karl Lehmann, *Der Tod bei Heidegger und Jaspers. Ein Beitrag zur Frage: Existentialphilosophie, Existenzphilosophie und protestantische Theologie* (Heidelberg, 1938), p. 77.

been lost. It is "the whole tragedy of self-reliant man that he can only have his 'authentic possibility-of-being-whole' guaranteed to him by death! Here Dasein itself has disclosed that the thing which shapes its life is death."[22]

This point exhibits the post-Christian twilight surrounding Heidegger's discussion of death and explains the singularity of his philosophy. What we actually have in his thought is autonomous Dasein cast upon its own resources, seeking to interpret itself, and thereby running into death as the immanent force, the limiting boundary which dominates it. And yet this consistently immanent and autonomous interpretation is not the product of immanence and autonomy itself. Instead this product will always carry the mark of repression on its brow, and consistently so, because human Dasein on its own—for whatever reasons—is self-concealing, self-evasive, and in refusing to acknowledge this fact, it also bypasses any knowledge of it.

Expressed more precisely, it is inherent in the nature of Dasein's autonomy that it cannot conceive of itself as subject to death and terminating in death. It is logically presupposed in this autonomous self-interpretation that there is a prior act of transcending whereby the empirical Dasein elevates itself beyond the empirical and assumes the position of agent for that unconditional *nomos* which evaluates human temporal existence. But in this transcending move it makes itself immune to the category of time.[23]

Inherent in autonomy's own pathos is its inability to acknowledge its situation of self-incarceration and banishment to the confines of temporality. Therefore it also remains ignorant of the fact that by not willing to have these be true, it does not allow them any credibility. For this very reason Kant is logically consistent in positing the extratemporal character of the unconditioned moral law since this is the only way that it can prove to be universally

[22] Ibid., p. 78.

[23] It is for this reason that such a logically consistent immanent interpretation is present in Kant. Kant's interpretation includes the same act of transcending and thus also participates in this consistent inconsistency of autonomy. See Helmut Thielicke, *Das Verhältnis zwischen dem Ethischen und dem Ästhetischen* (Leipzig, 1932), pp. 99 ff.

valid. Simultaneously however he hypostatizes a supraindividual self as the agent for that autonomy. Such a transcendental self as an intelligible entity is not intrinsically subject to space and time, to individuation; it is subject to them only in its phenomenal form, in the sense data of an empirical I. Intrinsically the transcendental self is above and beyond these categories and consequently not implicated within the boundaries of death.

Therefore Dasein is not illuminated consistently on the basis of immanence since any autonomous immanent interpretation undergoes the twist described above and forcibly breaks through the confines of immanence. This twist, however, signifies that Dasein does not want its own self-incarceration to be true, does not acknowledge it[24] although it is true, and therefore the moment of illusion, the illegitimate breakthrough into immortality, is necessary in Heidegger's view if Dasein is to endure this constant self-incarceration.[25] The greatness of Heidegger's interpretation of Dasein lies in the fact that it does not itself fall prey to this illusion, which he has clairvoyantly unmasked in man's normal understanding of his existence.

Our assertions about the possibility of an immanent interpretation of Dasein, however, seem with all of this to have run into a curious contradiction. On the one hand we said that if existence were illuminated from its own indigenous immanence consistently and without illusion, death and Being-toward-death would come into view as the final dominating powers of life.

However, we have also stated the apparently contradictory thesis that death and Being-toward-death cannot logically be elevated from the immanence of Dasein to the status of ultimate realities since Dasein by nature is self-concealing, refusing to acknowledge the truth about itself, that is, its creatureliness, its Being-toward-death, etc.[26]

[24] Concerning the relationship between knowledge and acknowledging in the interpretation of existence, see Helmut Thielicke, *Kritik der natürlichen Theologie*, 2nd ed. (Munich, 1938).

[25] Once more it is the same logic that compels Kant to move on to a doctrine of immortality from this same premise.

[26] See the corresponding Pauline assertions about human Dasein in Rom. 1:18 ff.

How can this contradiction be resolved? Death and Being-toward-death are not visible to immanental interpretation until immanence learns to understand the truth about itself better than it does by its own nature. The source for such a better self-understanding, or expressed more pungently, such illumination of immanence in the midst of its attempts to retouch its own self-illumination, comes from exposure to the radiance that exceeds all natural sources of light, namely, contact with biblical realism. Such realism about Dasein arises from the exposing action of the message of the law, and in Heidegger's interpretation of Dasein—as we have said—this very contact with Saint Paul is apparent.[27]

To use another illustration one might say that in entering the room of Heidegger's philosophy, it is as though one stepped into a hall of uncanny brilliance which is at first blinding, but then as one's eyes gradually adjust, the room withholds none of its terrors. Despite its size the eye sees all its cold stone walls. There are no dark corners which give any hope of a hiding place, no entries or passageways for flight into other rooms or even out into the open. Even the door is barricaded. When fully opened the eye sees in the distance the absolute emptiness of the room. No object invites one's gaze to rest for a moment or hints at anything external to the room. A prisoner in a normal cell can always tell by the pictures he has brought along or by some art object or by some memento that the cell is not the ultimate, but that it is embedded in a world that surrounds it, pointing beyond it. This "world" keeps the prisoner, as it were, in constant remembrance that he is not a prisoner only, since he nevertheless still possesses a certain and continuing share in that world which is more than his cell. Man in Heidegger's world is more imprisoned than this prisoner, and he sees the stark reality (even though previously confined to darkness and twilight) as soon as he has accustomed himself to this uncanny and surprising brilliance.

[27] See the literature just mentioned above. It is interesting that on the basis of this extensive substantive proximity to basic categories of Pauline understanding of existence, Bultmann seeks to reverse the direction and interpret Paul with the aid of Heideggerian concepts. See his article "Paul" in the collection of his essays, *Existence and Faith* (Cleveland and New York: World Publishing Co., 1960), pp. 111-46.

But now comes the most important item. The source of the light itself remains hidden. The room of existence which one has entered is bathed in a mysterious *indirect* light. One gets the impression that this light could not originate from the room itself, and this is only too true. The room of Dasein is like this. That we have learned as the light has unmasked it. And even if the man should some day get out again, he will be unable to forget the truth he has seen or accustom himself any longer to the comforting twilight of his illusions. But what forced him to see the room of Dasein the way it really is was only a supernatural light source transcending all human reality. Since it was indirect, the light source itself was hidden from the eye.

Only one thing must yet be said. It is a light without grace. It is the light of the law, but not that other light of the gospel.

Thereby we have conjured up secularized man's own vision of Dasein. In the secularization process he has transposed the light source into the category of indirectness. He can no longer forget this true view free from illusion, despite the fact that in daily life he is so concerned to repress it. But he no longer knows where the knowledge came from. And now he is the helpless victim of his own knowledge. This is the second thing that knowledge does. It curses him and compels him now to persevere in it. Perhaps it is accurate to say that this is the curse of the departing Christ shaking the dust from his feet. His penetrating X-ray eyes cannot be forgotten even though one no longer has his blessing. It is the judgment of the departing word; it is man abandoned to his death and to his knowledge. For this reason Freedom-toward-death is to be seen against the background of despair, and this time even against the background of an unrepressed and illuminated despair. This freedom is heroic nihilism as only the apostate Christian knows it, but not the heathen. "Wake up" and "Be brave" is all that remains as its motto.[28]

Ernst Jünger stands out among those who interpret our age from its own resources. As one perhaps most directly involved with the data he sees this awakening of modern man in the same

[28] Ernst Jünger, *Das abenteuerliche Herz,* 1st ed. (Hamburg, 1929), p. 93.

way that Heidegger does. Man has been roused from the process of repression, wherein he concealed the gruesome nothingness of his death that bodes no comfort and offers no exit. However, in Jünger this awakening does not occur primarily from contact with the message of the law (at least not in such direct contact as is demonstrable in Heidegger), although it too surely stands in the background. On the contrary this awakening occurs by means of dreams whereby knowledge once suppressed into the subconscious is brought out into the open. A typical example of this is his dream about swallowing the "fat green-black viper."[29]

[29] Ibid., p. 85. Jünger's later development in the very explicit direction of primitive Christianity is beyond our discussion here.

7.

The Divided "I" in Kant's Ethics

The chief trademark of the attempt to suppress death and pursue the dreamlike phantom of human immortality is, as we have seen, to divide the I. The secularized thought that Heidegger represents constitutes an exception to the rule. Yet before we leave this line of thought, we must at least take note of one other form of such I-division, namely, the I-division in terms of ethics classically presented in Kant's *Critique of Practical Reason.*[1] What is at stake here is the following: If the previously noted division of the I sought primarily to sidestep death's threat and juxtapose to it an insoluble, enduring, immortal region for the I, then Kant's I-division in terms of ethics signifies an attempt to sidestep the threat posed by the moral law as its unconditional demand lays claim to the total man.

The details of this tactical maneuver appear somewhat as follows: According to the biblical view man, by virtue of the fact that he is created by God and belongs to him, knows himself obligated to his Lord or at least knows that he ought to be so (Rom. 1:18 ff.). The law gives expression to this claim of God when it lays its hand upon man claiming him as God's property,

[1] See at this point the extensive analysis and critique in Helmut Thielicke, *Geschichte und Existenz. Grundlegung einer evangelischen Geschichtstheologie* (Gütersloh, 1935), esp. pp. 68 ff. What follows here in brief is indicative of the fuller treatment presented there.

commandeering him, and quite simply drawing out the consequences of the fact that God is God. As a creature who has received himself intact from the hands of God, man senses that he owes God his entire self and above all that he owes it in the same form as he originally received it from God's hands. At the same moment he is forced to discover that he can never balance out this obligation, that it rests upon him as "guilt." For he must admit that he is thrust into an existence which surrounds him on every side with evidence that he is already emburdened. At no moment does his existence present him with an open possibility by means of which he might yet take control of his own existence and shape it autonomously and self-creatively.

Although he recognizes the shape of this existence encompassing him and casting him into guilt, he cannot possibly detach himself from it, as does, for example, the aged harpist in Goethe's *Wilhelm Meister,* by viewing himself merely as the passive object of fate that overtakes him and overpowers him with its guilt but removes from him any blame or responsibility for guilt of his own. No, he is unable to pinpoint the boundary line between himself and the guilt that burdens him. He always knows himself to have been the doer, the subject, of the guilt that intrudes into his existence, guilt that he has appropriated and concretely executed. He can indeed *provisionally* attempt to isolate himself from his guilt. He can say with Saint Paul, "It is no longer I that do it, but sin which dwells within me" (Rom. 7:17), as though this sin were another power separate and distinct from him. But when in the very next moment he confronts the will of God with its sights set on him and him alone, then the two are identified again. "Wretched man that I am (i.e., that sin is me)! Who will deliver me from this body of death?" (Rom. 7:24).

Thus the most profound experience man has when the law confronts him is that he cannot get out of his own skin. He cannot, as it were, forsake himself or dissolve his identity, and therefore his existence is marred by a deep and unavoidable split. It is the split between what he *wills* and what he then factually *does* as a consequence of the encumbrance he carries with him (Rom.

7:1 ff.). He is forced to learn that the effect of God's commandment is not to attune him to it and make him obedient to it. Consequently it does not produce a uniform movement of his person toward God, but instead casts him into an outrageous conflict with himself expressive of that split. The contenders in this conflict are on the one side the will, which wishes to be obedient and intends to perform the law, and on the other side what Jesus labels the "thoughts of the heart," the sepulcher of evil desires camouflaged under a whitewashed cover, which Luther called concupiscence, the desire to be oneself.

This situation of man in the face of the total claim of God's will is hopeless for two reasons. In the first place, the net result of the works arising from such action is always ambivalent. For these works are the manifestations both of the desire to be oneself (and thus lead to Pharisaic work-righteousness in the midst of an externally worthy act) as well as of an intended act of obedience. Therefore, in essence, they are no fulfillment of the will of God. Secondly, work and action never lead to the sort of victory that would remove the root of man's rebellion against God. What is achieved on the ethical level is only an intensification of the ethical conflict for which there is no solution. This becomes apparent in the example of Luther's monastic struggles and that of Saint Paul's struggles in Romans 7. (Both the apostle and the reformer are experiencing vicariously and in intensified form what validly applies to all.) Seen from this perspective every action of obedience to the demand is never more than a reworking of the raw materials of concupiscence, a concession wrested from it or a process of sublimating it; in any case it is always something that presupposes concupiscence as a given and indeed as a constant given.

It must be noted that these consequences only come to the surface when the unconditional character of God's demand is taken seriously as it lays claim to man's totality, for example, in the form it takes in the Sermon on the Mount. Only when confronted with God's demand do we see the totality of man as a fallen creature. Only then do we see man's identity with himself to be a prison from which he is unable to escape.

It is also important to note the thoroughgoing consistency of biblical anthropology. Even in the context of ethics, that is, under the law of God, the same totality and indivisible uniqueness of the human I is proclaimed as in the context of the doctrine of death.

In the face of this threat from the radical demand which confronts and condemns man totally we now see autonomous man taking refuge in the same artifice that we detected in his attempt to render death impotent. (It is not accidental that the opponent of biblical anthropology is equally consistent.) This artifice is present in an especially vivid manner in Kant. Let us sketch very briefly the following points of his position.

The unconditional law as it is formulated in the categorical imperative is not an outside entity confronting total man with its demand for obedience, but resonates within man himself, just as certainly as he in his personhood is himself the subject and by no means merely the object of the demand. From this now several consequences follow.

1) "Ought" and "can" are completely correlated to each other. This means that an ought would be meaningless if there were not a corresponding measure of ability to obey correlative to it. If man did not possess this possibility for obedience, then he could not be held responsible for his disobedience. Then the ought could not appeal to man's responsibility and thus the demand for obedience would become untenable.

Kant goes on to qualify this ability to obey in a twofold manner. On the one hand, the ability to obey consists in man's possessing a formal freedom in the face of the causal nexus operative in the natural world; he is thus exempt from every fatalistic compulsion. "Freedom and unconditional practical law reciprocally imply each other."[2]

Secondly, the ability to obey, the "can," arises from the fact that the demand of practical reason does not lay claim to the

[2] Immanuel Kant, *Critique of Practical Reason,* trans. and ed. L. W. Beck (Chicago: University of Chicago Press, 1949), p. 140.

entire I, but only to that segment of the I which is available to human freedom. For example, the natural endowments, with which man finds himself blessed or burdened, are presupposed as ethically neutral and untouched by the demand. Man is not told that he must become completely different or that the totality of this change must reach to the foundations and roots of his being. Instead he is able in fact to detach one segment of himself and consider it something bestowed by fate for which he cannot be held responsible and which is thus ethically neutral.[3]

The demand consequently applies only to that segment of the I which can be mobilized for action as it develops from the foundation of those given natural endowments. In other words, face to face with the ethical demand my responsibility does not begin with the question, "Who am I, I together with all of my natural endowments?" On the contrary, responsibility begins with the question, "What shall I do with these given qualities?" "What shall I make of them?" For strictly speaking, "I" am not the one who bears these endowments, but the one who exploits them, who has to make something out of them. As a personal entity "I" am responsible only in this narrow sector as one who utilizes his given resources. By no means therefore am I identical with my self, but only with a segment of my self. The demand arising from human autonomy in no way applies to man in his totality; consequently it is unable to call him into question. A reality that is identical with itself (which is what we have here in the personal union of man as the one making the demands and the one of whom the demands are made) cannot call itself into question. This contradicts the essence of autonomous demand. Kant's way of expressing the impossibility of ethical man calling himself into question is the previously mentioned correlation between ought and can, that is, his fundamental thesis "you can, for you ought." For this thesis signifies that the demand of the ought is measured and limited by the extent of human ability, that is, by the extent of that I-segment which can be mobilized for action, is in charge of itself, and utilizes its given endowments.

[3] Thielicke, *op. cit.,* pp 74 ff.

2) Therefore, the autonomy of the categorical imperative entails a division of the human I into an I-segment that is responsible and one that is not. This duality is related to the two worlds in which man stands and which impinge upon one another in him. One of these two worlds is called *mundus sensibilis.* It represents the world of physical sense data, and the laws of nature, the world of "must." As such this world contains those component segments of the I which the I assumes almost as hereditary goods, as physical endowment from the operational law of causality and which thus are ethically neutral. By the same operational law of causality these appropriated I-segments continue to live on in man. Either they are untroubled as are his natural endowments, the self-regulated aspects of his animalian biology; or else they become the object of his ethical exploitation as man's other I-segment seeks to make something out of them. This other I-segment is a member of the *mundus intelligibilis,* that is, a participant in that moral world manifesting itself in practical reason.

3) This ethical bifurcation of man then logically leads to a conflict and a split. It is the conflict of man with himself inasmuch as he is partly flesh and partly spirit. But this conflict is now no longer a sign of that painful awareness achieved by Saint Paul in Romans 7, that awareness of the split which taught him that man is never able to be in unanimous total movement toward the will of God, but that he is always simultaneously antagonist and dissenter. By contrast, for Kant this conflict is an expression of man's dignity. He evaluates it as the exact opposite of what Paul says: Man in distinction to all other creatures is the only one who has not succumbed to the instinctive necessity of the laws of nature, but is able to rise in protest against them.

From this one might draw the following conclusions: When law no longer confronts man as the manifestation of the will of the Lord who possesses him, who creates his origin and his destiny; when it is instead internalized into man himself as an expression of his self-formulated legislation, then the conflict taking place within man no longer expresses a curse, but a blessing. It is no longer the sign of a destiny that he has failed to achieve, but rather of one that he has attained.

Thus it becomes plain why the division of the human I just described signifies that the demand has been rendered impotent. On the one hand, the I prescribes to the ought the radius of its legitimacy, and it does so on the basis of the I's ability for moral action and its consequently limited responsibility. Having made this prescription it simply declares the other I-segment, which could endanger the moral I, to be ethically neutral, and the commandment invalid for it. Secondly, the demand no longer calls the I into question at all, but by the very conflict created within the I, it leads it toward its destiny.

8.

A Biblical Basis For Viewing the Philosophical Perspective on Death

We have just seen in the area of ethics the same artifice in operation which we saw functioning when man faces the necessity of dying. Any division of the I aims at insulating the I from the unconditional threat posed either by death or by the divine imperative and does so by proclaiming an unassailable I-zone in which the I itself is God. Simultaneously what lies behind that artifice is brought out into the open, although it still needs clarification by considering the biblical perspective on man and death. For the artifice is a symptom of man's existence, an existence in flight from God that does not want to acknowledge the truth of God or of its own self, does not want to let God be God, and consequently plunges into rebellious illusions.

Denial of the unconditional commandment and denial of the unconditional law thus does not rest upon a misreading of the significant data of human life, which might then be corrected by a more rigorous search for truth. In both cases, it is not a truth at all that is involved, that is the object of contemplative cognition and thereby dependent upon the perfection or imperfection of the process of contemplation.

On the contrary, what is at stake here is the fact that human existence in its misunderstanding and repression is itself in untruth. It does not want to acknowledge that it is, indeed, an existence that has bolted from the divine fellowship, but which God nevertheless demands back *in toto;* it is an existence separated from God by the boundary of death. Here is man unwilling to accept the truth of his creaturehood, of his guiltiness, and of his limitations. Thus it is man who really does not know the truth of his own existence. By not acknowledging the facts of his existence he is led to false knowledge. Any cognitive actions which arise from such an existence in untruth are themselves under the sway of untruth.

What is at stake here is not a misreading of certain phenomena of human existence. If that were so, then a Christian philosophy of existence might engage in discussion with other interpretations of Dasein and clarify issues. On the contrary, at stake here is a misreading of existence itself. Just what is the truth about this existence? This is the central question at the bottom of our biblical reflections and it is to be expected that an existence which knows the truth about itself and above all acknowledges this truth will then also automatically read the phenomena in the proper light. For these phenomena are not so much objects of our knowing as they are of our acknowledging. Consequently they are accessible only to an existence that is itself in truth. Only he who is of the truth hears in them the voice of God.

At the same time it becomes apparent from this vantage point that in our analysis of secular ideology our discovery was not that the artifice of I-division is a technique of philosophical thought, but rather that a specifically assumed stance toward existence utilizes such a technique for its own intellectual consolidation and, although highly concealed, expresses itself in it. Yet inasmuch as we are here examining man's existence in its flight from God and its repression of his judgments, it becomes apparent that our analysis from the very beginning was accompanied by the knowledge of the truth about this existence as it comes to light under law and gospel.

Thus what we were engaged in was nothing less than a critique of natural theology especially in the light of Romans 1:18 ff. and pursued in terms of a concrete problem presented by the reality of death. Consequently it was not a philosophical substructure that we wished to create for our biblical considerations, but a retrospective view carried out in the light of this biblical consideration and presented first only for methodological reasons. We have looked at the world under the illumination of the "light of the world" (John 8:12).

We will now see in Part Two how the Bible protests against such attempts to divide man and thus flee death. For the terror of death to which men are sensitive in the Bible does not reside in any anxiety about being roasted in some other-worldly hell—as some cheap critics would have it, if for no other reason than to get a facile opportunity to sidestep the problem posed here. No, the terror of death resides in the fact that here man is simply a totality and therefore in death is totally dead. He cannot find a substitute for himself in some immortal powers whose individual transitional stages he then would be. At issue here are not the powers but man himself as he is addressed in his person, forsaken—if one would have it that way—by everything which belongs to him in this world and which seems to give him greatness, worth, and immortality. The man standing behind all this is the one God means and calls. The man standing behind all this is the one who must die. And the man standing behind all this is not simply nothing, is not a mere individual transitional stage for transsubjective powers, but he is something, yes, someone, who has a name before God and in this very name cannot exterminate himself. "If I take the wings of the morning and dwell in the uttermost part of the sea, even there thy hand shall lead me, and thy right hand shall hold me. If I say, 'Let only darkness cover me' . . . even the darkness is not dark to thee, . . . for darkness is as light with thee" (Ps. 139:9-11).

This is why death is a problem in the Bible. For here man is not simply a piece of life or of spirit or of the nation, but behind all of these and apart from all of them he still also has a self which bears an indelible character for which he must give account. Because of this self death is a problem. For seen in this light death is no longer an event of transition, the self going over into something else; it is rather destruction, the self going under like a sinking ship. For the same reason redemption from the bondage of death is not to be found in the dream of some alleged immortality, which is after all nothing else than a transition; redemption is to be had only in the resurrection of the dead, that is, in that reality whereby I am caught up and carried through the very destruction by that one whom death was unable to smother in its vortex. Resurrection is the shattered grave (but nevertheless a previously occupied grave); immortality is the denial of the grave.

Perhaps at this point we already sense from a distance that in this undenied destruction of the equally undenied self lies the basis for the curious biblical thought that death is connected with sin and that this is where its terror lies. For sin likewise is connected with that self with which death is so curiously involved. And even when secular thought on its own comes to some knowledge of these subsurface connections, it fends off both of these threatening powers by the same technique of dividing the I. Not only with respect to death but also with respect to sin the self strives to step out of the picture and push the grisly power off onto something or someone else.

Thus apparently everything that makes both death and sin so serious in the biblical view depends on this inextinguishable self of man. And apparently death and sin in the myth of our days are given so little serious attention because we have argued that self away into nonexistence. All we still see is the overarching power in which this self is only an apparently nonessential transition point caught up and supplanted by death. (The sum of such I's without selves is called the collective, the masses.) Apparently the fact that man has lost his self and has become personless is the reason why he is unable to take sin and death seriously; in addition, by means of his flight into personlessness he wills not to take them seriously.[1] He is unable and unwilling to take them

[1] We might recall here the words of Fichte in 1794 (in his *Grundlage der gesamten Wissenschaftslehre*) embedded in a decidedly metaphysical context and yet reminiscent of this: "Most men could be convinced more easily that they were a piece of lunar lava than that they were an 'I.' "

seriously until the hour of death itself when the physician dare not tell him that he must die because he suddenly begins to have a presentiment of death as something more than transition, because he realizes that "I" must die and that he has a self which death is here calling into question.

Just what is this self of man, this irreplaceable reality, the understanding of which is apparently what everything depends on? This is what we must now take up. But we should not like to close this first part of our investigation without pointing out that even in our day the secular man whose personhood is lost now and then has a vision as if in a daydream which lets him see that all his bravery and all his consciously assumed postures and achievements may in certain circumstances be nothing but flight from his own self, flight from that self which really would be in danger if he were ever to get serious about it. Therefore man has to talk and be active in order to drown out and anesthetize the deadly silence or that screaming accusation that arises from the very silence. And even Heidegger's Freedom-toward-death appears at this point to be only a caricature of the human countenance, mortally frightened, knowing itself lost—not in nothingness but in judgment. Such a waking dream is portrayed in the poetic view of Gerhard Schumann[2] who conjures up the terror of the lost self and the lost God:

> We are the world and create everything!
> We ate from the tree. Now we know.
> In the pit of the self we encounter ourselves pure.
> We saved ourselves from the happiness of dreams.
> We dare the most difficult paths alone.
> . . . We talk aloud in monologues. . .
> And often we sneer at ourselves: How anxious you are!
> Have we possibly deceived ourselves about our salvation?
> We are very proud, but anxiety lurks within.
>
> We created according to our own image the grand,
> The proud world of man in his glory.
> Our palaces towered into the clouds.

2 "Lieder von der Umkehr," *Wir aber sind das Korn* (Munich, 1940).

We burrowed into earth's deepest abyss,
And even the air we subdued for travel.
Yet suddenly we froze, and crashed hard
Against the wall of loneliness—strangers in our own home!. . .
Oh lost God, will you let us find you again?

As we departed from him, we were the ones deserted,
A withered branch to be broken from the tree.
. . . We talk, because it is deathly silent around us.
We pursue, cursed by anxiety to action,
Which only portrays our own caricature.
We already hear the march of judgment.
We act as though we are eagerly seeking something—
And we already know: we will only find nothing.

Now comes the time of dying most ghastly.
We doubt our own selves—and gurgling flows
The water of despair through the fragments
Of the last shattered dams. . . .
Yes, Lord of the world, you would have to condemn us,
And every plea is but presumptuous scorn.
Mute we reduce our proud fortress to rubble,
And descend in poverty from our throne.

We let the reins be taken from our hands
After a wild and imperious chase,
And take the purple from our loins.
Threatening rebellion arises—now we stand naked
And freeze, cast into complete emptiness
And without the comfort of our own sacraments—
Beaten, dark, and cowering
In endless despair. And that is the end.

We do not plead. Strike, oh God, strike!
We quench our light, now you shine forth!
It is impossible—yet you can do it!
Bowed down we kneel. Now let our tear-filled
Weary eyes rest in the light. . . .

Now do not judge. Now you restore us!
Now bind us with your arduous fortune.

Give us to the stream, to blood, to the course of the worlds!
Forgive us, Lord, and give us back to you,
And let us weep in the castle of the night.
It is impossible, Lord!—It is finished.[3]

[3] See Appendix I on the idea of palingenesis in Romanticism.

Part Two

The Biblical Disclosure of the Reality of Death

"What an infinite reality this human self acquires by being before God! A herdsman who (if this were possible) is a self only in the sight of cows is a very low self, and so also is a ruler who is a self in the sight of slaves—for in both cases the scale or measure is lacking. The child who hitherto has had only the parents to measure himself by becomes a self when he is a man by getting the state as a measure. But what an infinite accent falls upon the self by getting God as a measure!"

—Kierkegaard[1]

"He who believes in me, though he die, yet shall he live."

—Jesus Christ[2]

[1]Søren Kierkegaard, *The Sickness unto Death,* trans. Walter Lowrie, together with *Fear and Trembling* (Garden City, N.Y.: Doubleday & Co., Anchor Books, n.d.), p. 210.

[2] John 11:25.

9.

Death and Human Personhood

In biblical thought human death is simply unnatural. At no time and in no place is it the expression of any sort of normality of nature, as if it signified the necessary ebb in the rhythm of life. Death is rather the expression of a catastrophe which runs on a collision course with man's original destination or, in other words, directly opposite to his intrinsic nature. This catastrophe intruding into God's creation simultaneously becomes the boundary line between God and man, between him "who alone has immortality" (1 Tim. 6:16) and him who has forfeited life.

This boundary line can be eliminated by neither of the two possible viewpoints we have already discussed: neither by saying that man possesses an immanent immortal quality which relates him to the life of God (even if only with a limited segment of his I); nor by saying that the divine itself is subject to the fate of death. In the latter case, it is irrelevant whether this fate of death is the Greek notion of a *Moira* that sets the limits or the Germanic idea of a twilight of the gods. The first viewpoint (dominated as it is by the presupposition of a certain immortal quality) tries to obliterate the boundary line between God and man by maintaining the similarity of the quality of life on both sides. The second viewpoint (twilight of the gods, *Moira*) tries to annul the boundary line by means of a common fate setting an end both for man and for the divine.

In contrast to this, God alone—biblically viewed—has life. Even his Old Testament name "I am, who I am" points to God's life by designating his eternal present tense (Exod. 3:14). The divine majesty is incompatible with any creaturely life designed toward eventual termination; God "has life in himself" (John 5:26). Indeed, he is "the fountain of life" (Ps. 36:9). His life simply cannot be subject to any termination. Rather he is the end himself, just as surely as he stands both at the beginning (Gen. 1:1) and at the end, as surely as he *is* both beginning and end, Alpha and Omega (Isa. 41:4). According to the vision of Psalm 90 he is, as it were, the shore of eternity where the breakers of the seas of time come in from all sides.

Related to this is the fact that God is the only one who bestows life in that creative and unconditional sense appropriate to him as the Lord and Giver of Life. The use of the Hebrew term *bara* exclusively for God's creativity as in Genesis 1:1, illustrates this. Wherever God is, there is life. Where God is not, there is death (Ps. 104:29-30; Job 34:15).

Thus life in the authentic sense can be found only where God's own breath of life flows. Here too, however, it is particularly characteristic that such donated life is not like the popular image of man being endowed with a divine spark, which now burns of its own energy within him. Instead it is like the breathing process in that the breath is either flowing or can be interrupted (Ps. 104:30).

God's impartation of life is not to be understood as in deistic ideology whereby God winds the clock and lets it run on its own according to the energy invested in it. On the contrary, God's impartation of life is a present-tense creation that retains its present-tense character.

Related to this is the fact that the only person who has life is one who lives in contact with or, more precisely, in fellowship with God. Whoever does not have this contact with the breath of God, whoever lives in protest against him or in internal detachment from him, is already dead regardless of how much vitality he might have externally (Eph. 2:5; Rom. 5:21; 7:10; 1 John 3:14-

15). His life is disconnected from its actual source of power, though still rolling along "in neutral" according to the law of inertia.

The notion of God's present-tense creation, which is either constantly occurring anew or not occurring at all, no doubt possesses a substantive connection with the doctrine of justification as it has been classically formulated by Saint Paul and Luther. Actually such an internal connection can be seen by the very fact that God's justifying action is also a bestowal of life. It is God taking man out of his separation and alienation and receiving him back into the original living fellowship with himself.

The Pauline-Lutheran understanding of justification gives a clear picture of this analogy with present-tense creation, with the life-giving breath of God. This view, in contrast to the traditional Roman Catholic idea of justification, sees that God's impartation of grace is by no means the impartation of an immanent quality, a *gratia infusa,* but an act of God which man always asks for anew. God remains the exclusive subject of this act. Forgiveness and renewal are also creative actions that remain subject to his disposal and his refusal. Just as no creature on the level of death and life has any inherent qualitative immortality, so also on the level of sin and justification no man has inherent qualitative righteousness.

Even faith is not such a qualitative possession; according to Luther's exegesis of Psalm 90 it is an unexpanded *punctum mathematicum.* It is no extended psychic area which man might possess in the same way that he possesses his "feelings." Faith is purely and simply man's subjecting himself in trust to the justification granted him in Christ, producing the countersignature to God's assurance of grace; this is truly all. Consequently faith is not some daring decision to believe, by which a man might achieve God's righteousness and to that extent control his destiny with God. It is really just the opposite, for by believing man subordinates himself to God's control. Expressed still more precisely, faith does not mean that by my decision to believe I could make myself the subject of my relationship with God, but the other way around: I decide to be the object of God's gracious actions.

With this we have now summarized into a few precise formulas the entire line of thought which we were trying to show. It is the line that runs from the creative living breath of God who alone controls life, while the creatures apart from this present-tense bestowal possess no independent life at all, on down to the final point, the divine act of making righteous which also remains in the present-tense control of God. Strictly speaking, the formula pertains: Where God is, there is life; where God is not, there is death.

Thus it becomes clear even here that death always indicates divorce from God and thereby an ultimate disorder. Death and separation from God go together. Death is un-nature; death ought not be.[1] To this extent death is not a component part of life, but life's diametrical opposite. Thus to this extent death is the enemy. In fact it is even called "the last enemy," and it remains life's opponent to the very end (1 Cor. 15:26; Rev. 20:14). And in order to testify against this terrorizing enemy, who nevertheless must finally surrender to the divine victory, Jesus steps into battle against it here and now in anticipation and promise of the future: healing, raising the dead, rising himself—a first distant sign on the horizon of the coming glory when God will be all in all and therefore "death shall be no more, neither shall there be mourning" (Rev. 21:4).

Indicative of the way even the Old Testament sees death as the symptom of man's ultimate disorder with God is the situation of the psalmist in Psalm 49 (v. 11). He has great difficulty and doubts in coping with the fact that the righteous must die just as the unrighteous do, although they are "in order" with God and thus strictly speaking ought not be exposed to the clutches of death.

This much then is certain: Viewed biblically, death is the symptom of an inscrutable distortion of life. Life created by God is indestructible of itself—or more precisely of God's self—so long as it remains under the influence of the divine breath and in fellowship with God.

[1] See in this connection, e.g., Deut. 30:15-16; Eph. 2:1; Rom. 7:10, 13; John 5:24; Jas. 1:15.

To be sure, there is still another kind of life which continues to flourish even when the connecting link with the ground of life has been broken. But this is no longer authentic life; it remains only a life "in the flesh" (Gal. 2:20; Phil. 1:22).[2] The disruption which death signifies for this life in the flesh consists not only in the fact that death terminates this life, but even more in the fact that as life runs its course, it is affected by this end and qualitatively altered by it. "If in this life only we have hoped in Christ, we are of all men most to be pitied," for neither the extension of this life nor its content has any durability (1 Cor. 15:19). Just how much this life marked by death has sacrificed its durability is illuminated by our treating it over and over as though it were hopeless, and in view of this hopelessness, we act accordingly: "Let us eat and drink for tomorrow we die."

Therefore for "life in the flesh," death is not only the boundary line behind it, but also the shadow above it, that is, above the course it runs. Death is not an unmotivated, sudden punctuation mark placed at the end of life's sentence, but it is the target which determines the flight of the arrow even ahead of time, that is, during its flight. Insofar as I live "according to the flesh" I am living under the rubric of this terminal annihilation which of necessity already determines the curve of my life. Jean Paul gives expression to this in the apocalyptic view of his *Rede des toten Christus vom Weltgebäude herab, dass kein Gott sei.* "Death appeared to me as though it set my watch; I heard it chewing on man and his pleasures, and time seemed to crumble away into the abyss in a stream of decay."[3]

Life does not regain its durability again until "life in the flesh" becomes a "life in Christ." Then the connection with the divine

[2]In both passages the concept of life *en sarki* appears in clear contrast to authentic life, life determined by Christ. If one thinks thereby of a life cut loose from God and seeking to be self-determined, it would be more precise to consider the notion of *zēn kata sarka* (analogous to *sophia kata sarka,* 1 Cor. 1:26, or to *kauchasthai kata sarka,* 2 Cor. 11:18). For the preposition *kata* points toward the flesh as a normative concept and determining factor of life (except for its usage to designate genealogical factors, *Abraam ton propatora hēmon kata sarka,* etc.), while *en* frequently has the meaning of location.

[3] Jean Paul (Richter), *Sämtliche Werke,* ed. E. Berend (Berlin: Propyläen Verlag, n.d.), 1 II:445.

power of life is restored, then "though we die, yet shall we live" (John 11:25). In this case life is no longer characterized by an impending death casting its shadow back upon it (we "sit in the shadow of death," Matt. 4:16; Luke 1:79), causing us to live in hopelessness and succumb to an eleventh hour panic. No, then we are in the circle of the Lord's power, who has overcome the forces of disruption and of the entire divine-human catastrophe by joining our hand to the hand of God again. For in him the whole fullness of the deity has come bodily to us (Col. 2:9) and eternal durability has settled upon our life anew. Death's unnaturalness is victoriously countermanded by our new destiny.

UNNATURAL DEATH AND HUMAN UNIQUENESS

With this we have already struck an entirely different keynote from the one given by secular views of death which would incorporate it into life as something normative and proper, and thus finally trifle it away as insignificant. (The clearest symptom of such a trifling treatment was indeed the myth of immortality.) It is now important to see that any view of dying as unnatural, as an antithesis to what properly ought to be in life, can be understood and made meaningful only under one condition, namely, when we consider man under the aspect of his personal I-Thou fellowship with God, that is, when we consider seriously that man belongs to God and that consequently I can only speak about this man *sub specie Dei,* that is, only by realizing that man is constantly cast upon God (Ps. 22:10).

We can express the same thing more crassly and clearly by saying: the unnaturalness of death becomes apparent only when we speak of it in connection with God. We can also formulate the statement negatively: The unnaturalness of death does not become apparent if I isolate man, if I observe him apart from this divine context. To envision man in and of himself is an untruth, an imagined product of man's own hubris, as expressed most sharply in the premise of Cartesian thought.[4] For this reason, every

[4] Augustine described the untruth of this presumptuous attempt to put oneself in the center in *De Trinitate* 12. 11. In this connection see Walther Rehm, "Ex-

assertion about the death of man-so-conceived is also untrue.

The unnatural character of dying remains equally unapparent if I relate man to some "it" of a neutral law of nature rather than to the divine "Thou." Then man becomes an indifferent representative of biological life and the extinction of his individuality is the law of life in action substituting for him a new form which then represents him. In this case, dying is a law of nature.

As we have said, all of this changes immediately if we view man as conditioned not by some material connection with nature but by personal fellowship with God. Then we see that it is within this fellowship that man dies, or else it is at the rupture of this fellowship that he dies. Then death really becomes a sudden demolition, a brutal fact for which no concept of natural law can give me any comfort. Although we shall not yet seek to get at the meaning of such dying to God, or in connection with God, we can at least illustrate in a preliminary way the unnatural quality of dying which becomes apparent at just this point.

It is helpful for a preliminary understanding if we acknowledge that death appears as an alien even in our purely human relationships. The more intimately I am bound to another human being, the more icily and disruptively his death touches me. The well-known psychological effect on me when a close friend dies is but a testimony and reflection of a much more profound reality, namely, the fact that something unique and irreplaceable—or more precisely, something for which there is no substitute—has been destroyed. I sense that threads have been ripped apart once for all. An emptiness surrounds me that cannot be filled. A loss of wealth can indeed result in a collapse of my entire standard of living, my environment, my position, and my relations with my fellow men, a collapse which is externally much more vivid. But such an economic loss is still something that I can recoup, at least theoretically. It is an ebb in the rhythm of life and to that extent it is a recognized part of the normal regularity of the law of life. Nor am I helplessly at the mercy of this rhythm, as

perimentum suae medietatis. Eine Studie zur dichterischen Gestaltung des Unglaubens bei Jean Paul und Dostojewski," *Jahrbuch des Freien Deutschen Hochstifts* (Frankfurt a.M., 1940), pp. 237 ff.

though I were absolutely dependent on it. I can defend myself against it and in large measure take the law of my destiny in my own hands. Such a blow can be repaired. It does not destroy anything unique.

When my neighbor dies, however, it is different. This actually is the loss of something unique. And all the feelings described above dare not be misunderstood as though the secret of the event of death lay on the psychological level. Those feelings are only the psychic reflexes generated by the uniqueness of the loss. Since here something sinks into oblivion which cannot be replaced and does not return, we are confronting a fact that has no analogy in nature (which assuredly does replace everything), and to that extent it is unnatural. It is not accidental that this unnatural quality of death within the personal I-Thou relationship of man to man appears only (and perhaps remotely) in the psychological reflexes it produces, themselves also in need of interpretation. Symbols and myths make this subsurface sensation of unnaturalness clear enough—at least in significant zones of Western culture. We need only think of the skeleton of the grim reaper who mows, cuts down, and disrupts and who in the very figure he strikes testifies so simply to the finality of the fate he seals. He is simply death, the grim reaper, and not merely a "winter's sleep," a rhythmic transition that will lead to a new spring. Perhaps this is a symbol which could be created only in the context and under the influence of Christianity's knowledge of death.[5]

The myth of reincarnation speaks its message with equal clarity. This doctrine is nothing but the attempt to eliminate the uniqueness of human living and dying by taking from nature the analogue of repetition and transferring it to human events.[6] But in this very way it testifies indirectly to the unnaturalness which is implicit in the loss of a unique personhood. For the purposes of preliminary understanding and illustration we conclude that death

[5] This uniqueness appears not only at the death of my neighbor, of course, but also in thoughts about my own death which will remove me from my neighbors and from the environment which binds me to them. See the Hoche citation on p. 16 above.

[6] See my book on Lessing, *Vernunft und Offenbarung* (Gütersloh, 1936).

within the context of personal fellowship occurs as unnatural demolition.

From this point we at least see the orientation by which death appears as unnatural in an even more radical sense, namely, the orientation toward the fellowship in which God and man belong to each other. Even many prayers in the Old Testament lament the petitioner's exclusion from the word of God and God's congregation. "For Sheol cannot thank thee, death cannot praise thee" (Isa. 38:18). "Is thy steadfast love declared in the grave, or thy faithfulness in Abaddon?" (Ps. 88:11). "Save my life . . . for in death there is no remembrance of thee; in Sheol who can give thee praise?" (Ps. 6:4-5).[7] The fellowship between God and man appears therefore to be broken by death.

To be sure, there is no direct analogy here between fellowship with men and fellowship with God; it was for this reason that we spoke above of a merely "preliminary" illustration. For death is not to be understood as the cause of a precipitous unnatural rupture of man's fellowship with God, but as the consequence, the symptom, and attendant phenomenon of such a breach. It is an expression of that separation from God which we normally designate "sin."

In this sense the New Testament in numerous connections calls death "the wages of sin."[8] Death is a trademark of Adamite existence cut off from God. By the same token, however, it is a reality that has no more force in that new existence before God which is bestowed by Christ. Death really is unnatural. Death ought not to be. But insofar as it nevertheless is, it constitutes only the symptom of a much deeper unnaturalness, namely, that we have torn ourselves loose from God, that we are no longer in the Father's house (Luke 15:11 ff.), and that we have thus alienated ourselves from our intrinsic nature of being God's children. Sin and death are to be understood as an internally connected event in this God-

[7] See also Ps. 28:1; 30:9; 88:5, 10; 115:17; Isa. 38:11.

[8] Most often the New Testament uses this designation when it connects the fall of Adam with the death of his progeny resulting from it. See Gal. 6:7-8; John 8:21; 2 Cor. 7:10; 1 John 5:16 ff.; see also 1 Cor. 15:22; Rom. 5:12, 17; etc. For the entire subject see Bultmann's article in Gerhard Kittel, *Theological Dictionary of the New Testament,* trans. G. W. Bromiley (Grand Rapids, Mich.: Eerdmans, 1964 —), 3:15 ff., esp. the passages there listed in n. 67 on p. 15.

man destiny. Discovering how they are connected is the task of our further investigation. In the context of this preliminary exposition our purpose was only to understand that death's unnaturalness must be seen at the level of personal fellowship, both man's fellowship with other men and man's fellowship with God. This is all we have attempted to accomplish to this point.

As preliminary results we may thus list the following.

1) Death is unnatural since it most assuredly conflicts with man's original destiny to be near God; for wherever God is, there life reigns, not death.

2) The unnatural character of death can be expressed only by relating it not to a neutral "it" of some law of nature but to the personal fellowship between God and man.

10.

Death as Personal Catastrophe

In order to work out the specific character of *human* dying, we must bring into still clearer focus the uniqueness of the human person. The contrast between man's death and the demise of animals, and thereby the inadmissibility of all biological misunderstandings of human death, is connected to this notion of uniqueness.

The gravity of human dying, as we have seen, does not stand out until I come to understand, on the basis of this uniqueness, that I am endowed with personhood and that it is absolutely impossible for other persons or suprapersonal entities to take my place. I am simply unique.

This is not evident, of course, when we view man as a mammal or as a leaf on the tree of the world—falling off, blown away, but replaced; in other words, if I consider myself a piece of nature (in view of which the individual organism recedes in favor of the species). But it is evident if I understand myself as a piece of history.

This thesis needs to be understood more precisely. Indirectly it is also evident in secular observation of historical reality—somewhat as a final dotted-line continuation of the Christian understanding of life—when we consider, for instance, that Windelband calls history an "ideographic" science of events which in contrast to natural science is concerned with the unique and unrepeatable.[1] The same thing can be seen when Heinrich Rickert ascribes to history an "individualizing" conceptual framework in contrast to natural science which tends to "generalize."[2]

THE PERSON IN HISTORICAL ENCOUNTER

When we speak of man in these pages as the bearer of a history, it must be understood right away that the original for all history is our history with God.

Two things make that clear. In the first place, history occurs only in relationship and encounter with other people. It arises whenever I relate to another person or when I break away from him, in short, whenever I come to a decision with reference to him. Therefore the history of a human being does not consist in reporting how the stuff of his life developed through childhood, adulthood, and old age or even how he may have responded to things like some solipsistic Robinson Crusoe. Everything that I might be able to determine in this respect would still be, despite the precise truth of it, the artificial isolation of man as a phenomenon of nature. Consequently, it would reveal nothing at all of his intrinsic uniqueness. Paul de Lagarde relates such a series of true but nevertheless "unhistorical" facts in the life of Hellmuth von Moltke in order to demonstrate the nonsense of such an unhistorical sort of biography.[3]

I have history only when I have freedom and responsibility, not if I am a transition point in the flow of causality. Therefore I have history only when I encounter another who confronts me as a person. This becomes clear in one's history with God.

This history begins with the word addressed to me, "I have

[1]Windelband, *Geschichte und Naturwissenschaft* (Tübingen, 1894), pp. 26 ff.; *Präludien,* 3rd ed. (Tübingen, 1907), pp. 355 ff.

[2] Heinrich Rickert, *Die Grenzen der naturwissenschaftlichen Begriffsbildung* (Tübingen, 1896-1902), pp. 36 ff.; *Kulturwissenschaft und Naturwissenschaft,* 2nd ed. (Tübingen, 1910).

[3] He says, e.g., "Hellmuth von Moltke, born in 1800 at Parchim, frequently gave rise, as long as he lay in the cradle, to complaints abcut his uncleanliness" etc. "Die nächsten Pflichten deutscher Politik," *Deutsche Schriften* (Munich, 1934), p. 465.

called you by name, you are mine" (Isa. 43:1). That means that God lays claim to me for himself. I am not simply a functioning biological organism living on the resources of my own immanence, but I am an organism that belongs to someone else, in such a fashion that I can be committed to this belonging or deny it and break away from it. If this freedom of decision were eliminated, in a roundabout way man would once more become a phenomenon of nature despite any apparent religious foundation to his life. He would become an effect of the divine primary cause. If God were such a primary cause, then there would be no such thing as an encounter with him in freedom, no appropriation or rejection, but only blind dependence.

History with God does not come about unless the freedom of encounter is there, unless I am a person vis-à-vis God. This personhood God brings into existence by addressing me and making me a Thou, thereby calling me to decide whether I would have him be my Lord or whether I want instead to be my own Lord. Personhood means to be addressable,[4] to exist by virtue of another Thou and thus to stand in responsibility toward him. I have history only in the medium of my addressability since history occurs only between an I and a Thou and in the last analysis runs its course between God and man. This is stated well by Kierkegaard in the quotation cited above on p. 103.

If man ceases to understand himself as person, as one addressed by God and called into a history with God, then the rest of his existence also becomes ahistorical. So-called world history then becomes the sum total of ahistorical power struggles as they are fought out also among the animals in nature. Encounters in the

[4] Kant also considers this addressability to be the essence of man's personhood (or man's personality—see the next footnote). First of all, man becomes a person through the rational *logos* which operates within him and speaks to him (*Critique of Practical Reason,* trans. and ed. L. W. Beck [Chicago: University of Chicago Press, 1949], pp. 193 ff.). One can appeal to man's responsible personhood no matter how much he is also a creature of instinct, even if his instinctive reactions are as predictable as a solar eclipse in nature (ibid., pp. 203-4). Secondly, since in Kant's thought practical reason propounds the "fundamental law" that man should act so that "the maxim of your will could always hold at the same time as the principle of a universal legislation" (p. 142), it thereby places human personhood within the context of I-Thou relationships. In short, practical reason conceives human personhood in community with other persons.

form of treaties, pacts, and binding values (which can come to pass only under the rubrics of a third party that binds both partners together and to which both are subordinate) then no longer exist, at least not to the extent that they possess the significance of ultimate responsibility and commitment toward the other. Treaties and pacts, of course, continue to be made but their internal validity has underhandedly been changed. They are undoubtedly signs of a pause in the power struggle, but nothing more. The ceremony accompanying their ratification and the attendant promises ("for all time") are not meant seriously. They simply have transitory psychological significance. In reality, for the man who is separated from God, for the man who has thereby become personless, there exist only power conflicts. But these are natural phenomena which always intrude into history (even into the history of the man who wants to have God condition his life) just as certainly as man himself is part of nature. Yet they do not constitute what is specifically historical about history. And it is only natural and consistent that such a history that has become ahistorical—merely the sum total of power conflicts—finds expression in the biological world view of Nazism, in an understanding of the self that views history in analogy to nature.

We summarize: History, strictly speaking, arises only in encounter, in being addressed by God. This is where human personhood is created, by virtue of which man is no longer the apersonal product of a first cause, but is called to a commitment in freedom and responsibility.[5] Not until we realize this can we see clearly the other fact that we focused upon before, namely, that I, as such a historically existing being, am unique.

[5] One must be aware here of the distinction between person and personality. Personality is a typically Renaissance concept and signifies one particular human value among other ones. It represents not man per se, but one particular level within the human scale of values. Person, by contrast, means man per se in terms of his ability to be addressed and to make response. That is why the notion of person circumscribes the point of human solidarity where, by virtue of the very nature of personhood, there can be no preeminence of one man over another. To that extent no one should make person and personality into varying stages on a line of development. Each term stems from its own distinctive conceptual realm. Kant, by the way, crossed up our contemporary use of language by designating as "personality" what we understand as "person." At the same time, "person" for him is a synonym for the human I per se, which belongs equally to the *mundus sensibilis* and the *mundus intelligibilis*. See *op. cit.*, p. 193.

HISTORICAL UNIQUENESS ARISING IN JUDGMENT

When it is God himself who addresses me, I am pinned down to myself and cannot be represented by anyone or anything. This is most easily seen when God's address is the "Stop!" of the judge, when, for example, God calls to the guilty man who is fleeing from Him: "Adam, where are you?" (Gen. 3:9). Confronted with this call, Adam experiences how useless it is to try to have Eve take his place under judgment: "The woman whom thou gavest to be with me . . ." (Gen. 3:12). And it is equally useless for Eve to have the serpent take her place: "The serpent beguiled me . . ." (Gen. 3:13). It is in this moment when they are addressed, when they become responsible, that they experience their own uniqueness and the impossibility of having someone else substitute for them.

It is equally impossible in the moment of God's judgment for us to substitute suprapersonal entities for ourselves as, for example, our milieu or the spirit of the times. If, for example, a man had betrayed his convictions for the sake of his career, he might be able to say, "It is not *I* who sinned, but the age in which I live that demanded it," or (especially in an age of mass suggestion), "I sensed that my own personal decision made no difference and I floated willy-nilly, unconsciously carried by the billows of the masses and the intoxication of it. Momentarily my own indigenous personhood was extinguished."

But this sort of disengagement does not exist. The biblical message teaches everywhere that I am separable from all the powers that surround me and support me, that in this ultimate dimension of my personhood I have to become singularly alone. Thus, the rich young ruler of Mark 10:17 ff. is challenged to sell all that he has so that his riches can no longer substitute for him. For Jesus had looked deeply enough into him to see that this man's piety was calculated on the presupposition of his standard of living, which he needed as much as air to breathe—at least much more than he needed God. Separated from it he considered himself to be nothing. He was completely identified with his wealth and its ups and downs. For this reason, Jesus challenged him to break away from it and to become singularly alone.

In the same fashion Jesus can demand that under certain circumstances we be prepared for his sake to leave behind our entire kinship connections. In other words, he proclaims that we should be separable even from that (Luke 14:26 and parallel passages). When "goods, fame, child, and wife" are gone we are not then simply nothing; indeed, in certain circumstances we then for the first time become something. That is, we become people who exist entirely by God's address and in obedience to him.

According to our line of thought, even the eschatological words of the Apostle Paul, "having as though they had not" (1 Cor. 7:29 ff.), signify the distance between ourselves and the things which actually have *us* and would devour us. They signify that even though we stand within the natural orders and are dedicated to them, we dare not let them become substitutes for us; we dare not totally identify ourselves with them. For our existence does not derive from these orders, but from God's address, and therefore we are both called into them as stewards and called out from them, as persons who are separable from them and singularly alone.

God drags us out, as it were, from everything we have sought to hide behind and turns into bright daylight the night in which we have tried to become personless and eliminate our responsibility. Behind the trees where Adam hid himself and into the night of our extinguished selfhood rings out the arresting call of God: You are the one I mean, I have called you by your name; you are in a special way responsible to me, that is, you are loosed from everything that apparently conditions you and takes away your responsibility. I do not mean you as "man in general," or as representative of "the human all too human," or as twentieth-century man (who can blame everything on the spirit of the times). I mean *you,* you who bear your *name,* that name that responsibly underlies whatever you undertake as an agent for the spirit of the times or for the orders in which you stand, even if you maintain a hundred times that all of this is not your action or that in all of this you have no personal responsibility, that is, that in all of this you are personless and merely the plaything of the powers that possess you and that operate through you. By no means are you excused by the orders (e.g., the state or the economic order), nor by generally accepted binding norms (e.g., concerning our stance toward worthy or unworthy life, toward fellow countrymen, or toward what is alien to the race). By no means are you excused by what according to your account forced you to act, but you yourself are the active agent and responsible executor of these orders.[6]

Only when man understands himself as one addressed in this fashion does he also know of his irreplaceable character as one who is unique and singularly alone. And only when he understands his irreplaceable character in this way does he perceive himself as a phenomenon of history rather than nature. At this point history is, above all, history with God and thus simply that event which creates history in the first place.

This notion of being singularly alone, which is not without connections to Kierkegaard, has of course nothing to do with individualism. As we have worked out the concept, being singularly alone becomes evident precisely in the midst and on the basis of man's connections with things and with human fellowships. In order to make the antithesis to individualism graphic, we can say that the singularly alone one is not the individualistic *subject* of a world event; he is, in the midst of the world events that pass through him and sustain him, the *object* of the divine address.

One dare not get the two mixed up. Individualism is one particular perceptible form of historical existence that occurs among men. To be singularly alone signifies being isolated *before God,* which is another dimension entirely.

DEATH AND PERSONHOOD IN THE AGE OF ORTHODOXY

It is a distinctive characteristic of orthodoxy that it did not highlight this quality of man's historical being and therefore it

[6] See the corresponding sections on the doctrine of the orders in my book *Geschichte und Existenz* (Gütersloh, 1935), which still represents the basic contours of my position.

constructed a distorted doctrine of death. This distortion is reflected above all in the terribly short-circuited connection it made between sin and death. In simple fashion it labels death as a consequence of the fall into sin; the fall is the cause and death the effect.[7] Thus death simply becomes an evil, the reaction, so to speak, of divine righteousness to man's rebellious provocation.

Two things remain unclarified here. In the first place, why is God's answer death and not some other evil? Could death not also truly be understood as the manifestation of some biological law? On what grounds does man simply deny that death is the effect of this obvious biological law and instead make it dependent upon that metaphysical cause?

Secondly, the specific character of *human* death remains perforce unclear. The simple causal connection—death regarded as the effect, of which sin is the cause—apparently brings the entire cosmos into an excessively short-circuited subordination to man's fall. Completely apart from this difficult problem of subordination—which we will deal with later[8]—the death of man and the death of animals are here once more relegated to the same level. The specific character of man's dying in contrast to that of the animals is denied, as in the biological materialism of our own day.[9]

As a rule Lutheran orthodoxy is satisfied with the simple assertion *that* (but not how or why) death is a consequence of sin and that man is guilty of death. Johann Gerhard deduces three causes (it is significant that he designates them *principales causae*) of death. "The first is the wickedness of the devil and his temptation; the next is the guilt of man who committed the transgression; the

[7] Within the systems of the orthodox theologians, the doctrine of death is treated under various headings; sometimes under the *status integritatis,* sometimes under the heading of man's corruption and its consequences, often also in connection with the doctrine of providence under the question of the relationship of evil to God's governance of the world. Finally, especially in later orthodoxy, it is treated under the heading *De novissimis.*

[8] See Appendix II on "Death in the Cosmos."

[9] The dogmatics of the Reformed tradition, especially that of Johann Heinrich Heidegger, at least gives a hint of this concern by treating death in its concrete significance for man's relationship to God. See, e.g., his discussion of the separation from God occurring in death, the significance of the separation of soul from body as a sign of the original integrity being broken and as the sign of an unnaturalness which cannot be deduced from man's nature, in Heinrich Heppe, *Die Dogmatik der ev.-reformierten Kirche,* ed. Ernst Bizer (Moers, 1935), pp. 238, 260.

third is the wrath of God in his vengeance." Hafenreffer expresses the same connection this way: "Since man has truly transgressed God's commandments, death came into the world by sin."[10]

Theologically, there are two criticisms to be made of this commonly held Christian opinion about the origin of death.

At the outset the argument for deducing death from the sin of the first man is subject to the same criticism that is validly addressed to the orthodox form of the doctrine of original sin. In both cases man is viewed in a fatalistic subjugation (reminiscent of natural law) to some given that has occurred outside of him, and as a result, despite all the theological and metaphysical decoration, he is not treated in terms of his history with God, but as a phenomenon of nature. However, there is no aspect of living or of dying in which man can legitimately consider himself only as an effect in a causal naturalistic cause-effect relationship to divine activity. On the contrary, his life is always—even in the midst of its subjugation to God and Satan—historically responsible. Luther worked out this problem with special clarity at that most extreme point of human existence where the subjugation appears total, namely, in the realm of the *servum arbitrium,* the enslaved will. In order to highlight here too the personal historical responsibility of man, Luther emphasizes that the posture of subjugation, in which man after the fall into sin is forced to act, never has the character of a coercion, but rather of a necessity.[11]

With this, Luther means to say that if such subjugation did possess the character of coercion, then man would be standing in a fatalistically determined situation of compulsion that would remove all responsibility from him. He would then be only the impersonal effect of a cause that determines him, which, as it were, operates through him without himself being in any sense an active subject. For this reason Luther introduces the concept of necessity as a corrective. This necessity, to be sure, also expresses the compulsory character of man's actions, but in a way that still derives the actions from man himself as the active subject. Man

[10] See the respective sections of Heinrich Schmid, *The Doctrinal Theology of the Evangelical Lutheran Church,* 3rd ed. (Minneapolis: Augsburg, 1961).

[11] For the references in Luther see my *Geschichte und Existenz,* pp. 50 ff.

can do nothing but express in his actions what resides within him, develop his own self in his actions and to that extent include his own self in whatever he has done. "Hence it is that the ungodly man . . . wills, desires and acts according to his nature."[12]

From this perspective, to say that man knows about his original sin can only mean: I know that what I am has its origin within myself, that I really am as I find myself to be in my thinking, willing, and acting. I see no place in my own history in which I had myself in hand as a blank page and where I still possessed an open possibility within my control. I always see myself facing the reality of my own self. This reality is labeled alienation from God, and I must confess that this reality is my reality.

Only in this way does man stand in a history and not merely in natural causal subjugation to transsubjective powers. If this is forgotten and if, for example, original sin is understood in analogy to a causally deterministic natural law (i.e., as the product of some doctrine of heredity regardless of its metaphysical substructure), then man becomes personless and to that extent exempt from responsibility.

In practice this leads to a well-known consequence. A consistent orthodox doctrine of original sin entails a concomitant attitude of indifference toward actual sins, and to that extent it tends toward irresponsibility. Human existence stands summarily under a minus sign. The concrete negative actions that occur, my offenses against God, lose thereby their specific weight and are only the symptoms of a fateful destiny, a pressuring coercion, that overarches my entire existence. Sin, so to speak, is no longer "mine and mine alone." It becomes the "human all too human" in which I share. And in the face of this weightlessness of sin itself, the redemptive work of Christ, ostensibly for the sake of removing that sin, appears as an excessive and unnecessary expenditure. Consequently it too becomes incredible. This can be seen in the reductionist Christologies that followed orthodoxy. (It would lead us too far afield at this point to move to the easily documented connection between this fact and the wholesale and thereby trivializing

[12] *WA* 18, 709. *Martin Luther on The Bondage of the Will,* ed. J. I. Packer and O. R. Johnston (London: James Clarke & Co., 1957), p. 204.

confession of sins in the Protestant service of absolution.)

The same fateful consequences of the orthodox cause-and-effect way of thinking naturally become apparent in relation to the phenomenon of death just as in relation to original sin. Since death is simply a punitive consequence of the first fall into sin, it befalls me in the same way as the natural occurrence of a thunderstorm or a hurricane, both of which come upon me without any effort on my part. And even the recollection of that distant "whence" of death is unable to remove its character as an impersonal happening.

The characterization of death that arises from this perspective we could express graphically as follows. In orthodoxy's way of thinking death becomes an occurrence of natural law but ceases to be anything that I have incurred. It amounts to the death of "man," but ceases to be "my" death.

When the character of death as "mine and mine alone" is lost, it becomes clear that a fact of history—always striking me as an individual, irreplaceable and responsible—is transmuted into a fact of nature to which I am subject as to any coercively deterministic law. Man under the shadow of death as viewed by orthodoxy becomes just as personless as he does under the fate of an original sin that is viewed hereditarily and deterministically. In both cases he is but the impersonal point of intersection for a transsubjectively functioning law that works through him.

From this arises the second consequence, that death does not strike man in his personal relationship with God. Failing to see God's hand and arrow aimed at him personally, man is consequently placed on the same level as the rest of nature. From this then follows the further conclusion (erroneous, though it seems so self-evident) that death in the animal world derives from the sin of man. An act of judgment always occurring anew and concretely in the personal relationship between man and God is transformed into a theory of the origin of death which then comes into competition with the biological theory. Indeed, it must compete with the biological theory because it has put itself on the same plane.

The pattern persists. As soon as an event originating in God is depersonalized, that is, as soon as it has lost its historical mine-and-mine-alone character, it becomes some sort of pseudoscientific theory or world view.

This symptom is even more obvious in the doctrine of creation than in the phenomena of sin and death. The danger of seeing Genesis 1 as a theory of the world's origin or of setting up one's own theory in conjunction with the biblical creation account arises when the event of creation is neutralized. This occurs when I forget that through his creative act God has not simply set me on my feet like the young lions or calves, but has created me to be his possession so that I owe myself to him and am obligated to give him an accounting of what I have made out of his work. Therefore Luther's words in his interpretation of the creation ("I believe that God made me") constitute the keenest safeguard against such depersonalizing of creation into a mere cosmogony. And how he achieves that safeguard is quite characteristic. He does it by designating creation as a personal historical event to be understood only from the perspective of mine-and-mine-alone. I am created by God and thus obligated to him.

In summary, we might say that orthodoxy changes death from a fact of history into a fact of nature, even if metaphysically disguised. The manner in which it unites sin and death is by an illegitimate causal connection, that is, a connection which makes the man whom death strikes personless and sees him as a victim of a suprapersonal natural law.

Here a disastrous implication becomes apparent. When orthodoxy makes man so personless and views him as an entity of nature, it puts its doctrines of original sin, death, and creation—and by no means only these doctrines—on the same plane as biology and natural science. Thus it enters into a completely illegitimate competition with them which leaves it defenseless in the hands of the advancing knowledge characteristic of the forward march of science. The fact that science and religion have been considered antipodes in the recent past, and to some extent even now, is basically traceable to this erroneous development beginning in the period of orthodoxy.

11.

Death as Personal Event

We now have our task clearly defined: to analyze death as a personal historical event and not as a natural one. Of course we will also have to reflect on the way the two aspects of death are related to each other, the personal and the biological or medical. But the priority for the initial task is simply to demonstrate that the historical and personal aspect is the intrinsic character of the reality of death.

Even secular observers note that human death is different from animal death in that man knows about his dying. To be sure, this knowledge of death can be interpreted in radically divergent ways; and here we will also see the chasm between secular and biblical thought.

Animals know nothing of cemeteries nor any of the other reminders of death that accompany man on the path of life. Man however is compelled to know that some day "holy Troy will pass away," and this knowledge lies like a shadow over his entire life. He cannot follow the arrow of his life without being mathematically certain that this arrow at some specific point will have to strike down upon the earth. One cannot even mention this human knowledge of death without immediately understanding it as part of the content of man's life.

It is conceivable, of course, and experts credibly assure us, that animals too possess a certain measure of knowledge about their death. In any case it frequently appears to be so, if one is affected by their presentiment of death and their anxiety about death. Sometimes dogs, for instance, seem to have an extremely sensitive premonition of the impending death of their master while the human relatives do not yet suspect it at all.

But this knowledge, which may indeed be present, is different from human knowledge in that it is acute and arises only in the temporally immediate circumstances of danger or of actual perishing.[1] Human knowledge of death however consists in knowing that I *am* toward death, long before death chronologically comes upon the scene. Hence knowledge about death is a characteristic of human life. Only in this way—that is, only when we see the shadow of death thrown back across our entire life—can we understand the biblical picture of man sitting in the region of darkness and in the shadow of death and at this point being sought out by Jesus (Luke 9:1; Matt. 4:16; Luke 1:79). It is not only the end of life but life itself that is characterized by death. Thus Pascal can say with profound insight, "Death is easier to bear without thinking of it, than is the thought of death without peril."[2]

If we interpret this thought in terms of what we have just established, we already know that the factor which makes death frightful is by no means its being a physical moment, the end point of life, for that can whisk me away without terror if I succeed in duping my consciousness or in some other way switching it off. Neither is death's horror in the process of destruction that precedes it, for example, in severe injury or illness. For all such things can be just as frightful, yes, even more frightful apart from any fatal termination.

No, the gruesome aspect of death is the thought of death, that thought which casts a shadow across man's entire life and characterizes this life as Being-toward-death. Thus death's horror consists in its being a constituent of life, of life all the way back to

[1] This is how Luther characterizes the difference between death of animals and death of man. See *LW* 13, 107.

[2] Blaise Pascal, *Pensées,* Modern Library Edition (New York: Random House, 1941), p. 59.

the moment of birth and not merely some temporally datable moment of acute mortal danger. In a similar sense Luther, in view of the anxious awareness of death that accompanies life, related death to life itself: "This terror is truly the poison of death."[3] If death belonged only to life's final moment and not to all of life, then it would no longer be fearsome. This is why there are so many attempts to render death harmless by making it the phenomenon of such a moment or of such a last hour. We saw this in the first half of the book in Barbarin's statistical approach to death.

Hölderlin in his ode "Der Mensch" had a special view of death as the power that overshadows life itself when he spoke of the birds, unencumbered by knowledge of death, breathing more freely and thus taking life in stride quite differently:

> More freely breathe the birds of the woods, although
> The breast of Man more proudly may heave and he
> May see into the future's darkness,
> Death he sees too and alone must fear it.[4]

It is entirely in line with this when he calls the child, who is still not conscious of himself and thus also unaware of death, "immortal": "It is immortal for it knows nothing of death."[5] This would be nonsense if death were comprehended as an end point; for obviously Hölderlin too knows that the child does not stay a child, but becomes an old man and thus fulfills the laws of his own mortality. It makes sense only if the essence of death is seen in the influence exerted by our knowledge of it upon our entire lives. Only in this sense is a child still immune to death.

As far as the nature of death's influence upon our lives is concerned, this is again a matter of common knowledge among men. Either life's futility becomes transparent (with the frequent consequence of indifference) or man suppresses the knowledge of that

[3] *LW* 13, 115. Luther's own lecture notes (not the final printed copy) read at this point, "This fear of death, this despair, this horror is death itself." *WA* 40^{III}, 550, 1.

[4] Michael Hamburger, trans. and ed., *Hoelderlin* (New York: Pantheon Books, 1952), p. 99.

[5] Friedrich Hölderlin, *Hyperion* (Ulm: Aegis Verlag, 1946), p. 14.

futility by living as though life were eternal: by deifying his own work, delaying the inevitable, and gaining more time. In the words of Shakespeare:

> That we shall die, we know; 'tis but the time
> and drawing days out, that men stand upon.[6]

And the rich farmer viewing his filled granaries said to himself, "Soul, you have ample goods laid up for many years" (Luke 12:19)—you are, so to speak, immortal.

Even if in contrast to the animal realm knowledge of death extends oppressively across man's entire life, and therefore as a rule is repressed, there are still within the human realm fundamental differences in the nature of this knowledge and the value assigned to it. Such a difference exists between natural secular knowledge of death on the one hand and faith's knowledge of it on the other. Without wanting to anticipate our later discussion of this matter, we might simply say in a preliminary way (as Luther said) that the heathen of course know of death in the fact that man dies, but they do not know the why or the wherefore. In technical terms they do indeed know death's formal and material causes, its external causes, but not its efficient and final cause, the inner causality and teleological purpose. "It is common knowledge to all men that they must die, and that we all travel the same road, and see death both before us, alongside us, and behind us; wise men even among the pagans have bemoaned this tragedy of the human race. But the cause of death and whence it comes, that they have been unable to perceive. Most people think that it happens by chance, that we die like cattle, as though man were created in such a way that he must necessarily die."[7]

What is initially of paramount importance in the biblical doctrine of death is that it keeps the knowledge about death open and in overwhelming monotony admonishes man to take it seriously, thus preventing the usual repression and the custom of closing one's eyes to it. As the Bible thus puts a finger on the knowledge of death, it also lays a finger, as it were, on the human

[6] *Julius Caesar,* act 3, scene 1, ll. 100-101.

[7] *D. Martin Luthers Werke,* Kritische Gesamtausgabe (Weimar, 1883–), vol. 22, p. 284. [Hereinafter cited as *WA.*]

quality of death. For knowledge about death, according to our previous insight, is a specifically human affair, distinguishing man from the animal realm.

It is equally important, however, to note that the Bible by no means nurtures knowledge of death for its own sake. The Bible has no interest, for example, in reminding man that he may no more ignore the reality of his dying than he would forget eating and drinking and the other life functions. Such a *memento mori* would be a piece of practical wisdom, which in its aim and its one-sidedness is quite alien to biblical thought, yes, even contradictory to it. For looking fixedly at some ostensibly important point of our life (in this case the end point) would soon bewitch and captivate a man the same way as a spellbound fascination with any other realities of life, such as with eating and drinking ("Let us eat and drink, for tomorrow we die") or with mammon. It is not only the radiant luminous powers of existence that can be deified, but also the dark and ominous ones. Any absolutizing on one side would be just as much idolatry and bewitchment as it is on the other. (Those all-too-facile critics should take note of this when they ridicule Christianity's somber bells ringing out an open knowledge of death and yet do not know where the bells are hanging. Here as everywhere in life we must see not merely the symptoms, in this case the weight of Christian knowledge of death, but above all the reality standing behind the symptoms and producing them.)

No, when the Bible emphasizes man's knowledge of death, the point is not merely, nor even primarily, the fact of our having to die, but the why, as Luther indicated. It is in this dimension that the human aspect of human death first becomes evident. For only this dimension gives us an insight into that disorder between God and man, as death reveals it. Here lies the genuine background of human dying; here the issue at stake is an answer to the "why."

We could also express it in the following way. When the Bible speaks of knowledge about death, or more accurately, about the "why" of death, it means the background of personhood operative in death, that which points to the relationship between God and man manifesting itself in death. Consequently it does not consider death to be a biological event; neither does it consider knowledge about death to be simple clarification about life's biological limits.

The biblical message about the knowledge of death makes human death, as it were, doubly powerful in comparison with that of animals: first, by even taking up the issue of the knowledge of death which distinguishes man from the animal, and, secondly, by further distinguishing between the universal human knowledge of the fact of death and the biblically revealed knowledge of the why. It is in the latter that it expresses the personal character of dying, as we have already shown in our preliminary outline.

Now since we have clearly specified our route into the biblical knowledge of death, let us be even more precise in our understanding. As far as material goes, two references are sufficient although they could be multiplied almost at will. In Psalm 90:12, the psalmist asks for clarity about the knowledge of his own death; he asks that God would guard him from suppressing that knowledge: "So teach us to number our days that we may get a heart of wisdom." Similarly Psalm 39:4 says: "Lord, let me know my end, and what is the measure of my days; let me know how fleeting my life is!" The psalmist requests this open and constantly clear knowledge about death for three reasons: in order to achieve a proper relation to the world, a proper relation to God, and a proper relation to time, or more precisely a proper relationship to the directional movement which characterizes our time line. We shall deal with the first two of these reasons here and then come back to the third in Chapter 13.

OUR RELATION TO THE WORLD REVEALED BY DEATH

Since I know about the end of my life, I can no longer constantly live on the basis of things. For death terminates this relation to things even if it is incomprehensible and rather discomforting for me to know it and even if I consequently seek to override it with intensive clamor and concentrated self-anesthesia.[8]

[8] See once more the citation from Hoche, p. 16 above.

Of these things mammon is the one we naturally think of first as representative of those creaturely powers by means of which I seek to make myself secure and "draw out my days." This self-security is so vain that the believer, by virtue of his eternal reliance on God, no longer needs to fear when he sees his godless enemy rich and ostensibly secure, "for when he dies he will carry nothing away; his glory will not go down after him" (Ps. 49:17). Just as we brought nothing into the world, so we also take nothing away with us (1 Tim. 6:7). We do not consist of these attributes, these almost artificial stuffings of our existence. For these are the very things that have no durability, but fade away in death.

What we do have is a self that exists beyond all these things and is separable from them. And it is this self which is the subject of blessedness and contentment. At the same time, however, this self is the object of that history that God has entered into with us which even death cannot fracture. It is not as though we ourselves were not fractured by death (we are indeed!). It is not as though we were immortal (we must indeed die). It is not as though we had more than that "house not made with hands, eternal in the heavens" (1 Cor. 5:1) (we must indeed pass through death). But God holds "our heavenly dwelling" (1 Cor. 5:2) ready for us. He holds it ready despite all the death that really does surround us.

Paul does not say that God has given us some immortal substance which would victoriously break through our mortal fate. No, not a bit of us breaks through this fate. But God has given us the hope that on the other side of the great fissure he continues to be Lord and does not allow his history to be ruptured, that he is for us a God of life and resurrection, that he remains the Creator *ex nihilo*—and his initial installment of this hope is the Spirit (2 Cor. 5:5). This Spirit is not some immortal spirit of man or an unquenchable divine spark, but the Spirit of God himself, who remains under his direction. In relation to the Spirit, we are always petitioners and worshipers; we are those who persevere at a distance and do not revere ourselves in that Spirit. The petitioner's posture prevails: *Veni creator spiritus.*

OUR RELATION TO GOD REVEALED BY DEATH

The biblical conclusion that "in death we must leave behind everything that we have relied on here below" is not made in the name of some weary skepticism or some annullment of all life's values. That would be true only if we held exclusively to the negative part of the conclusion: "Everything is wiped out." The goal of the biblical admonition is rather something eminently positive; instead of annulling all values, it seeks a proper ranking of all values before God. This becomes especially clear in the controversy between Jesus and the rich mammon-worshipers.

We can see it already in the previously mentioned parable of the rich farmer. His life consisted in "time and drawing days out." With his granaries full, he retires content: "Soul, you have ample goods laid up for many years; take your ease . . ." (Luke 12:19). Then comes the sudden call from God: "Fool! This night your soul is required of you; and the things you have prepared, whose will they be?" God's call does not simply mean to certify the vanity of everything earthly and make the man a skeptic in the last moment. It seeks rather to rub his nose into the fact that he has neglected the one and only enduring reality, namely, his history with God; he has neglected this enduring reality because he has cherished and falsely committed himself to what perishes. The parable itself expresses this contrast between the durable and the perishing in the words, "So is he who lays up treasure for himself, and is not rich toward God." Whoever neglects this "richness toward God" loses in death not only the treasures, but above all his self, insofar as he has forgotten to capitalize on his history with God, though he has been offered acceptance into it. "Richness toward God" is nothing but being rich in hope for the "heavenly dwelling." It means being bound to the Lord who will not let death have its prey, since he is the Lord of life. Only insofar as we participate thus in God's history do we have a self that, to be sure, does not outlast death, but is a participating member of the resurrected head, who stands out above the night of dying and does not desert his own.

It is all too plain that the rich farmer did not lose his self—

in view of our earlier terminology we can simply say his person—only in death; he had lost it all during his lifetime, in the midst of his satiated ownership of the granaries he had filled and admired. He was already a ghost, a personless shadow without genuine existence. He was already in judgment (John 3:19) regardless of the fact that this was concealed from men's vision. For men's vision regularly focuses on a person's appearance, not on the person himself (Matt. 22:16; John 7:24; Rom. 2:11; Gal. 2:6; 1 Pet. 1:17).

What was at stake with the rich farmer was by no means merely the question of other-worldliness to which death was the passageway. At stake was also his personless, hollowed-out existence in this world, the upshot of which was death. Death merely exposed the fate of a life that "though he lived, yet he had died." From this vantage point it is quite clear that the proclamation about death is not part of a skeptical, relativizing negative philosophy, but that it reevaluates all values according to their highest criterion—we might even say according to the only criterion.

Consequently it is wrong or at least inaccurate if we speak of death only as the end of our riches, our possessions, the content of our lives. That is not at all the main viewpoint of the Scriptures. Riches as such are of no consequence. They are things, valued as things, and in a certain sense they are also an expression of order (e.g., the order of property) which we should not simply dismiss, but in which God permits us to stand (Eph. 6:1 ff.) albeit within the bounds of "having as though we had not" (1 Cor. 7:29). Biblically death is important not as the end of our treasures, but insofar as it marks the end of the gods we have made out of them, whereby those treasures have assumed the place of "richness toward God." It is not the treasures themselves that are significant in connection with the reality of death, but the position they occupy for us, the throne they have ascended and upon which they function as "other gods before Him." The loss of treasures as things of value is certainly a psychological problem, as Hoche expressed so well (see p. 16 above). It is not until we experience the end of treasures as our gods, that is, as illegitimate competitors of God, that the theological problem arises. Treasures become gods when we possess them as though we possessed them forever.

When death separates us from our treasures, it is all-important that we look not to the treasures. They are of interest only to moths and rust, but otherwise neither to God nor to man. What counts is that we keep our eyes on the relation which we have to those treasures, or to express it more directly in terms of our concern, that we keep our eye on the personal relationship into which such treasures place us. This personal connection can be toward them as gods or to our actual Lord under whose eyes we have them as though we had them not. For this reason the Bible never speaks of riches per se, but always of rich men, that is, those who are characterized by their wealth alone, since they draw their life from it and are, as it were, possessed by it, their wealth having become their god. If Luther says God per se has nothing to do with us, but only God in his *quoad me,* his relatedness to me, then the same could be said of our riches and the entire content of our lives. They are not significant theologically as things of value, but they are significant in their *quoad me.* This *quoad me* however is nothing less than the personal relationship in which I let these things put me, whether in the midst of them I belong to God or to mammon. (Of course it is obvious that instead of mammon I can take any idealistic values. These of course can also be lodged at the wrong spot in the ranking of values and consequently render me personless in living and dying. We need only mention the values *Geist* and *Volk* to catch an immediate glimpse of these consequences).

Therefore let us be clear in our formulation in order to steer clear of any skeptical or negativistic misunderstanding. The boundary line of death is important insofar as it is the limit of the deceptive jurisdiction of our gods. At the same time it points us toward the Lord who awaits us at the boundary line and for whom we have to be prepared. Death's boundary line makes our personal existence evident.

But what is there about this Lord who awaits us at death's

boundary? Having discussed the false gods whose end is our death, we must now consider the connection to Him.

Psalm 90 teaches us to pray for a clear knowledge of death "that we may get a heart of wisdom." This wisdom consists, according to vv. 7-8, in the awareness that we are consumed by God's anger. Thus the prayer is that we might recognize the particular relation to God in which we actually stand, and as a result not become secure, not overestimate ourselves, not dream that we bear within us some substantive eternal life. To know this is wisdom, because it means that illusions and securities are removed and it imparts to us the necessary and drastically needed realism, namely, reckoning with and measuring all things by the one and only value.

Now of course it is important to note that this one and only value is no timeless entity (some *summum bonum,* e.g.) nor even God per se, as though he would be anything to us. On the contrary, this one and only value consists in a very concrete connection to, and encounter with, this God. In short, it consists in a personal act, an event. One could say it consists in the incarnation of Christ and my confrontation with him as my Lord in judgment and promise. An event is the actual standard of value! At stake here is a personal reality, not a thing at all.[9] This personal event, manifest in death and casting its shadow across all the things that fill our lives, is what the psalmist designates as judgment, the wrath of God.

God's wrath signifies the reaction of divine holiness to man's separation, hence to his sin. Death is the most exposed place in which that wrath of God is experienced. It signifies that human life cannot pass God's inspection. Human life is not God's eternal life.

"We must depart." That is, in a very explicit way we are dust, from which we were made and to which we return again. But for the thought-world of the psalmist dust is not simply symbolic of

[9] Hence the concept "value" is not specifically applicable for conveying our meaning, since the term in normal usage is laden too much with a sense of timelessness. Actually we used it only in a preliminary way in order to move forward to this point. From now on we shall drop it.

that perishable quality which also applies to flowers and grass (Ps 103:14; 104:29; 90:6-7). Of course their perishing too, as well as their growth, can only be comprehended in relation to God: "When thou sendest forth thy Spirit, they are created" and vice versa, "When thou takest away their breath, they die and return to their dust" (Ps. 104:29-30).

Not even the flowers and grass, nor any nonhuman creatures, ever have a self-contained finitude that grants them independent life. All their growing and perishing, even their death, is effected by God. But the flowers and the grass, the whales and the mountains know nothing of being thus related to God. Only man knows this. Only he with his solitary awareness of death protrudes above the creaturely realm and thus has a different form of perishability, as though his were raised to a higher power. He alone must pose the question of the meaning of God's action that comes to expression in his death.

Merely because he is able to pose the question—no, because he is compelled to pose the question, it becomes evident that man's returning to dust is qualitatively different from the simply physical returning to dust of a simply physical being. It is clear that here man experiences something in response to which he must pose the "why" question, simply because it is no obvious and unquestionable link in a process of natural law. He sees clearly a decision being made against him here with which he must come to terms.

What is the nature of this decision, this element that exceeds the natural law of physical necessity? If, first of all, we simply let the key thoughts of Psalm 90 speak for themselves, we come to the following conclusions: From man's vantage point death is his lot because of his guilt. From God's vantage point the death verdict falls on man because of His wrath.

Guilt and wrath must be seen together. The theological question is this: Why and for what reason should both come to expression in man's death?

From the example of Protestant orthodoxy we are sufficiently warned to take the "why" and "wherefore" question very seriously and avoid the short-circuited and over-simplified conclusion that death is simply punishment, period. Orthodoxy might even add that death was chosen as a disciplinary rod since it is so painful to man, a much harsher whiplash than those other punishments whereby pain accompanies childbirth, and sweat and tears are necessary for procuring the fruits of the earth. Such a line of thinking breaks off at the decisive point; with this sort of presentation we could not coax anyone out of his cozy comfort. For this would just be another instance of manipulating the causes of death. Our previous criticism of the error of such a procedure still stands. Questions of causality are solved much better and much more credibly by natural science. Thus, the cardinal question which we have now approached from all sides is why and in what sense the fate of guilt and wrath comes to expression precisely in man's dying.

No one can grasp the mystery if he has not first of all marveled at it. If we simply take the formidable opening verses of Psalm 90 by themselves we get an inkling of what human death and decay are all about.

> Lord, thou hast been our dwelling place in all generations.
> Before the mountains were brought forth, or ever thou hadst formed the earth and the world, from everlasting to everlasting thou art God.
> Thou turnest man back to the dust and sayest, "Turn back, O children of men!"
> For a thousand years in thy sight are but as yesterday when it is past, or as a watch in the night.
> Thou dost sweep men away; they are like a dream, like grass which is renewed in the morning: in the morning it flourishes and is renewed; in the evening it fades and withers.

The impression left by the psalm is something to the effect that the sea of time smashes onto the shores of eternity, that its breakers pound against him for whom a thousand years are like a day. One has the sensation that the sea of time is enclosed on all sides by the shore of eternity and amounts to no more than a modest ripple within it.[10] If one views death only in the light of these first verses, apart from what follows, death would seem to be explained in terms of the difference in the energy resources of time as contrasted with those of eternity. Death then simply represents human finitude vis-à-vis God's infinity.

But precisely here it is all-important that the issue remain in no sense at the level of a quantitative distinction between God and man, but that a qualitative category, namely, guilt and wrath, be introduced to describe the inequality between God and man. "By thy wrath we are overwhelmed" (Ps. 90:7). The issue is finally not one of quantitative disparity between two entities, but one of a qualitative breakdown between two persons. What is involved here is not the different sizes of two parties, but a juridical verdict. Death therefore is visible representation not of the disparity between the two, but of the judgment. It hovers, so to speak, right over the point of fracture in the fellowship between God and man. Our first task now is simply to formulate this quite remarkable fact clearly, before we then seek to comprehend it.

Naturally death also represents quantitative finitude. But it is important to note that this finitude and its inequality in terms of energy resources in the face of God's eternity is always permeated and colored by the disparity between the sinner and God's holiness, by the awareness of judgment. What is involved here is anything but a feeling of being still a long way off from some ideal, still separated by a (quantitatively) long path and thus still needing to postulate a (quantitatively) infinite progression beyond the limits of death.[11] On the contrary what is involved is awareness of my sinnerhood, awareness of my separation from God's person, in the face of which the sense of quantitative distance is but secondary and derivative. What is involved is therefore a thoroughly personal phenomenon.

10 See in this respect the eleventh book of *The Confessions of St. Augustine*, trans. and ed. John K. Ryan (Garden City, N. Y.: Doubleday and Co., 1960), pp. 277 ff.

11 Cf. Kant's doctrine of immortality, which quite typically and consistently is thought out in the name of such an ideal demand, namely, the categorical imperative. The qualitative distance between what is and what ought to be leads to a quantitative extension of the "proving grounds" so that the disparity between the two can be reduced.

A typical instance of this is Peter's confession in the face of the miraculous draft of fishes, "Depart from me, for I am a sinful man, O Lord" (Luke 5:8). The reason this confession is so meaningful is that the miracle which occurred seems initially to lie beyond any implications for Peter's person. It appears to be a dynamic demonstration of Christ's power playing off the omnipotence and omniscience of God against the unwitting helplessness and impotence of limited man. Yet we must take special note that this disparity in terms of physical energy resources between God and man is immediately experienced by Peter in the personal dimension and, as it were, transposed into a different key. He does not sense that he is a "small fry" in the face of such a power play, nor a minute "atom" in the face of God's cosmic dominion, as would have to be the case if it were merely at the quantitative level of comparative power. On the contrary his being a "small fry" and an "atom" is but the projected shadow of the actual reality, namely, his sinnerhood, cast across the plane of quantitative standards of measurement. Thus it is the shadow of the fracture in the personal dimension which becomes apparent here. Both always go together, like a body with its own shadow. Hence on the divine side miracle and forgiveness of sins also belong internally together (Mark 2:1 ff.). The act of power in the miracle is only the measurable expression (or better: a projection into measurable categories) of the event of forgiveness, hence the restoration of a previously broken personal fellowship.

The same phenomenon that we saw with Peter can be seen in the closing verse of Psalm 104 which, although frequently contested, is nevertheless in terms of content exceedingly authentic. This psalm appears to be a single hymn of praise to God's dynamic superiority over the world and to the quantitative disparity between Creator and creature. And right in the face of this disparity, the psalm concludes (apparently abruptly, and yet it is abrupt only for one who views the realm of comparative power for its own sake and not as the cast shadow of the personal destiny between God and man): "Let sinners be consumed from the earth, and let the wicked be no more!" It is the exact parallel to Peter's experience of fracture in the personal dimension.

Let us summarize at this point as follows. Death becomes visible at the point of fracture in the fellowship between God and man; hence it does not express a merely quantitative disparity of power between time and eternity, even less is it characterized by the autonomy of biological life which is bound to the cycle of growth and decay (in other words another *quantitative* standard of life), but it is determined by the personal dimension, namely, the separation of man from living fellowship with God.

The personal aspect which we have seen embedded in the death of man says that it is not a "thou must" of natural law which I encounter when my last hour comes, and thus no necessary process which makes of me an object, but death is an event that I have produced, of which I am the subject, and which I have brought about in freedom, that is, as a person responsible for his performance.

The wrath of God by virtue of which we pass away is no fatalistic destiny and no simple "shore of eternity," but God's reaction to our action which we as persons have responsibly undertaken against him. In other words, the personal dimension means I have to concede that God is right when this happens to me. With my death God wants to say something to me. In my dying he reacts to me and therefore in this dying there resides a message. I see God's hand and word aimed at me.[12]

Here we have found the point which is all-important to understand. What we have to do is show how the personal dimension of guilt and wrath operates in and behind the dying that quantitatively limits us, in and behind the dying that is tied to the phases of our biological life—once more quantitative elements.

We can circumscribe the answer in two sentences antithetically attuned to each other: (1) Death is the representative of the

[12] This view of the juridical connection between sin and death is indirectly confirmed by Saint Paul's central doctrine of Christ's death as the vicarious penalty and atonement for our sin. See Rom. 8:3-4; 2 Cor. 5:21-22; Gal. 3:13; Heb. 2:14-15; 9:27. In the same way John's Gospel points out the connection between wrath and death, in one case by its doctrine of Jesus' death "that takes away the sin of the world" (1:29) and in another by its view of the "prince of the world" who is simultaneously a "murderer" (8:44).

boundary, the representative of the fact that our life has an end and that there is a measure to our days. (2) Man in revolt—and that means empirical man, man separated from God, man "on the loose"—is the representative of the fundamental boundary infraction.

As a gloss to the last sentence we might add that, biblically, sin is always described as a boundary infraction. It always means that man seeks to "be like God" (Gen. 3:5), that "man has become like one of us" (Gen. 3:22), and that he elevates himself —as in the episode of the tower of Babel—into God's own sphere (Gen. 11). Sin (separation) is thus never something purely negative, a simple parting company. On the contrary, this parting company may be said to occur implicitly in man's no longer wanting to be man, but to be God, in his wanting himself and not God to be the measure of all things and the measure of God too. Therefore the demand to have a God who is congruent with our image of man very vividly expresses this sinful hubris and draws a strict and substantive extension of the line that runs from Genesis 1 to 3. Idolatry above all is the most prominent manifestation of this endeavor to shape ultimate reality according to the image of man (Rom. 1:18 ff.) and make man the measure of all things and values. The same applies naturally to the essentially unaltered tendency of idolatry when it is transposed into the impersonal realm, as is expressed, for example, in the worship of an idea, or in the worship of pleasure, or in the worship of mammon. These differences in divine images arise only from the differences in the human types who are making these gods in their own images—regardless whether the term "god" is expressly used or not.[13]

In our juxtaposition of the two assertions—death as the boundary and man as one outside the boundaries—we see clearly the

[13] As an expression of just such a movement toward hubris and toward violating the boundaries see the rather indicative title of Ernst Bergmann's philosophy of religion *Die Geburt des Gottes Mensch* (Leipzig, 1938). Precisely because Bergmann gets in way over his head—in terms of philosophical competence as well—and thus cheerfully and uninhibitedly chatters away about heaven and hell, he presents everything quite distortedly and in the manner of a simpleton, but thereby betraying a lot. I recommend the book highly even if it does not possess the class and the demonic character of the story of the tower of Babel.

personal character of death within and behind all its biological aspects and its physical power factors. It must befall man on the same day that he eats of the forbidden fruit hanging beyond his boundary: Man "out of bounds" is shown his boundary. The first boundary, that between God and man, was left to the freedom of his obedience to respect; in this very freedom he wantonly transgressed it. So the second boundary is held out before him, one which is insurmountable and constitutes an unavoidable dividing line between perishing man and eternal God: this boundary is death.[14] The one who was called to living fellowship with God but sought to take his life in his own hands is shown that this life is nothing but death, that it must collapse into itself.

We can also circumscribe the decline from creation to fall as follows. The "likeness of God" which God created into man consists in man's being permitted to live with God; it is a kind of deathlessness.[15] By contrast the stolen "equality with God" which wants to surpass this bestowed life and strives to escape obligatory commitment in exchange for independence, leads directly to death. It is death. "The wages of sin is death."[16]

The terror of death thus consists not in its being the end or boundary in a quantitative temporal sense, but in its being the

[14] "We see that God speaks for us in our conscience from the fact that death carries out the verdict already spoken in our conscience—and we see that death comes from God in the fact that because of our sin we stand in fear of death." Carl Stange, *Luthers Gedanken über die Todesfurcht* (Berlin and Leipzig, 1932), p. 8.

[15] We are purposely avoiding the term "immortality," not only because it is metaphysically freighted and points in a different direction, but also in order to avoid falling into the trap of making dogmatic metaphysical assertions about man's primeval situation with the concomitant illegitimate historicizing assertions that this entails. It goes without question that the assertions of the Bible in Genesis 3 posit a profound and thoroughgoing difference between man's original destiny in life and his deathlessness (Gen. 3:3 ff.) on the one hand, and the immortality (Gen. 3:22) which he thought he had gotten or could get on the other hand.

[16] "This verse reveals in striking fashion," says Luther, "that death in man is in countless ways a far greater calamity than the death of other living beings. . . . But the death of human beings is a genuine disaster. Man's death is in itself truly an infinite and eternal wrath. The reason is that man is a being created for this purpose: to live forever in obedience to the Word and to be like God. He was not created for death. In his case death was ordained as a punishment of sin. . . . If Adam had not eaten of the forbidden tree, he would have remained immortal. . . . Therefore it comes to man as shocking news to hear that he, who had been created as a good and perfect being for life and who was to have his dwelling place in God, is now destined for death." *WA* 40III, 513-14; cf. *LW* 13, 94.

boundary for one who from the very beginning has been out of bounds. Or stated more tersely: in death we see manifest the one eternal God contradicting finite man in his attempted self-elevation beyond his boundaries.

This is the character of death as it becomes visible *coram deo.* One dare not therefore isolate it as a biological phenomenon, but must view it strictly in terms of the history between the I of man and the Thou of God in which it is framed. As we urged previously, one must take death as a fact of nature and make out of it a fact of history.

This fundamental theological understanding can be made clear by some additional amplifying statements. The significant aspect of death is not *that* it is the boundary, but rather *who* it is that is being bounded, namely, man out of bounds, man who has elevated himself from God's likeness to equality with God. In addition it is significant who *sets* the boundary, namely, the one who alone is holy and tolerates no other gods beside himself.

We can formulate this understanding as follows: Death in the biblical sense is not the death of man the mammal, but the death of man who wants to be God and who must learn that he is only man.

However, since man is both mammal and personified vehicle of hubris, in personal union as it were, death also has its biological side. But this biological termination that resides in death is not what is uniquely intrinsic to it, just as little as the fact that man is a mammal constitutes what is uniquely intrinsic to his humanity, but is only the physical basis of what is uniquely intrinsic. Uniquely intrinsic to man is his personhood. Uniquely intrinsic to death is the fact that via a biological medium it contradicts man's person, a person out of bounds.[17]

This duality of man in being both person and biological creature is also expressed in the curse imposed upon him by the death

[17] See Michael Schmaus, *Katholische Dogmatik,* vol. 3^{II}, 1st and 2nd ed. (Munich, 1941), p. 493: Physiological laws are allowed "to exercise their dominion all the way to annihilating life," as "punishment imposed by God upon sinful man." "In the operation of physiological laws something happens which no experiment and no experience can determine, but only faith can affirm, namely, the execution of an act of divine judgment."

verdict in Genesis 3:19. The curse condemns man to eat his bread in the sweat of his brow and still endure a variety of suffering untii he once more becomes the very dust from which he was taken. And then follows the reason for it: for you are dust, and to dust you shall return.

In this sentence both items are found. "You are dust," that is, you belong on the earth, belong in that subordinate realm under God, above which you have elevated yourself and will continue your self-elevation by building the tower of Babel as a link in the chain of your rebellion.

"And to dust you shall return," that is, since your death is such a return to dust, it remains a reminder that you will eventually be driven back behind the barrier you broke through. Your death is thus confirmation of the fact that you belong on earth and not in the heaven which you have sought to snatch.

Therefore it hurts to have to return to dust, since it gives us a reminder of the fall and the divine reaction to it. Thus Paul says in 1 Corinthians 15:56, "The sting of death is sin." That means in terms of what we have just learned that what really hurts in death—that reminder, that reaction of God—is sin. Sin gives death its right to me. Sin is death's foothold in the preserve of my person.

Simultaneously another thing becomes apparent, namely, how the biological and the personal event inseparably interpenetrate one another. To return to dust means both, of course. It does not merely mean being thrown back into the zone where man is once more behind boundaries, but at the same time also physically becoming dust, decomposing. That which qualifies the living man, namely, his personal and biological duality, qualifies also his end. In both cases both aspects must be viewed together.

The following objection might be raised: Is biological dying, the dehydration of cells, the decomposition of the organism therefore supposed to be made dependent upon that incident? Would the biological process have been different without this incident? How could that make sense at all?

The question and assertion inherent in this objection move in the wrong direction. For it once again introduces the erroneous and inappropriate causal connection for which we faulted orthodoxy, by disengaging the physical facts from biology's own laws and bringing them into causal dependence upon a metaphysical datum. The accounts of the creation and fall, however, are not seeking to chronicle history nor to deduce the fallen world from some first cause. The accounts of primeval man and his fall into sin are not concerned to present the datable chronological sequence of the earliest epochs in the history of mankind. These accounts are much more intent on describing *our situation* and interpreting the faith which confesses that God made me. It is not the factual truth of the world, but the factual truth about me that is at stake here. I am supposed to see myself as the one who comes from the creative hand of God and is indebted to him for my entire self. I am to see myself as the one—demonstrated by Adam, the prototypical exemplar[18]—who breaks away from this creaturely life and its existence under God. Creation and the fall into sin stretch, so to speak, like a horizon all the way around my existence, impinging upon me from all sides. If one wanted to present the theological intent of those accounts in some pictograph, he dare not chart them as the first segments of a time line which historically precede the twentieth-century time segment that I am now living through, as if they had occurred outside my existence in an era beyond the reach of memory. On the contrary, they must be presented as a circle that is drawn around me, the horizon encompassing my personal world.

[18] Luther likes to use the concept of "exemplar" (in the sense of prototype or archetype) in such texts, especially with reference to Christ, whose righteousness is my righteousness, whose humanity is my humanity. See his sermon on Matt. 11:25 ff. of 24 February 1517 (*LW* 51, 28-29). "The same thing that has been said of Christ will be understood as said of us for Christ's sake" (*LW* 27, 282). "Mine are Christ's living, doing, and speaking, his suffering and dying, mine as much as if I had lived, done, spoken, suffered, and died as he did" (*LW* 31, 297). See also *LW* 26, 163, also his lectures on the epistle to the Hebrews in James Atkinson, ed. and trans., *Luther: Early Theological Works,* Library of Christian Classics, vol. 16 (Philadelphia: Westminster, 1962), p. 46. It is first of all from this point that the Christ's being *pro me* reaches its highpoint. Similarly I can of course relate myself to the counterfigure of Adam as my archetypal exemplar. Adam's creatureliness is my creatureliness, Adam's fall and sin are my fall and my sin. See my theological analysis of our identity with Adam in *Geschichte und Existenz* (Gütersloh, 1935), pp. 239 ff.

On these grounds we can rule out the direction in which the objection above was raised. I cannot distinguish causally the personal and biological aspects of myself, as I might distinguish between cause and effect in a known quantity that can be comprehended and defined objectively. I cannot stand detached from myself in this sense, but as the nonobjectified subject of my responsibility I experience the inseparable interpenetration of my person and my biology or (to transpose it to the plane of idealism and thus already to modify it) the inseparable interpenetration of causality and freedom, of *mundus sensibilis* and *intelligibilis*. On the plane of just such idealism Kant described a similar factual situation when he said that to objective observation the mystery of the human person is totally incomprehensible—simply because it is being approached from the wrong angle. For in objective observation I simply have to view everything in subjection to the category of causality and consequently never catch sight of the phenomenon of freedom—or of responsibility. The phenomenon of freedom and responsibility I experience only as a nonobjectified reality, namely, by being confronted with moral decisions. There I experience—despite all the derivative causality in the things that are not "I"—that I am free, that is, that I am not causally determined in the actions that are assigned to me, but am myself the first cause.

Thus I assume an illegitimate and inappropriate position (namely, that of objective thinking, disregarding myself) when I try to bring my personhood and my biology into causal dependence upon one another, or when I refuse to let the personal phenomenon and the biological phenomenon of my death be two sides of the same coin, and instead dismantle them and derive one from the other. For this reason we used what seemed to be the most fitting formulation: that via the medium of biological dying a personal act pointing to the God-man relationship occurs, namely, the bounding of man out of bounds. We cannot and ought not try to get behind this union of biology and person, since we can only attempt it at the cost of our personal involvement, yes, at the cost of our personhood itself. We can and ought not try to get behind it any more than on Thanksgiving Day we ask what we should thank God for in the harvest and what thanks belongs to the farmer. Here, too, the farmer's labor is a medium in which—and inseparable from which—God's blessing occurs. In the words of Matthias Claudius, "It passes through our hands, but comes to us from God." In just the same way our dying passes "through the hands" of our biology, "but comes to us from God."

It is true that we die biologically the same death as animals do, and yet for us it is totally different, because we are simply different creatures. (See in Appendix II our treatment of the connection of animal death and the "groaning of creation" with man's fall). And if we should once posit—but only for illustrative purposes—a death of man apart from the wrath of God, beyond the personal fatefulness operative in death, then such death would in fact be something totally different; it would be in Luther's words only "a sleep."[19]

[19] See the Luther citations in chap. 12.

12.

Death in Luther's Theology

In working out the personal character of human death as we have just done, we find ourselves in essential agreement with the basic thoughts of Luther concerning this problem. We may note briefly how his thoughts parallel our own on the subject. This is especially clear in Luther's exegesis of Psalm 90 and Genesis 3.

Although he naturally operates with a different terminology, Luther observes very precisely the distinction between the physical and the personal side of dying. He works out the distinction by explicating the physical side in terms of the death of animals, and the personal side in terms of that quality in man which makes his death something more than the demise of animals.

In particular there are three rubrics under which Luther works out the distinction. (1) The natural quality of an animal's demise and the unnaturalness of human dying. (2) The constant contemporaneity of man's dying by virtue of the awareness of death that accompanies our entire life. (3) The illegitimacy of man's despising death.[1]

NATURAL ANIMAL DEATH AND UNNATURAL HUMAN DYING

An important statement of Luther which we shall be inter-

[1] Those sections of Luther's thought in which death is used parabolically for spiritual processes (e.g., the dying of the old man and rising again with Christ) lie beyond the scope of our present line of thought and are therefore not considered here.

preting as we go along begins with the significant words that "death in man" has its own uniqueness when compared with the death of animals. Note the suggestive formulation, "death in man" (*mors in homine*).[2] It is not simply "the death *of* man," but death which now—in contrast to the mortality of animals—overtakes man, death as it appears in the human sphere and is thereby—even though biologically identical to the death of animals—transformed. "*Mors in homine* is in countless ways a far greater calamity than the death of other living beings. Although horses, cows, and all animals die, they do not die because God is angry at them (*irascente Deo*). On the contrary, for them death is, as it were, a sort of temporal casualty, ordained indeed by God but not regarded by him as punishment. Animals die because for some other reason it seemed good to God that they should die."[3]

Luther can also say that the death of animals in contrast to that of men is nothing more than the operation of "a law of nature."[4] Naturally, Luther is by no means so blind about nature that he is unaware of the creatures' own anxiety and suffering at the time of death. Thus he does not arrive at his conviction about the contrasting gravity of man's dying by virtue of his oversimplified ignorance about the death of animals. "A hog that is slaughtered expresses its revolt and distress by its squeal. A tree that is cut down does not tumble to the ground without a creaking noise [the equivalent lamentations of botanical creation]. Therefore, how can human nature bear to think of God's wrath [namely, that wrath which stands as the particular fate behind men's dying] without tears, without muttering, without the most vigorous objection?"[5] This citation indicates the particular element in human death which makes it so much more painful than death

[2] See p. 144, n. 16.

[3] *LW* 13, 94. The word "temporal" might here be interpreted as follows: The death of animals refers only to their temporally delimited life's curve, but has no reference to anything beyond that.

[4] The death of human beings is, therefore, not like the death of animals. These die because of a law of nature." *Loc. cit.*

[5] *LW* 13, 107; cf. 106.

in the creaturely and animal world. Although the latter too has its own kind of distress, the former is qualitatively different by virtue of the relationship to God which becomes apparent in it.

"The death of human beings [in comparison with mere animal death] is a genuine disaster. Man's death is in itself truly an infinite and eternal wrath."[6] The word "eternal" when applied to death does not merely designate an unending death in hell which follows man's earthly life, as it were, a death beyond the grave. Rather eternal death already possesses us in the here and now. Carl Stange's interpretation is doubtlessly correct: "The word 'eternal' does not convey the meaning of unlimited time in contrast to the limited temporality of earthly life. The reason death is called 'eternal' is rather that the wrath of God expressed in death is invincible to anything else in the world. Nothing exists which can liberate us from the wrath of God and abolish that wrath. In this sense it is 'eternal.' "[7] Hence the reason why human death is infinite and eternal is this: Man is a special creature inasmuch as he was created with the goal of living as an image of God in obedience to the Word. Thus he was not created to die; death enters

[6] *LW* 13, 94. For Luther's understanding of the concept "eternal death" see his listing of the various kinds of death in Wilhelm Pauck, trans. and ed., *Luther: Lectures on Romans,* Library of Christian Classics, vol. 15 (Philadelphia: Westminster, 1961), pp. 179-80. "There is a double death, namely, the natural or, better, temporal one and the eternal one. Temporal death is the separation of body and soul. But this death is a symbol and a parable; it is, in comparison with eternal death (which is spiritual), like a picture of death painted on a wall. This is why the Scripture very frequently calls it sleep, rest, or slumber.

"Also eternal death is twofold. One is a very great good. It is the death of sin and the death of death, by which the soul is freed and separated from sin and the body from corruption, and the soul is united by grace and glory with the living God. . . . Thus sin dies, and also the sinner when he is justified, for sin does not ever return, as the apostle says here: 'Christ dies no more,' etc. (Rom. 6:9). . . . Therefore, God brought about the death of death and the sin of sin, the prison of prison [sic! should read "the poisoning of poison"—Trans.] and the captivity of captivity. As he says through Hosea: 'O death, I will be thy death; O hell, I will be thy bite' (Hos. 13:14). This is symbolically represented in the Old Testament by all the wars of the Children of Israel in which they killed the Gentiles.

"The other death is eternal and a very great evil. It is the death of the damned. Here it is not sin and the sinner that die, while man is saved, but it is man that dies while sin lives and remains forever. This is the 'very evil death of the wicked' (Ps. 34:21)."

[7] Carl Stange, *Luthers Gedanken über die Todesfurcht* (Berlin and Leipzig, 1932), pp. 15-16. See also the direct quotation from Luther footnoted at p. 155, n. 13.

the scene only as punishment for sin.[8] Man's character as image of God was expressed among other ways in his not knowing death and in his sharing God's own eternal life. It is "as though he said: 'Adam, and Eve, now you are living without fear; death you have not experienced, nor have you seen it. This is My image, by which you are living, just as God lives. But if you sin, you will lose this image, and you will die.' "[9].

The terrifying quality of man's death consists thus not merely in his loss of physical life, but in his forfeit of the living fellowship with God. To use our earlier terminology, death is not merely a quantitative boundary, but the imposition of qualitative limits; it is a fateful event in the personal relationship between God and man.

Should one seek to contemplate death apart from this fateful personal event, that is, apart from the wrath of God—in other words, should one seek to comprehend death either as something original in man's creation or as a component of his animal being, then death would be only a sleep, a viper whose poisonous fangs had been removed. It would be literally harmless. If the terror were gone from death, if we could simply ignore our dread of the wrath of God, then "death would truly be a kind of sleep. For just as a dead serpent retains the form of a serpent but is without poison and can do no harm, so death would be truly dead if it no longer struck terror into the hearts of men; for this terror is truly the poison of death."[10]

Hence death, without this dimension affecting our personhood, would itself be dead. It would be nothing. At the present, however, death still carries the poison of wrath and thus remains a living reality focused on us, a power holding us spellbound.

[8] "Man's death is in itself truly an infinite and eternal wrath. The reason is that man is a being created for this purpose: to live forever in obedience to the Word and to be like God. He was not created for death. In his case death was ordained as a punishment of sin." *LW* 13, 94.

[9] *LW* 1, 63. Cf. also Luther's statement: "Therefore it comes to man as shocking news to hear that he, who had been created as a good and perfect being for life and who was to have his dwelling place in God, is now destined for death." *LW* 13, 94.

[10] *LW* 13, 115.

We could also express it as follows. If a man is aware of his own personhood and if he takes seriously the reality of God, to that same degree must he take to heart the thought of death. Here, as elsewhere in the Christian faith, the rule applies: Since redemption from anxiety, from guilt, and from distress is a gift to us, since we are "raised with Christ," we must at the same time take seriously that distress, anxiety, and guilt, and must face up to the grim reality of truth. The Christian faith does not offer comfort by keeping the dark truths about life and death veiled. It actually unveils these truths and bestows comfort in spite of them.

This is possible only because as we confront the many heads of this Medusa-like terror, there appears before it the Head crowned with thorns, upon whom rests the threat meant for us. Any other comfort is purchased by illusion. The cold-blooded stance of pagans confronting death stems from the fact that they see only death's biological mask, the segment that is the law of nature, while the efficient and final cause of death remains hidden from their eyes.[11] They are as blissfully undisturbed as a child who is unbothered by the genuine danger in which he finds himself.

Luther is naturally just as aware as are the pagan thinkers that one can face physical death with composure. "If we were compelled to look forward only to this [namely, physical] death, we might say with the poet [Martial]: 'Neither fear, nor long for, the last day.' "[12] However, this bodily death which man can look in the eye with cool composure is not the real enemy at all, but merely its vanguard. When a man catches sight of the actual forces advancing toward us, his composure may indeed evaporate. Of course physical death is a temporal reality, but we are never helplessly delivered up to temporal reality, never in the sense of Schleiermacher "totally dependent" upon it. On the contrary we are able to resist it, even though it calls for hardship and toughminded heroism. However, that aspect of death which affects our personhood, approaching us via the medium of the biological, is eternal. It simply cannot be remedied regardless of the temporal

[11] *LW* 13, 77-78.

[12] *LW* 13, 78.

means one might employ, either external exertions or internal convictions. The net result is that no mortal can cope with the wrath of God. Hence the dread of mortal man when he hears the Most High say, "Here shall your proud waves be stayed" (Job 38: 11). "We however [i.e., we Christians who have been compelled to face up to the knowledge, who have been stripped of our pagan illusions] are subject to eternal death, namely, the wrath of God, which it is impossible for us to conquer [as we can bodily death]."[13]

AWARENESS OF DEATH AND DEATH'S CONSTANT PRESENCE

The fundamentally different evaluations of death held by pagan illusion on the one hand and Christian realism on the other also affect the role they ascribe to death as it casts its shadow back into the days of man's vitality and good health. One might express it as follows: These differing evaluations affect the extent to which we see death as a reality in the here and now.

By way of illustration we may note how Luther calls attention time and time again to the crassly opposite impact which the awareness of death has among pagans and among Christians. His thought goes as follows. Although as natural men we are constantly reminded of dying by cemeteries and the death of others around us, we do not relate death to ourselves.[14] When we really do relate death to ourselves and reckon with it as our death, most often it is already at the door. A person does not really take notice of death (which means knowing it as his own death) until he has already lived his life and is now on his deathbed, just as one does not notice sleep until he has awakened from it.[15]

Therefore it is no wonder that natural man represses death and refuses to let it play any role in his life. Death is nothing more than an episode of the last and final hour, of what Martial meant

[13] *WA* 40III, 487, 20-22; cf. *LW* 13, 78.

[14] Cf. the quotation from Tolstoi at p. 65, n. 11.

[15] "And do we not know that sleep is something which leaves us faster than we can become aware of it? Before we become conscious that we have gone to sleep, sleep has already left us. Therefore our life is truly a sleep and a dream. Before we discover that we are living, we have ceased to live." *LW* 13, 102.

by "the last day." Therefore death, as mere death of the body, is for natural and pagan man entirely parallel to the death of animals, for whom death likewise has no meaning until the very last moment arrives.[16]

The practical consequence of banishing death from human life in this fashion and confining it to the last day is that by nature man lives as though he would never die at all. The premise behind all men's effort and thought leads them to act as if they would live forever and to make of their life an eternal life.[17] Thus man bases his life on the deceptive and illusory energy of an "as if" and not on the harsh truth about genuine death. He always interposes between himself and death an insulating wall made up of the decades he ostensibly has yet to live. And all of this is quite logical since on this false basis death does not become acute until the very end of his life span.[18]

Thus we get the grotesque situation that with reference to his own death man is struggling for minute particles of time, for puny decades—as Shakespeare said:

> That we shall die, we know; 'tis but the time
> and drawing days out, that men stand upon.[19]

In the process man forgets the eternity that surrounds him on all sides precisely with respect to his death, and in relationship to which his life is out of joint. Taking another cue from Luther, we might describe him as the man who is exclusively concerned about protecting his own private property during a time of great national crisis without any sense of the greater totality. While thus engaged in this petty exercise of private self-help, he forgets that

[16] See *LW* 13, 106 ff.

[17] "This is the reason why everyone organizes his plans and projects as though he were going to live forever. Because of this common practice people transform their life into an eternal life." *LW* 13, 100.

[18] "Today a person dies who yesterday had hoped to live another forty or more years. Even if such a person had actually realized his hope, even then he would not abandon the desire for a still longer life." *LW* 13, 100. "Just as Moses set down as a general limit seventy years, so we set down for our day forty or fifty years. The number of those who get to be sixty years old is exceedingly small, and these few are thought to have attained an advanced age." *LW* 13, 122.

[19] See p. 130, n. 6.

his property, too, goes to the dogs if the greater totality falls. Consequently it is precisely here where he ought to pitch in and work with all his might. This man has lost all sense of measure and proportion in the same grotesque manner as that natural man who strives to gain a few more years when eternity is at stake, who struggles to be calm in the face of his minuscule microcosmic bodily death when what is really at stake is the macrocosmic fact of his being torn asunder from God, the overwhelming fact of bounds being imposed on one who is out of bounds.

Only the Christian is cured of such distortion in perspective—and that only with fear and trembling. Only for the Christian does death move out from its chronological confinement in the last day and become something that leaves its mark upon his entire life, stamping his life as a life that is separated from God and thrown back behind its boundaries by God. Thus death becomes "ever present,"[20] a palpably real death in the here and now. "In the midst of life we are in death."

Therefore that temporally ascertainable moment when physical death actually arrives is far less important than that fear and trembling with which I relate to death my current life. It is this anxiety-ridden relating of my life to death, rather than my physical departure, which in a very real sense is "my death." For in this action of relating the two I am conscious not only of my body, but now also of my soul being claimed by death. Thus this action touches that dimension of death which affects our personhood.[21]

CONTEMPT FOR DEATH PROHIBITED

From this position it is only natural and logical for Luther to launch a sharp polemic against the heroic pagan ideal of despising death. For it is impossible to hold anything in contempt unless I can degrade that thing and elevate myself above it. And this is

[20] *LW* 13, 128.

[21] In the words of Luther's own manuscript (not the printed lectures which are translated in *LW* 13, 115): "But fear of death is the death of the human soul. This fear, despair, horror is death itself." *WA* 40III, 550, 1.

precisely what happens in contempt for death, which is blasphemy and hubris.[22]

The bad thing about it is that, strictly speaking, contempt for death does not at all mean subduing (as contemporary slang would say) the "chicken" which rises in all of us as we face death, which the physical drive for self-preservation brings to the fore again and again. No, contempt for death is after all contempt for him who allows death to happen to us. It is contempt for death as a divine measure. It is a matter of wanting to hear the message that God wants to speak to us in death. Thus contempt for death takes place only by man's degrading God and elevating himself above God. This is the frightening background to contempt for death. And whenever this direct tendency toward blasphemy against God is absent (e.g., in Epicurus), then contempt for death is based on ignorance of the true cause of death, a foolhardy security which is possible only when one is ignorant of the real danger. "Both Gentiles and monks have indeed said a great deal about the need of scorning death. But what they said was wrong. As a result of such prattle men become either hardened sinners or blasphemers, since they discard all reverence for God, become angry with Him, and regard Him to be a tyrant, who for no reason whatever abandons man, this poor creature, to death.[23]

As a rule such contempt for death is less often a conscious opposition against God than, as in the case of Epicurus, an ignorance of God. As such, it appears objectively to be madness; but subjectively too, as a heroic impulse, it has scant value since it is concerned only with the biological aspect, that is, the most insignificant aspect of the event of death. Thus contempt for death is possible only on the basis of an illusory security, not on the basis of a firm realistic stance in the face of the frightful truth about death. To that extent, then, contempt for death is no longer any great feat; it is by no means the expression of genuine bravery. Such bravery could be conceded only if it were demonstrated in face of

[22] "Since reason is determined to escape God's wrath, it proposes either the way of disdain [*contemptus*] or the way of blasphemy." *LW* 13, 107.

[23] *LW* 13, 98.

the real danger. "What of it when Epicurus [who professes contempt for death] dies? He not only does not know that there is a God, but also fails to understand his own misery which he is experiencing."[24] This heroic contempt is based of course on ignorance.[25] Like that fabled horseman riding across Lake Constance, one's imagined security abruptly collapses when he looks back over his shoulder with genuine knowledge and is forced to see the unwitting sham in which he lived out his Being-toward-death.

We can summarize Luther's thought as follows. Death is not to be conquered by the illusion of security that comes from ignorance, nor by downgrading God and elevating myself above him in fearless and wanton contempt for death. On the contrary, it can be overcome only by acknowledging him who has ordered it, that is, by acquiescence to this decree of the wrath of God. Only by doing that, willing to have the truth be true, do I surrender myself entirely to God. In such self-surrender I admit, "Fighting against you is senseless. There is no help for me against your wrath. The only one who can save me from you is you yourself. The only thing superior to your judgment is your grace." God alone can heal the wounds which he has inflicted.[26] Everything else is illusion and blind obstinate defiance. Everything else must always operate on a fallacious hypothesis, as if there were something greater than God that could be set against him, as if man in his contempt, for instance, were greater than God. As those who have really been called to order by God's word, addressed and awakened by it, we are "not to look frantically for help anywhere except to him who caused the evil. 'For He who has torn, the same will also heal' (Hos. 6:1). This is the name of our God: 'He kills and restores to life; He brings down to hell and raises

[24] *LW* 13, 112.

[25] See Luther's introduction to the argument of Psalm 90. *LW* 13, 76.

[26] We dare not arm ourselves against God's blows by indulging ourselves in thoughts of security (which come straight from the devil). No, we must let even our security be smashed by God. "Christ would comfort those whom the devil wants to frighten and dishearten, and, on the other hand, He would intimidate those whom the devil makes smug and presumptuous. After all, these two must always contend against each other. What the devil ruins and destroys, Christ must build up and restore; and what the devil establishes, Christ destroys." *LW* 24, 15.

up' (1 Sam. 2:6)."[27] Thus the real issue is that we, in contrast to the Epicureans and their intellectual efforts, do "not attempt to find a way to mitigate an inescapable evil. He [Moses] rather teaches us to refer both good and evil to the one God and to learn how these evils [especially death] may be overcome."[28]

In connection with these thoughts on contempt for death Luther arrives at a graphic definition of the concept "barbarism" that is worth remembering. "Barbarism," that is, stupidity, brutality, presumptuousness, is not at all simply the opposite of aesthetic culture and its concomitant refinement in one's style of life. Genuine barbarism actually permeates all stages of mankind's cultural development. With reference to the attitude toward death, for instance, one would be compelled to see it precisely in the elegance of the Greek cultural world "inasmuch as this is conjoined with disdain and ignorance of God,"[29] that is, with that hubris and unawareness of ultimates which is otherwise designated "barbarism" when it occurs in conjunction with cultural primitivism and gross unrefined behavior.

It is clear what Luther meant here in view of his attitude toward Epicurus indicated above. And it is just as obvious that we, who claim to know more accurately than Luther "how devout the Greeks were," can concur in this reproach of the Greeks only if we do not confine our attention merely to the subjective structure of their devotion (which is obviously not Luther's concern either), but to the objective fact that they bypassed the God of judgment and grace. When this God is taken seriously a transvaluation of the concept barbarism does in fact take place. We find its characteristics (disdain and ignorance of God, *religio sine cultu et affectu*) not only on the level of primitive culture, but just as much on the intellectual heights of mankind amidst the shell of aesthetic culture, which from this perspective is truly nothing but a shell. And frequently the opposite of barbarism, namely, ultimate knowledge and ultimate fear and awe, is to be found in the ranks of the despised and lowly, who as the despised and the lowly

[27] *LW* 13, 97.
[28] *LW* 13, 96.
[29] *WA* 40^{III}, 459, 22-23.

have been the ones specifically chosen by God (1 Cor. 1 and 2). It is of course a fundamental teaching of the New Testament that the gifted and the mighty are in the greatest danger and that man at the peak of his humanity is by no means closer to God, but can (in Luther's sense) still be in the depths of barbarism.

We can summarize Luther's teaching about death in its relevance for the issues we are considering as follows.

1) Human death is qualitatively different from that of animals since it is not an instance of order as in the case of the latter, but a disorder. It is the consequence of a shattered relationship to God, a sign of man's escape from the life of God, and a threatening signal of the wrath of God. Man's death is thus more than one might suspect from its physical parallel to universal creaturely death. Behind the foreground of a biological occurrence which it shares in common with the animals it is simultaneously and essentially an event of human personhood, which makes sense only in terms of man's fateful relationship with God.[30]

2) Since death is a verdict of God upon our life, it then also qualifies the entire course of this life. Death is not the terminal point of life, but a qualifying characteristic of life. Consequently I am not living in the truth unless in my awareness of death I relate my entire life to the action of God manifest in my dying.

3) On this basis contempt for death is forbidden whether it arises from defiance or ignorant security. I am not to elevate myself contemptuously above death and its author; I am attentively to acknowledge it and submit myself to it. Only in this way do I allow for the fact that there is nothing (myself included) that is greater than God, on the basis of which I might nourish the hope of overcoming his blow and his punishment. Only God himself can heal the wounds which he has inflicted; only God's love is greater than his wrath.[31]

30 See in this respect Paul's words in 1 Cor. 15:56 where he draws a distinction (but not a separation) within death itself between the mere physical suffering on the one hand, and on the other hand the experience of God's judgment which strikes at man's person and awakens aching guilt-feelings and fear of punishment. Not until "sin" and "law" come on the scene, does death as all men experience it come into being, and without this "sting" there is no human death deserving of the name.

31 See Appendix III on "The Biological and Personal Dimension of Sickness."

13.

The Directional Character of Time

Up till now we have essentially been describing two aspects of the personal character of death. One was the solitary isolation of man vis-à-vis people and things that death reveals. In dying we must forsake them all, for death reveals that our personhood is separable from all things and all people. Secondly, in dying our personhood is at stake; man clamors for boundless existence, but God confronts him with the fact of his finite limits. In our dying God's person encounters us, primarily in his wrath. Thereby we ourselves as well as our death take on the qualities of personhood. Luther's thinking followed the same perspective in numerous variations.

Before we leave these two aspects in which we have related personhood and death, we wish to take a brief look at the manner in which this doctrine of death is to be preached, proclaimed at the graveside, and propounded in conversation with other philosophies.

By no means should one simply set up on one side the idea of death in terms of personhood and the bounding of the man attempting boundlessness, and play this idea off against the profane concepts of perishability, the spring-autumn rhythm of all life, and the insignificance assigned to the dying individual. All this would do would be to illustrate two different worlds of thought. But they would be only illustrated, or at best defined one in terms of the other. But that can never be the task of proclamation. An awareness that death is the boundary set for our life by wrath is no more demonstrable than, for example, sin is, for the simple reason that in dealing with death and with sin we are not dealing with phenomena existing per se which could be observed objectively in the manner of natural phenomena. Neither phenomenon stands by itself, therefore neither is comprehensible by itself. Both are relational entities, and the one to whom they have reference is God. Sin means separation from God; death means being limited by God. Apart from this "from" and "by" both phenomena are incomprehensible. Above them both stands God as the common qualifying factor. Only because the modern world has lost sight of this factor has it also lost sight of the essence of death. Apart from its relationship to God death cannot be described as a reality of human personhood.

Consequently one should preach about death only by preaching this Lord who wills to have us under him and whom we by nature continually refuse to have over us. The proper teaching about death then comes about as a by-product, so to speak, as an emanation from this center of the message. Our proclamation becomes erroneously dogmatic and irrelevant, despite its apparent doctrinal accuracy, when we play off the individual assertions of faith frontally against the corresponding assertions of unfaith by outsiders. To do this is but to play the fallacious and disastrous game of apologetics.[1] To use a military analogy, the proclamation, from its position far out on the front line of faith's truths, must continually retreat to the inner defense perimeter.[2] That means retreating to the center of the message of the Lord who judges us and raises us up, who sets limits to our existence and yet in Christ brings us home again. All the other truths are credible, that is, they are apparent as truths relevant to me (and not merely dogmatic propositions) only when and insofar as they are obviously sorties made from this inner defense perimeter, and are

[1] See Helmut Thielicke, *Jesus Christus am Scheidewege. Eine biblische Besinnung* (Berlin, 1938), pp. 49 ff.

[2] I have developed this basic theme elsewhere in "Brief an einen feldgrauen Theologen," *Deutsches Pfarrer-Blatt,* no. 42 (1941), pp. 381-82.

thus intimately connected to it. This is not a special method for proclamation, but part of the core content of the proclamation itself.

This core content and the method appropriate to it is given classic expression in Luther's explanation of the Ten Commandments. If we want to follow through with our metaphor of the defense perimeter we would say it as follows. The vanguard truths that man ought not kill, commit adultery, and lie, are not discussed out on the front line itself. Thus, for example, no attempt is made to show that principles of moral or natural law are at stake here, the violation of which would lead to such and such consequences, although without a doubt this is indeed true if only in the sense of a vanguard truth. Rather, the truth of the other commandments is championed from that inner defense perimeter, from the first commandment, that is, from their relation to the author of the law himself. The truth of the individual commandments follows only from the fact that we should fear and love God. Or expressed the other way around, when we do fear and love God, when the center is in order, the norms of our behavior and attitude follow automatically.

Preaching about death is no different. Right here is the opportunity to test that principle of the "inner defense perimeter," since death is a reality contemplated and explored by both church and world, by the message of Christ and by the secular myth. The church's proclamation about death is under special attack, since it is so timely, and thereby it also stands in special danger of being sidetracked into a peripheral front-line discussion about the phenomenon of "death per se." We dare not counter the world's thesis, "Death is a transition form in the rhythm of life" with our own antithesis, "Death is a consequence of the fall into sin." Expressed in this manner the dogmatic accuracy of this assertion is nevertheless a lie, since it occurs in the wrong field and at the wrong level. Many signs of such skirmishes in the church's pamphleteering and similar things suggest that the church's proclamation time and time again gets itself sidetracked at the wrong level and thus loses sight of its connection to the center, to the inner perimeter.

Since in this work we intend to reach out from such a central position into the controversy about death, which permeates all times including our own, we could not very well bypass this opportunity to draw some homiletic implications.

But now let us return to our main line of thought. By understanding human death in categories of personhood, we take it seriously and thus gain not only a new perspective on our relationship to the world, vis-à-vis which we are the "lonely ones" forsaken by the world's own gods, but we also achieve a new perspective on our relationship to God, who shows us our limits when we die. However, through this new perspective on both of these relationships we also finally gain a new and different relationship to time, understood as our time for living. Of this subject we must now speak.

THE CONSCIOUSNESS OF TIME REVISED BY DEATH'S BOUNDARY

Our life is constantly moving toward its boundary. One might also say that it is constantly approaching this boundary, never standing still for a moment and never reversing direction—even for a moment. "Lord, let me know my end, and what is the measure of my days; let me know how fleeting my life is!" (Ps. 39:5).

The clock is a poor symbol for this time line hastening to its end. The movement of the hands on a clock describe a circle returning to its starting point in order to begin anew. The hour which the clock ticks off is not the once for all traversed segment of a directional time line; it is endlessly repeatable and always returning. Time as the clock portrays it is cyclical, curved time. Leopold Ziegler has shown that this is the concept of time functioning in the world of myth with its notions of the "great year" and of world time.[3] Such a concept of time thus holds sway precisely in that intellectual climate in which man's personhood

[3] Leopold Ziegler, *Ueberlieferung* (Leipzig, 1936), pp. 343 ff.

recedes, in which man becomes an exemplar of the genus, a non-unique, replaceable representative of suprapersonal powers.

Therefore we must abandon the clock as our time symbol because the clock never runs out; it can always be rewound and started over again from the beginning. It is significant that the man who is bound to the cyclical time pattern of the clock is not conscious of the flow of time whenever the clock strikes, but only at the decisive hours of his life, for example, his birthday or New Year's Eve. Here we see how deceptive is the message of the clock's circling hands. The hours of the day may indeed return, but the elapsed year nevermore. Here it can suddenly dawn upon a man—frequently in such a frightful fashion that with no other available consolation he will grasp for narcotic means to forget—that we do not march along a time circle which always goes on and on in the same way, but on a time *line* which moves forward straight to its end.

As my life hastens to the end of its line, two things become apparent that condition my existence most profoundly. First of all, I always carry myself with me. I am and I also remain coextensive with my own past, in just the same way that I can never give up my identity with myself. And secondly, I can never start myself all over again as cyclical time suggests. No, my time line is irreversible. It is unequivocally directed toward its end. In the words of the psalmist, our years "are soon gone, and we fly away."

These are the two assertions applicable to our life in time as a consequence of the reality of death. Both truths, which point reciprocally to each other, are kept open and protected from being repressed only if one takes seriously the Lord to whom that irreversible line is hastening. For only by encountering him do I become a person, that is, unique, irreplaceable, and responsible for myself (as surely as he has entrusted this very self to me). Related to this is the fact that I cannot give up my own identity; I cannot push my self away from me and shift it over to someone else in order to start all over again. Rather I must remain standing before him as one who is called by name—that signal of identity!—and is supposed to be God's. From this existence as a person before God follows the directional time line of the course of my life.

The procedure is not reversible. This must be emphasized in order to ward off all the approaches of natural theology. I cannot speculate about cyclical time and linear time—for example, in connection with some such New Year's Eve experience as mentioned above—and from that point work my way up to knowledge of my uniqueness and my existence as a person before God. All natural knowledge of God is still suppressed in unrighteousness and, although it is there, it is kept from any revolutionary eruption. It is repressed.[4] As a result, the normal consequence of the New Year's Eve experience and any growing presentiment of the linear character of man's life line is some flight into illusion which suppresses the truth: "You only live once"—"After us the deluge"—"Let us eat, drink, and be merry, for tomorrow we die."

In this very example it becomes clear that the thought of uniqueness as we have explicated it cannot be grasped by man himself. Instead this thought remains a grotesquely distorted fragment that leads to a consequence quite the opposite of that to which the uniqueness of personhood leads, namely, to dispensing with all responsibility. "With death it is all over." (At this point those who understand themselves in idealism's categories and who do not have this New Year's Eve experience of existing but once in linear time have a greater responsibility, qualitatively measured. They see their insignificant individual existence taken up into a suprapersonal context of meaning for which they have responsibility.) There simply is no such common denominator of uniqueness that is even formally the same for the godless man and for the man whom God addresses and calls by his name. In each of these cases it is something qualitatively different. In the first case death becomes the preacher of uniqueness in its meaninglessness ("With death it's all over. . ."). In the other case death becomes the preacher of the *kairos,* the unrepeatable segment of time for God's grace and God's call ("Now is the acceptable time"—

[4] There then develop "complexes," as is the case with everything that is repressed. One might very well designate the gods of the ersatz religions as just such complexes.

though, to be sure, it is hastening to an end). And simultaneously death preaches that. God's history with us does not terminate but that we stand under the power of resurrection and life. But again, the latter makes sense only as a consequence of a fellowship with God in personhood, for it is surely not *our* life and *our* power of resurrection that shatters death, but it is God's history into which we have been taken and in which we have become persons, God's continuing history with us.

Our uniqueness in terms of personhood and the concomitant directional cast it gives to our time line becomes apparent by virtue of death, but only under the condition that death itself is viewed as an event in our history with God, understood not simply as a formal boundary line but rather God's setting bounds to our person.

THE MYTHICAL NOTION OF TIME

If the directional character of our time line becomes clear in this sense, we then notice a new and important connection between sin and death. We come to realize, namely, in what sense death stands guard over the guilt of our life and how it keeps this guilt out in the open and prevents its repression.

The two assertions which I had to make about my time in the face of my death, in the face of my own movement toward termination, were these: (1) I always take myself with me; (2) I can never start myself over again in the sense of cyclical time.

Both assertions imply that I can never recoup my guilt. The moment my still open future becomes the present and my not-yet-made decisions become completed decisions, my guilt cannot be undone. To state it crassly, as a person I am the sum total of all my decisions, including all the past decisions I have made. And I stay that way. However, since we must understand our personhood strictly in terms of God and his address to us, this means concretely that with God my past life is not passed away, but it is present before him. For this reason "my sin is ever before me" (Ps. 51:3). It remains in the present tense, because it is the same road down which I am still traveling right now. This explains the petition in Psalm 25:7, "Remember not the sins of my youth," for the time in which they occurred is not obliterated, but is the same time that I am now living through.[5] Practitioners of pastoral care and psychiatry know very well how concretely this truth is manifested in particular people. I cannot escape myself. I cannot forsake the path on which I travel. I cannot leave that time line. I remain identical with myself. I must follow this path to the end and confess that the segment lying between the end and the beginning belongs to me. "I am my time," as Rudolf Hermann said. Death is the inexorable watchman over my irreplaceable life's course and the irreversibility of my time line. Naturally this applies only under the presupposition that I understand death in terms of personhood. The sting of death, which now also means the sting of this time line with its irreversible and irreplaceable movement, is sin.

At this point we are able to make an important observation about the implications this has for one's world view. It is not accidental that the following two phenomena always appear together and necessarily reveal their internal substantive connection.

On the one hand, the viewpoint that posits a supraindividual complex of meaning into which my personal uniqueness is absorbed to be made immortal always occurs in connection with a cyclical concept of time. In the biological world view of Nazism this fact becomes especially patent: Insofar as I am only an exemplar of my nation or of my race, I personally am insignificant. For this reason my death is also insignificant, since I am absorbed into that meaningful entity anyway and live on in it. Related to this is the fact that the essential segment of my I, namely, the I

[5] Although the expression "irreversibility of the time line" [*Nichtumkehrbarkeit der Zeitlinie*] originates with Karl Heim, who regularly emphasizes it very effectively with reference to the experience of guilt, we see ourselves at odds with Heim at least at the point where he presents this irreplaceable aspect as a phenomenon of existence which I must necessarily acknowledge because it is objectively demonstrable. We deny that categorically. The natural evaluation of the New Year's Eve experience can also turn out to be completely different as we noted above. It all depends on whether one acknowledges the personhood structure of our existence and of our boundary at death. And this in turn depends solely on the revelation of the God who encounters me, addresses me in Christ, and thus makes me into a person. See my response to Heim in the article, "Jesus der Weltvollender," *Theologische Blaetter,* June/July 1938.

in me which represents that meaningful entity, participates in cyclical time. The nation and the race seek to realize themselves in new beings, they are always producing new exemplars. And since it is only in such realizations that they exist and take shape at all, my essential supraindividual I lives on in those exemplars yet to come. In them it starts all over from the beginning, just as the nation and the race do. The mythical biological concept of eternity, even as it is popularly understood, is an eternity of such continuing self-renewal, such starting all over again from the beginning, and to that extent it is totally representative of cyclical time. Consequently, personlessness and a cyclical concept of time—and now connected to them, deathlessness—belong essentially together.

On the other hand, it is also significant that for biblical thought man's irreplaceable personhood which arises when God addresses him, is connected with an irreversible linear time line—which means that death is taken seriously. This connection could be demonstrated much more amply than we have done within the limited perimeters of our problem. For this directional time line applies not only to the microcosm of individual life, but also to the macrocosmic fate of the entire world which is itself conditioned by the judgment day, that is, by its own end, its eschaton. This macrocosmic time line is equally conditioned by God's address to the human race in his word, for it constitutes the interlude of grace in which God's message is proclaimed. It is the "acceptable time," the time of God's patience. Any awareness of the end of the world and the death of the world is strictly oriented to this call. The end comes when the time allotted for the call reaches an end, when the counterproclamations of men and the concomitant travail of history have exceeded the measure set for them. And the end of the world in the form of judgment day is itself nothing but a final summation of the call and the response given to it. It is nothing but the harvest of history in which the chaff is separated from the wheat.

Thus with regard to the death of the world the directional character of the time line becomes manifest again. God's call sounds forth, qualifying the world too as something that has its time and must come to its end. It is a sort of macrocosmic personhood bestowed on our aeon. Related to that again is the fact that the world's death and judgment can occur time and time again in certain anticipatory episodes here and now. Even here a piece of world, such as a nation or a region, allows the call to pass by and prematurely comes to its end as though it were dying the world's death in advance. This happens when it lets what Luther labeled the "rainshower of the gospel" pass over and stays behind unblessed. Luther frequently saw himself as the spokesman for this apocalyptic thought and his own native Germany was the piece of world to which he especially applied it.[6]

Death, both of persons and of the world, is the inexorable watchman over the directional character of the time line, the path of time that runs toward its end straight and true. In the parable of the rich man and Lazarus (Luke 16:19-31) this character of death as the watchman over the uniqueness of our time line is made inescapably clear. Even more inescapably, however, the parable expresses the fact that awareness of this temporal uniqueness does not stem from mere observation of death's end, but only from the call of God and his word. If the rich man's five surviving brothers would not hear "Moses and the prophets," that is, if they were to play deaf in response to the call, then they would not be helped even if one should rise from the dead. That is to say, no matter how vivid the demonstration of death and what follows it is, it does them no good.

The watchman over the unique character of our time line, therefore, is not simply death as such, but only the death whose secret I have perceived in God's addressing me. In fact, death as boundary and judgment is itself this very address by God.

[6] See Hermann Dörries, *Luther und Deutschland* (Tübingen, 1934).

14.

Death and Security

Ignorance of death, or expressed better, wanting to forget death, according to the Bible means not wanting to see the boundary and finally actually closing one's eyes to it. From such action arises security. When the psalmist prays, "Lord, let me know my end, and what is the measure of my days; let me know how fleeting my life is!" (Ps. 39:4), his petition is synonymous with the request that God would actually shatter his security. After all, it is the false and deceptive security of such men who "go about as a shadow" (v. 6) and live in the same unconcern as the passengers of the *Titanic,* dancing, eating, drinking, and flirting—and in the next moment crashing into the iceberg and perishing completely.

Now it is important to notice that this security is procured with considerable unrest. "Surely for nought are they in turmoil" (v. 6). How are these two related to each other: security and unrest?

Security consists in men's understanding themselves in terms of the goods and values of this world and clinging to their presumed durability. Thus they try to derive their significance and protection from what they have "heaped up" (v. 7) as presumably valuable. Or as the psalmist says (Ps. 49) in view of his persecutors (vv. 11 ff. following Luther's translation): "Their inward thought is that their houses shall continue forever, and their dwelling places to all generations; they call their lands after their own names. Nevertheless man cannot abide in his pomp, he is like the beasts that perish. This is the fate of those who have foolish confidence, the end of those who are pleased with their portions."

The internal disaster of that security consists in its being founded upon flesh, which means it is founded upon something that is specifically of unconstant worth. It deteriorates, taking along to its own fate those who have deified it and found their security in it.

Precisely for this reason the security sought in this fashion is constantly permeated by secret unrest, however contradictory that may appear on first glance. The unrest consists in the constantly new selection and undergirding of those goods of life, by procuring more money, honor, and power, since these additions appear to be identical with acquiring expanded security. However, since this unrest is always animated by the hope that by acquiring those goods I can satisfy my life and give it peace, it is an unrest founded on security. Seen from this perspective, therefore, even Faust's unrest is security. It is a case of willing to live without death.

SECURITY AND REPRESSION

Now, of course, one must not lose sight of the fact that security does not actually exist, either in the objective sense or in the subjective psychological sense. The unrest itself already indicates that. It seeks to achieve security precisely because it *is* unrest, and constantly remains such. The fact that unrest remains itself indicates that no one can genuinely ignore the threat of death's end. The New Testament, in fact, illustrates that there is no such thing as ignorance toward any of the divine truths that condition our existence. There is no ignorance, only a suppressed knowledge. The classical example for this is Saint Paul's portrayal of the wrath of God upon the Gentiles and their idolatry (Rom. 1:18 ff.).[1] Although we have occasionally referred to this passage before, let us now examine it more closely.

The factual circumstances pertaining to security here are actually quite the same as those pertaining to death. The only difference is that here the security of the Gentiles is related not to the threat coming from death's end but to the threat from God himself.

[1] For a more extensive study of the entire issue see my *Kritik der natürlichen Theologie,* 2nd ed. (Munich, 1938) and *Christus oder Antichristus,* 3rd ed. (Barmen, 1935).

The line of thought is as follows: The apostle observes how the heathen pray to images of men and animals, thereby finally sinking into self-worship. The theological question here is this: Do the heathen do this because they know nothing of the true God, either because this God is too hidden or because the heathen are too irreligious, too unreceptive to perceive him? Or do they go to the false gods because they do indeed know something of God but have suppressed this knowledge for some reason and do not want to have God's truth be true?

In the first case the heathen could not be held responsible, since a deficient organ for the knowing process or the excessive concealment of the object to be known can never be designated guilt. In the second case, that of repression, we must indeed speak of guilt, because a latent act of protest lies beneath the alleged ignorance.

Paul emphasizes unequivocally, as clearly as possible, that the latter is true of the Gentiles and that for precisely this reason the wrath of God is inflicted against such worship because it is willfully false. How does Paul arrive at this view of Gentile worship? In order to understand this we must look further into the pertinent verses of his letter to the Romans.

Paul documents the guilt of the Gentiles by saying that God can be plainly known "in his works." The entire creation is, as it were, an objectification of God in which one can grasp him with his hands and see him with his eyes. If this perception nevertheless does not occur, it cannot be because God—that objective reality—lives in darkness "which no one can approach," but on the contrary because the heart of men—the subjective side in that process of knowing God—is darkened.

What this darkening looks like and how it arises is itself described in order to eliminate every possible misunderstanding that would see Paul's statements as a generalizing dogmatic and apodictic verdict about the "wickedness of man." The darkening is explained as follows: Man does indeed recognize the objectification of the Creator in his created world, but he "does not honor him as God or give thanks to him." In other words, man's attitude toward God is wrong, for he does not want to be dependent on Him. He refuses to acknowledge that he is a creature. The reason for this is not difficult to determine in view of the total context of biblical thought in which Paul's thought is rooted. Man refuses because to be a creature means to remain under God, to see the boundaries God has placed and to acknowledge that as creature he is indebted to God. Man refuses in order to escape having to understand himself as a steward obligated to give an account of his existence. He refuses in order to be exempt from the commitment to obey God and acknowledge him in judgment and grace.

Because man refuses this and instead desires to be independent, he loses sight of God. Where the focus on God is faulty, man, as it were, does not even get his sights set on him. "Only he who is of the truth," that is, who acknowledges his existence under God as he acts and lives, is the one who hears God's voice and sees his objectification. Our knowing God does not depend on whether our organ of intellectual perception is intact; it depends rather on our relationship to God. Or one might express it as follows: The knowledge of God is always rooted in acknowledging God.

It is not as though I must first convince myself of God on the basis of some sort of proof—a process of gaining knowledge—in order then to acknowledge him; indeed, the reverse is true. It is in this sense that Blaise Pascal rejected the idea of trying to bring anyone to a knowledge of God by means of proving to him God's existence. One arrives at this knowledge only by coming to the truth about his own existence, which means having God bring him to this truth. "Endeavor then to convince yourself," says Pascal in the *Pensées*[2] "not by increase of proofs of God, but by the abatement of your passions." And again "'I would soon have renounced pleasure [excesses],' say they, 'had I faith.' For my part I tell you, 'You would soon have faith if you renounced pleasure.'"[3] The knowledge of God takes place only on the foundation of acknowledging him. It is thus an existential affair throughout.

[2] Modern Library Edition (New York: Random House, 1941), p. 83.

[3] Ibid., p. 85.

REPRESSION AND GUILT

The situation is as follows: Since man feels himself threatened by God, since man knows himself delivered up to him—the Creator of course is also the judge—therefore he does not even want to concede that God is; indeed, man wills that God not be. He represses God. He moves over to the gods created in his own image, the gods with whom he consequently feels himself affirmed and confirmed, in the knowledge that he is secure in their company.

It would of course be fallacious for us to envision these actions as quite conscious actions, or even as occurring in the upper levels of consciousness at all. While the Gentiles repress the fact of God, they really do think that the gods they worship are genuine gods. We have shown how the sequence "first knowledge, then acknowledgment" is invalid; by the same token the sequence "first knowledge, then nonacknowledgment" is not valid either. Nonacknowledgment is no subsequent act of protest, no conscious programmatic declaration with a clenched fist raised against God—at least I know of no place where this sort of procedure has taken place. On the contrary it is the secret protest and the inner turning away from God which then, and only then, give rise to an erroneous knowledge of God by virtue of this fallacious personal attitude toward him.

We all know of course how concretely such acts of repression occur elsewhere in human life. A sick person who refuses to acknowledge a particular symptom of an illness which he fears and therefore represses, will after a while not even see it any more. His eyes are caught fast, as it were, and he discovers and invents enough arguments to explain it away; finally he sees it as something else than what it truly is. The attitude which characterizes our existence shapes our knowledge. Thus the Gentiles do not know God because they want neither him nor their correlative creatureliness to be true, in other words, because they "suppress the truth in unrighteousness." Søren Kierkegaard expresses this insight as follows: "It is conviction that actually supports our reasons, not our reasons that support our conviction."[4]

[4]Søren Kierkegaard, *Der Einzelne und die Kirche* (Berlin: K. Wolff Verlag, 1934), p. 91.

For this reason the security of the Gentiles, which they seek in the shadow of their arbitrarily chosen harmless gods, does not rest on an authentic ignorance. If it did, they would have found genuine peace, like a child who is unaware of any danger. On the contrary, this security rests upon a repressed and restricted, yet undeniably present, knowledge which shows itself dimly in the restless whirlpool incessantly swirling up from the deep.

This is exactly how we must interpret the security man seeks in the face of death, over which he strives to gain control by means of those fleshly powers that provide his security. What we have here is not an authentic ignorance that fails to notice death but rather the nonacknowledgment and repression that are born of fear. The Gentile gods appear to be the object of genuine knowledge, though the protest against the true God certainly does not become explicit but remains latent and hidden in this knowledge. In the same way, philosophy's reinterpretations of death appear to be the result of authentic knowledge, but in the last analysis they are only repressions and willful refusal to acknowledge the genuine disaster of death.

We cherish the hope that our analysis of secularism's awareness of death (in Part One) brought some of this to expression, but now as a sort of postscript let us review the theological presupposition of these interpretations. I repress the awareness of death—I "suppress it in unrighteousness"—whenever I understand myself in terms of inner-worldly and supposedly durable value structures and goods. Or I suppress it by depersonalizing myself in Teutonic or Faustian or Hegelian fashion and transposing my intrinsic I to some supraindividual entity (tribe, the "traces of mine earthly being," the spirit) which is apparently durable. Or I can also simply refuse to connect death to "me," as we saw in the example from Tolstoy in Part One.

None of this is knowledge that has been gained; it is repressed knowledge. None of this is truth; it is a willful refusal to let something be true. None of this is genuine response to the reality of death; it is rather a response to a particular concern (natural man has a particular ax to grind) in the face of this reality. That is how this philosophical line of thought looks when viewed from the biblical perspective. Thus the first part of our presentation is illuminated by a new light which now becomes accessible at this point.[5]

GUILT AND ANXIETY

These attempts at making oneself secure against death, these acts of repression, do not bring any genuine peace or make it possible really to cope with death or conquer the world. One sign of this is the constant repetition of the self-securing action (e.g., Faust) and the continued care and unrest, both of which are animated by anxiety.

When death actually arrives, it absolutely shatters such illusions of security, since it suddenly becomes a reality that cannot be overlooked. In the face of its arrival there are two possible reactions.

On the one hand, there is open despair. One need only think of the scenes at many a secular burial or of the sinking of the *Titanic.* The people stand before this last enemy as if just roused from sound sleep by a burglar with whom they did not reckon and before whom they now stand befuddled.

On the other hand, there is also a despair that is suppressed behind clenched teeth. It witnesses to a new way of suppressing reality and willing not to let it be true; in this case it is focused upon a subjective condition that arises when the objective reality of death, namely, the end, occurs. This suppressed form of despair is usually called self-control. It is classically described by Spengler in the person of the "soldier of Pompeii" standing his ground against Vesuvius' impossible odds, and it finds its most consistent interpretation in Ernst Jünger's works, where such persistent self-control against impossible odds means having the support of nothingness in the face of nothingness.[6]

The biblical designation for the knowledge of God and of death

[5] With reference to this line of thought, we call attention once more to chap. 12, especially the section on Luther's prohibition of contempt for death.

[6] See his work *Das abenteuerliche Herz,* esp. the 1st ed. (Hamburg, 1929). In later years, to be sure, Jünger clearly overcame his nihilism. See also my book *Fragen des Christentums an die moderne Welt* (Tübingen, 1948).

being "suppressed in unrighteousness" is "security"; the despair which is "suppressed in unrighteousness" is biblically viewed as "defiance."

Another distinction also becomes clear here, namely, that between security and peace. If one erroneously begins from the psychological data, and thus in a sense from the mere shadow of what is really meant, he could conclude that both concepts express peace of mind in the face of threatening powers. However, behind these apparently similar psychological phenomena are concealed two completely different objective foundations. Peace means being objectively in order with God. Among other things (and really only one among many other things), in the face of death's boundary line peace is the pacification that arises from Christ's work of reconciliation. It is a personal reality through and through, namely, peace between two persons that, coming from the cross, bridges the chasm that had opened up between them. Peace of mind is but the shadow of this objective factual reality. But inasmuch as this peace of mind can take shape in the face of the powers that threaten us, such as death (or, expressed better, inasmuch as this peace is bestowed by God as a new fellowship between God and man), we see another facet of the fact that "only He is able to heal the wounds, who has inflicted them." God gives us the confidence that he will not allow death to fracture the history which was begun in Christ, but that we remain "friends of the resurrected one."[7] Peace in the face of death is bestowed only by that same one who is also the source of anxiety in the face of death. Only he who casts man into hell can lead the way out of it. This is the objective foundation of peace, constructed outside ourselves.

Security, on the other hand, remains an interior subjective entity. It is supposed to come into existence without even facing or restoring to order the ultimate cause of insecurity and terror. It is a kind of looking past the reality. Hence any concern devoted to it is, medically speaking, only treating the symptoms, which will always let the actual cause of the disease continue to manifest itself again and

[7] See the extended citation from Paul Gerhardt below, p. 202.

again. We traced this very process when we exposed the security that is founded upon unrest and the despair which animates it.

One can also illustrate both phenomena in relation to the doctrine of justification (although here to be sure we can only sketch its outlines). Wanting to be secure means to suppress the truth in unrighteousness. It means, for example, to repress the reality of death. Having peace, however, means to be set aright before God. For "the righteousness of faith," after all, means to say "yes" to God in his judgment and his grace. It means, for example, to acknowledge both death's boundary and God's faithful history with us which helps us cross over it. Wanting to be "secure" means to exist on the basis of untruth; having "peace" means to exist on the basis of the truth.

15.

Death in the Light of Law and Gospel

We have now drawn the lines of demarcation which distinguish the biblical proclamation of the reality of death from all the dimensions of secular reinterpretation and repression of death's reality. Hopefully we have done even more. We have sought to place that reinterpretation and repression into the light of truth and thus show how it is not only misleading but is merely the product of man's separation from God.

The real truth of death, namely, that death really means the end, that there really is about it a "knowledge suppressed in unrighteousness" and that there really is a despair and anxiety "suppressed in unrighteousness," was intelligible only on the basis of one decisive premise, without which one cannot understand the biblical coordination of sin and death. Indeed, apart from prominent exposition of this premise in the proclamation, one cannot even preach about death. This premise is man's irreplaceable personhood in both his living and his dying. Since, however, man's personhood, as we have noted, comes into existence only in his history with God and in God's addressing him, we could now speak of a theocentric understanding of human death instead of one couched in terms of human personhood. Both amount to the same thing, except that in the first case the divine and in the second case the human partner of the God-man history constitutes the vehicle for the perspective.

Before we conclude this line of thought on person and death, we should still illuminate the biblical concept of personhood from one last vantage point. We do this in order to hone out to its finest edge the concept which ultimately sustains our understanding of death.

The unique character of the human person comes to expression in a special way under the perspective of law and gospel. We have already noted this with reference to the law. One sentence suffices for us to recall it to mind. When God as the author of the law addresses man in judgment: "Adam, where are you?" Adam cannot make Eve represent him in his guilt, and she in turn cannot make the serpent do so for her. Both are compelled to be completely themselves. "None can by any means redeem his brother" (Ps. 49:7, KJV). It is in this dimension, where man is "alone, alone, all all alone," that human death takes place.

Similarly—and thereby we attain an important new perspective—personhood becomes clearly evident under the gospel. At the outset this applies to the gospel of the image of God. For being the image of God simply means that man is exalted above the other creatures and called into a special partnership with God by virtue of God's addressing him, his ability to receive the divine address, and his ensuing responsibility. Being the image of God means nothing else than being called into a history with God. That is what is meant when in the Sermon on the Mount Jesus says that we are "of much more value than" the lilies of the fields and the birds of the air (Matt. 6:26 ff.). We dare not understand this "more" quantitatively in the sense of our being higher on the biological ladder, more highly organized. Basic to this "more" is a qualitative difference. It consists in our being allowed to call God "Father" though the lilies and the birds do not (Matt. 6:32), and in our being the ones who should seek the kingdom of God (Matt. 6:33), who are called into personal fellowship with God.

The ultimate theocentric meaning of this personhood comes into view only in the cross of Jesus Christ. Paul speaks in Romans 14:15 and 1 Corinthians 8:11 of not injuring those people who take offense at something even on erroneous grounds (e.g., at foods, at eating meat sacrificed to idols, etc.). One could easily be tempted to run roughshod over such narrow-minded people. After all, what are they good for—except perhaps for being a constant impediment to fellowship. They are not distinguished leaders, irreplaceable and inexchangeable figures; they are simply the representatives of that anonymous group, the narrow-minded people. It is significant that not one of their names is transmitted to us. And yet they are not to be injured, since "Christ has died for them" and "they were bought with a price." Consequently every single one of them who socially or culturally might still be classified as a nobody, who could be replaced by anybody and very likely constitutes an encumbrance on the Christian community, every one of these is infinitely worthy and dare not be touched. But these nobodies have their dignity and their worth not from themselves, nor by the reception of some specially infused immanent quality. No, this dignity and worth comes to them from outside, as an alien righteousness which consists in the fact that someone died for them. This is their alien dignity. This constitutes their personhood and their uniqueness, their infinite value.

Luther works with the same notion in his teaching on baptism when he says that fathers and mothers are often just like other people. Yes, they even look like the Turks and the heathen and therefore might be exchanged or traded for them. Nevertheless they possess a unique worth which turns them into irreplaceable persons—if for a moment we use the interpretive terminology of our own line of thought. For they stand under the protection and the recognition of the word, "Thou shalt honor thy father and thy mother." Because of these words suddenly "I see another man, adorned and clothed with the majesty and the glory of God. The commandment, I say, is the golden chain about his neck, yes, the crown on his head, which shows me how and why I should honor this particular flesh and blood."[1]

Here the concept of personhood under the rubric of the gospel is given such pregnant formulation that in its light we get still another overview of the entire chain of thought. Father and mother are flesh and blood just as the mammals are. But they are elevated out of the creaturely row of undifferentiated exemplars by the word of

[1] Luther's *Large Catechism,* IV, 20; *The Book of Concord,* ed. Theodore Tappert (Philadelphia: Muhlenberg Press, 1959), p. 439.

God which has been spoken over them and has bestowed upon them that alien dignity portrayed graphically and exactly with Luther's parable of the golden chain of office.

They become unique and irreplaceable only under the word, and this means both under the word as law and under the word as gospel. Indeed this is what gives human death its peculiar significance, its extraordinary gravity—the fact that it focuses on and strikes such a person, the man addressed by the word of God.[2] Death therefore strikes something of infinite value: in human death a unique and irreplaceable being sinks to its end.

If for this reason Christian faith teaches man to understand life from the perspective of its end, thereby rendering it transparent in its nothingness and its movement toward nothingness, a remarkable contradiction arises here which Bernhard Groethuysen profoundly calls to our attention in his analysis of French bourgeois man's secular encounter with death. The last moment of life, in which we must shed all our deceptive illusions, in which the Being-toward-the-end and the nothingness of life is revealed, that moment receives "its significance precisely by virtue of the value that we have ascribed to life."[3] It is because death destroys something irreplaceable that it has this terrifying quality of negation. And the annihilating power of death must be understood all the more profoundly, the more we are aware of the worth of that which meets its end in death. And we are all the more aware of this worth—in fact, we are only aware of it at all—if we view man under law and gospel, thus understanding him as a personal member in God's history, the bearer of an alien dignity. Every attempt to get at man's value via immanent categories leads necessarily to viewing him as nonunique, namely, as though he could be represented by the supraindividual entities of meaning vicariously present in him.

[2] At the conclusion of this work, I discovered that Wilhelm Kamlah in his book *Christentum und Selbstbehauptung. Historische und philosophische Untersuchungen zur Entstehung des Christentums und zu Augustins "Bürgerschaft Gottes"* (Frankfurt a.M., 1940) traces the connection between man's knowledge of death as the boundary and man's knowledge of himself as an individual. See his chapter entitled "Die eschatologische Vereinzelung vor Gesetz, Gericht und Tod," pp. 47 ff.

[3] Bernhard Groethuysen, *Die Entstehung der bürgerlichen Weltanschauung in Frankreich*, vol. 1, *Das Bürgertum und die katholische Weltanschauung* (Halle, 1927), p. 83.

THE RELATIONSHIP OF PERSON AND DEATH SUMMARIZED

We are now in a position to formulate the connection between person and death and summarize our results to this point.

1) Man's dying is really a termination, not a secret continuation or living on in supraindividual entities of meaning. It is a definite termination, since at death boundaries are imposed upon man who asserts himself out of bounds against God and commits the primeval sin of hubris.

2) Since man as a human person always dies alone and irreplaceably, his death resembles a man's passage through the platform gate at the depot where only he can go, leaving behind his comrades, his neighbors, and his goods. We have already shown above why for this very reason a hero's death gives no particularly fruitful example of human dying; it can easily be interpreted—erroneously—as though in this case man were not dying alone, alone, all all alone.

> To die at home in one's own snug bed
> Is to enter alone the ranks of the dead;
> But great is the fellowship here, we say,
> In falling together like new-mown hay.[4]

We dare not let ourselves be deceived by the fact that when he is "falling amidst comrades" while mounting an assault on the enemy man's solitary isolation does not come to expression psychologically, his psyche in such a moment being obviously possessed. The solitude inherent in this sort of dying occurs in the minutes preceding the signal for attack, and again later on in the field hospital or in the desolation of lying wounded on the battlefield.

3) Although we live our entire life under the eyes of the judge (since we do indeed exist as persons), there is a truth to the common saying about a dying man that he "goes to appear before his maker." The fact that we are confined to ourselves does not become more apparent anywhere else than in the loneliness and irreplaceability of our dying.

[4] Jakob Vogel, 1584.

4) Since in dying we are the lonely ones, whom no one and nothing follow, it becomes clear that by letting us die God really means *us.* And he means us precisely as the ones who in remembrance of our fall must return to dust, from which—despite our attempts to get out of bounds—we nevertheless are taken. It is precisely we who are at the termination point; the hands of our clock stand still and we have no hope beyond the hope of resurrection. However, this is not a hope that stems from that same dust, but from heaven, from that other Adam, who is the "life-giving spirit."

5) Human death transcends biological death, therefore, to the same degree that man as a creature of personhood transcends his own quality as a biological being, as a mammal. Death viewed in the biblical sense consequently takes place in a different dimension from the biological, namely, in the dimension of man's history with God, which means in the dimension of personhood. Only if we begin here is it possible to comprehend in depth the notion that the wages of sin is death. We dare not twist this thought to mean that the cause is man's sin and the effect is his biological death. Such a misunderstanding would inevitably lead to the elimination of the personhood which underlies it. It would thus lead to a completely erroneous analogy with biological causality in nature. It would lead to understanding man's death in animal categories. No, it is only that God uses the medium of the biological to give his answer to man's rebellious urge. By this means God places boundaries on the one out of bounds. Biological phenomena and personhood dare not be linked together in a causal connection.[5] They are related to one another but it is impossible to go behind that relationship in a search for causes. According to biblical anthropology man is a totality that cannot be divided—not even in the sense of understanding his body and his soul as separable components of his I. Thus, for example, in Pauline anthropology body, spirit, flesh, soul, etc. do not signify parts of man, but in each case the total man in one particular aspect of his conduct.[6] By the same token one dare not separate the

[5] Bovet has traced the medical aspects of this factual situation.

[6] For Pauline anthropology see the very important article by Rudolph Bultmann on Paul in *Existence and Faith* (Cleveland and New York: World Publishing Co., 1960), pp. 111-46.

biological and the personal, or the biological and personal sides of death, as though they were mutually dependent component parts and building blocks of a man. The issue is that man should learn to see in his biological death more than merely a biological event. We have already seen that death goes through the hands of the biological, yet nevertheless comes from God. The biological is the medium of personal death. It is impossible to try to get behind this surprising perplexity. In fact, it is out of the question since every attempt to get behind it necessarily involves, by virtue of the very categories of our epistemological structure, an assumed causal relationship.

From all this we have seen that human personhood in its uniqueness is firmly connected to the call of God and man's history with him. Of course this does not mean that outside of Christianity there can be no awareness of such personhood, albeit in a different fashion. Indeed, we saw in our discussion of the problem of time that even in secular thought one can become aware of the linear character of time and its termination (in contrast to a cyclical idea). But this notion of time with a limit, since it is not understood as an imposition of limits by God, immediately takes on a qualitatively different character from the understanding of death's end in terms of personhood. This different character is expressed in the reasoning which says, "Therefore since the end is approaching, let us eat and drink, for tomorrow we die." By contrast, the biblical awareness of the end of man's time line leads to the conclusion (let us select a very graphic contrast), "Repent, for the kingdom of heaven is at hand." When God is eliminated the otherwise identical phenomenon of linear time immediately becomes something completely different.

The same thing also applies to the uniqueness of human personhood. In a sense it too can be experienced apart from God's calling in judgment and grace. But this uniqueness, despite the apparent parallels, immediately becomes something else when it is posited as a fact of experience rather than as something that one has lived through in the surprising encounter with judgment and grace, in that encounter which brings personhood into existence. As an example one could take Greek tragedy, in which man's experience of the uniqueness of life is basic.[7] However, it is not accidental that the consequence drawn here, in contrast to the consequences drawn by the Bible from a uniqueness experienced completely differently, is that of the tragedian, life's tragic man. Kurt Langenbeck is profoundly right when he says that "the Greeks were convinced that man's personal existence was unique and not capable of repetition [which led naturally to the necessity of Greece creating the tragedy]. It was within this life, which they received as gift once and one time only, that they were compelled to establish some kind of order in life itself. For no one whom Hades had once enfolded to itself could ever return, or ever have any further effect at all."[8]

[7] See Josef Sellmair, *Der Mensch in der Tragik,* 2nd ed. (Munich-Crailing, 1941). See also Thielicke, *Schuld und Schicksal. Gedanken eines Christen über das Tragische* (Berlin, 1936).

[8] Kurt Langenbeck, *Wiedergeburt des Drama aus dem Geiste der Zeit* (Munich, 1940).

16.

Death as the Contradiction of Eternal Life

Now that we have sufficiently developed the personal character of human death, we must still discuss more precisely the concept of life that is the antithesis of death. In the course of our presentation one thing has become clear. Biological life can by no means be regarded as the opposite of human death—whether understood in biblical or secular terms. As a matter of fact, on neither of these two views was death simply the opposite of life. In the secular understanding death was a segment in the rhythm of life itself, namely, the "ebb" phase. Or else it was but a transition from one form of life to another, for example, in the immortality myths. On the other hand, even for the biblical understanding, biological life is not the counterpart of human death, for death occurs through the medium of the biological laws of life and thus also through the medium of that rhythm of life which is also known to secular thinking. Everything now depends on our finding the direct antithesis to the biblical concept of death, since this is the only way that the personal character of human death can be set forth with ultimate precision.

To find this antithesis is not difficult if one recalls that personal death must correspond to a personal ζωή (*zōē*-life), a life definitively shaped by the history in which God engages man. In the New Testament this *zōē* is designated "eternal life" and thus clearly distinguished from mere biological vitality, which as a rule is designated *psuchē* (ψυχή) or "present life" (ζωή τῆς νῦν) (1 Tim. 4:8), "this life" (ζωή ταύτη) (1 Cor. 15:19), or "life in the flesh" (ζῆν ἐν σαρκί) (Gal. 2:20). This form of *zōē* can only be ranked as inauthentic life and in no case dare it be confused with God's own life or with human life in an eternal fellowship with God.[1] "This life" can even be lived apart from fellowship with God and thereby be lost and wasted. In fact, it is all the more lost and wasted the more it relies upon itself, and the more it is then compelled to reap the destruction coming from this flesh upon which it has sown[2]. Therefore beneath its attractive camouflage godless biological vitality is already dead (Matt. 8:22; Luke 15:24, 32; Col. 2:13; Eph. 2:1, 5). For this very reason death cannot be held to be the opposite of this sort of life, for this life is itself already characterized by death.

We can set up an authentic antithesis only in the following manner. On the one side stands our death, our limitation, in short the wrath of God. On the other side stands acceptance into living fellowship with God as Christ bestows it anew. Here stands the possibility that "though we die, yet shall we live." This is the authentic antithesis to personal death and to the boundary line of wrath between God and man. Here, as it were, the cherub with the fiery flashing sword is commanded to leave the gates of paradise, and those who sat in the shadow of death thus have a new access to the life of God. It is in this fashion that Romans 6:23 and 5:21 express the contrast. "The wages of sin is death but the free gift of God is eternal life in Christ Jesus our Lord." "As sin reigned in death, grace might also reign through righteousness to eternal life through Jesus Christ our Lord."

One could multiply such antithetical pairings at will from the statements of the New Testament. In every passage it is characteristic that the opposite of death is not physical life, but eternal life, life related to eternity with the barrier removed. The fact that the figure of Jesus Christ always stands where the barrier had been

[1] For insight into the New Testament terminology see the respective articles on life and death in Gerhard Kittel's *Theological Dictionary of the New Testament,* trans. G. W. Bromiley (Grand Rapids, Mich.: Eerdmans, 1964 —), 2:849 ff., esp. 863 ff. and 3:7 ff.

[2] See, e.g., our exegesis of the parable of the rich farmer in chap. 11.

placed and now has been razed, the fact that he is the prince of life who leads me through death's narrows—"and when I am departing, O part thou not from me"—makes it simultaneously clear that the conquest of the barrier does not occur by an upward movement from below, but by a downward movement from above. When man tries an upward movement from below, striving on the strength of his own hubris to break through the limits imposed upon him, the barrier is actually erected again, and death gets the upper hand. No upward movement of life from below is able to burst the bonds of death; instead it necessarily makes them more massive, more pervasive, and more invincible. Is it not a fact that precisely in secular culture and in the apparent celebration of vitality death becomes more icy, more mysterious, and more frightful, so that the lie about life must be enlarged even more in order to conceal it? Conquest occurs only in a downward movement from above, via condescension, via the incarnation of the word, via Jesus' comradeship with us in death on the cross. The secret of the existing barrier lies in man's attempted apotheosis. The secret of its removal lies in the incarnation.

ETERNAL LIFE AS PRESENT AND FUTURE

The way in which eternal life—as distinguished from biological life—is authentically opposite to the barrier of death becomes even clearer when we probe deeper into its nature. By no means does eternal life have only the significance of future life, that is, life after death. Of course this significance is also there,[3] for God does not break off the history into which he has entered with us. "Death cannot separate us from the love of God." Since he has called us by our names, we are and remain his, as surely as Jesus Christ is risen from the dead and in his role as head does not desert his members.

However, more significant for our train of thought in characterizing the nature of death is the other aspect of eternal life, namely, its present-tense character, its efficacy already in the here and now. For as surely as we even now participate in the resurrected life and

[3]See the New Testament references to *zōē mellcusa* in 1 Tim. 4:8; Mark 9:43, 45; Matt. 7:14; 18:8-9; 1 Pet. 3:7, 10; 2 Pet. 1:3. See the references to these passages in Kittel, *op. cit.,* 2:864.

are bound together with Christ in word and spirit (Rom. 8:23; 2 Cor. 1:22; 5:5), just as surely are we even now in possession of the new life, even if it is still "hidden with Christ in God" (Col. 3:3).

It is important that this eternal life be sharply distinguished from our natural vitality, although it does indeed come as we travel the biological path of life that is measured out to us. This distinction is already expressed in the sharp conceptual demarcation whereby the New Testament designates natural vitality as *psuchē,* and eternal life as *zōē.* The mere vitalism of life is "Adamite," for Adam was a living *psuchē.* Eternal Life, however, stems from the "new Adam," Jesus Christ, who is the life-giving spirit (*pneuma*).

The most vivid expression of this distinction comes from Johannine Christology where the two are distinguished from one another in the person of Jesus Christ. On the one hand he is a natural living man, and, as it were, shares our Adamite vitality; on the other hand he has *zōē,* which is "the light of men." The former he sacrifices into death for our sakes, thereby consummating the total gravity of man's existential destiny and doing so for our sake and in solidarity with us. His appropriation of man's existential destiny which already occurred in his incarnation is solid testimony to such solidarity (John 10:11, 15, 17).

By contrast the *zōē* of Jesus Christ, the actual content of eternal life, was not overcome by death. Instead it overcame death since death as the boundary, as the reminder of the fall, is meaningless in the face of God's own life. Death can find no flank, as it were, on which to attack him, just as death can no longer have any power over those who are "in Christ Jesus," in living fellowship with the Resurrected One, the one who has shattered death. And this kind of protective custody already exists here and now since already here and now Jesus Christ is Lord and bestows on men this fellowship with himself.

Thus *psuchē* is life that comes by nature; *zōē* is life in personhood which exists in our history together with God. Johannine theology expresses the element of personhood above all in that this life is lived only under the commandment of God, in obedience, in love.[4]

[4] See the entire thrust of 1 John.

To abide in him is to abide in love (John 15:1-17). It is precisely by such an interpretation of life as standing anew under God, a new obedience, that John shows that this life is not some intrinsic quality and natural substance, understood perhaps as some supernatural extension and elevation of the natural *psuchē*. (If this were so, it would turn out to be another analogy to natural biological existence and thus instead of removing the boundary would become a kind of natural medicine of immortality.) On the contrary *zōē* signifies that we are called anew into fellowship with God and now stand responsibly in that fellowship.[5] God is not some power of life which gets transferred to us; he is the author of law and gospel under whom we stand. To express it still another way: what is involved in *zōē* is not a neutral power but a demanding and bestowing Person. For this reason *zōē* is never something timelessly existing but a living fellowship which confronts us here and now in the call of God's word which we must either accept or reject.

In view of its present-tense character eternal life seems particularly meaningful as the opposite of personal death. For in exactly the same way that qualitatively unique personal death overtakes us via the medium of biological dying, just so do we already have God's eternal life *(zōē)* here and now in the medium of biological life (the *psuchē* life-span). Inasmuch as we possess this eternal life in the form of the Spirit's "first fruits" (Rom. 8:23) and "guarantee" (2 Cor. 1:22; see Gal. 5:5), personal death no longer has any power over us as the boundary that banishes and separates. It cannot separate us from the love of God which is in Christ Jesus, to which we "will cling forever" (Paul Gerhardt) and retain our history with God. What still remains is merely the biological side of death, *psuchē* expiring, which does indeed remain a reminder and a significant indicator, but an indicator which has already lost its sting, its poisoned fang. For biological death can no longer be understood in terms of the wrath of God, for the valid wrath of God has now been overcome by God's own condescension. Whatever may still remain of death's anxiety and its oppression even for a fol-

[5] For we are able to love God, of course, only because we have first been loved and thus have been called. See John 13:34; 15:12; 1 John 4:7-10.

lower of Christ, it is only the shadow of the biological drive for self-preservation. It is the universal creaturely sign of aversion to physical annihilation. But it has nothing whatever to do with the personal fate and that poisonous fang at the center of death.

When viewing the fact that personal death has been rendered impotent, the Epistle to the Hebrews is able to say that what Christ has conquered about death is not physical death—for that continues to occur just as it does among the birds and flowers—but rather "him who has the power of death, that is, the devil" (Heb. 2:14). And this devil exercises death's power by telling man, "With physical death it is all over, and therefore the goods of this world are ultimate values; these goods are gods." Did not this very devil picture these goods—the riches and the kingdoms of this world, even daily bread—as gods to Jesus when he was alone in the wilderness? And did he not say: If you would cling to these gods then you really would be the son of God?

This killing power has been taken from death. Those who stand in living fellowship with Jesus can no longer be enslaved to their anxiety about death. They can no longer be slaves of false gods and thus separate themselves from God even more by raising their primeval hubris to an even higher power. Death is not removed, but it is rendered impotent. In a certain sense even death's personal character of limiting and confining man is inverted into its opposite. For in the sphere of God's *zōē* death now becomes a parable of my dying to the fundamental thrust of my own animosity toward God. Thus by a kind of dying I get loose from the fate of sin and death instead of falling victim to it. "For you have died . . . therefore put to death what is earthly in you" (Col. 3:3, 5).

However, since death has lost its sting and had its poisonous fang removed, since it is no longer the personal execution of the wrath of God, it is now so to speak only a biological mask having no significance for those in fellowship with the risen Lord.[6] "He

[6] Michael Schmaus goes considerably beyond the notion of a biological mask: "What comes forth in bodily death is what has already been in man ever since his baptism. Bodily death is the completion of the death that man dies in his baptism." *Katholische Dogmatik,* vol. 3^{II} (Munich, 1941), p. 494. According to this, therefore, baptism is no longer only a parable of human dying, as it also is of the resurrection of Jesus Christ (Rom. 6:3-4). On the contrary, man's death

who believes in me [I who am the resurrection and the life] though he die, yet shall he live, and whoever lives and believes in me shall never die" (John 11:25-26). This means you can die in peace. What remains is only a "dying" in quotation marks, dying in a non-genuine sense. For the one in whose hands and for whose purposes death was a weapon no longer has anything on you. He can no longer use death to hand you over to the gods of this world and thereby tear you away from God's hand. And the fear that enslaved you can no longer get the upper hand on you, because anxiety about God—which roamed about in the guise of anxiety about death—has become meaningless since God has condescended and has become your Father.[7] He who believes has already passed over from death[8] into life[9] (John 5:24; 1 John 3:14).

IMMORTALITY AND RESURRECTION

Could we not ask at this point, however, whether this is not simply another form of that immortality and survival beyond death which we so emphatically rejected in view of the seriousness of death and which we were compelled to label theologically as flight

carries out and completes the dying implicit in his baptism. In the form in which Schmaus presents this notion, it seems to us unbiblical and systematically too shaky. In this way death loses entirely the sense of distress which it still retains as a biological mask. It no longer has the threatening character of a last enemy. And the defiant "nevertheless" with which Christians encounter death in the name of the risen Lord would make no sense. But Christians in their encounter with death do indeed counter it: "Death, I now defy thee."

The reminiscence of our fall remains. Our contrariness remains even if it no longer can separate us from the love of God. The moment never arises when we as the redeemed join death on the same rope pulling in the same direction. Even Saint Paul's joy at the prospect of his departure (Phil. 1:23) is not joy over the completion of the blessing of baptism, but joy over the fact that his existence which remains in discord—this existence of one still walking in shadows far from home—is finally coming to an end.

[7] See art. IV of the Apology to the Augsburg Confession on "Love and the Keeping of the Law," esp. secs. 126, 141, 147 in Theodore Tappert, ed., *The Book of Concord* (Philadelphia, Fortress Press, 1959), pp. 124 ff.

[8] We may well interpret this "from death" as "from Being-toward-death," "from Being-conditioned-and-determined-by-death."

[9] Only under one condition does the personal fatefulness of death remain; in fact it acquires the character of finality. That is when man refuses the fellowship God offers. In this sense the book of Revelation speaks of the "second death." On the whole, even in the here and now there is the reality of "being dead in sin" (Luke 15:32; Rom. 7:10; Eph. 2:1; 1 Tim. 5:6; 1 John 3:14; Rev. 3:1).

and as suppression in unrighteousness? No, here something quite different is at stake.

At two points this fellowship with the resurrected Lord, this "though we die, yet shall we live," is distinct from secular theories of immortality. In the first place, these theories constantly operate with an immanent quality in man, a suprapersonal substance residing in him, by participating in which he outlasts his own characteristic of being merely one specimen of the species. In contrast with this, the victory over death in fellowship with the resurrected Lord is an historical event. It is not a timeless substantive fact. *Zōē* is a quality of divine life to which I am recalled and in which I participate in the personal dimensions of obedience and love described above. Consequently this *zōē* is not a quality of *my* being, but of *God's.*

Secondly, the facts of the case here are different as can be seen in the strict analogy they provide to the doctrine of justification. The righteousness that is valid before God (namely, that validation which makes me a participant in God's gracious fellowship) is not a quality of my own by virtue of which I am righteous, but God's quality by virtue of which he makes me righteous. Luther described this factual reality in both respects (as righteousness and as life) with the notion of the *punctum mathematicum.* When viewed as the subject of faith, appropriating the righteousness of God, we are a "mathematical point." That is, we are not extended as though our righteousness encompassed a specific psychic space which we might designate as our possession or a quality of our self. We do nothing more than place ourselves in believing trust under God's own quality of being gracious. Thus our righteousness is the quality of someone else. It is an alien righteousness (*aliena justitia*).[10]

The same thing applies for the entire expanse of our life at the end of which stands death. This life, even if it lasts a hundred years, also resembles an unextended mathematical point and to that extent has no durability of its own; it has only the durability which resides in him who brings about the living and the dying. This is the only way that life can be viewed as having durability, namely as

[10] *LW* 12, 239.

zōē, which again is not my quality, but the quality of another.[11] Nor do these two qualities, the righteousness and the *zōē,* pass over into my possession in some conditional or secret way as the traditional Roman Catholic doctrine of infusion and substantive transferral of grace would have it. For if such a substantive transferral were accepted, a simultaneous consequence would necessarily be an acknowledgment of the possibility for man to be substantively righteous. This amounts to a more or less monumental notion of the ideal saint and therewith the very thing that elicited Luther's protest, namely, that man can make a claim upon God on the basis of the quality which he, man, now possesses—even if it was bestowed on him. Another consequence that arises is that man views himself in partnership with God, and even though he remains aware that God is the author of that righteousness, this partnership is the ultimate refinement of blasphemy for it sets God in analogy to man.

The notion of infusion also necessarily produces from the same root a new doctrine of immortality, which must operate with the idea that the soul now filled with the divine substance of grace, furnished with *zōē* as it were, cannot succumb to death, but must outlive it.[12]

By contrast the biblical faith rediscovered by Luther knows that both righteousness and *zōē* remain exclusively at God's disposal and that I participate in them only to the degree that fellowship with God in Christ is vouchsafed to me personally, that is, vouchsafed to me for no intrinsic reason at all.

The personal character of such fellowship stands of course in stark contrast to all notions of participation operating in terms of "substance." For personal fellowship means that in faith, love, and hope, I may live under God as one expecting everything from him as I continue to pray, "Hand that will last, hold thou me fast." It

[11] "Moses prays [in Ps. 90] that the Holy Spirit might teach us to count our days and to be disturbed by the terrors of death and other perils. He wants us to reflect on what we are and to equate even a hundred years of this life with a mathematical point and the smallest fraction of a second." *LW* 13, 128.

[12] See the work by O. Karrer, *Der Unsterblichkeitsglaube* (Munich, 1936), which raises the question from the Catholic side. See also the apologetic response in Konrad Gröber, ed., *Handbuch der religiösen Gegenwartsfragen* (Freiburg, 1937), pp. 583 ff. Additional bibliography is found in both works.

means that I have become the brother of Jesus Christ and that I may therefore take everything that applies to him and predicate it of myself because it is God's own will that Christ's vicarious existence should be valid for me.[13] This is certainly not the same as any mystical transfusion of qualities from Christ to us.[14]

It follows that I dare not regard my death, even under the aspect of biological mask, as something that no longer strikes the real me, since I am immortal, but moves on bypassing my soul. No, all of me goes down into death. Nothing gives me the right to reject the totality of man, which the Scriptures proclaim in connection with the disaster of death, and suddenly split him into body and soul, into a perishable and an imperishable I-segment. But as a Christian I go down into this death with the complete confidence that I cannot remain therein, since I am one whom God has called by name and therefore I shall be called anew on God's day. I am under the protection of the Resurrected One. I am not immortal, but I await my own resurrection. I am one with whom God has begun to speak. God will not break faith with me in the fellowship he has estab-

[13] The notion of vicarious representation carries with it the implication that someone else presents and constitutes a reality which we are not and never can be, and which even by virtue of the vicarious representation we do not become in substantive reality. Consequently Christ's vicarious righteousness also always remains an alien righteousness. Only in this sense can I take everything that applies to my representative, Jesus Christ, and predicate it of myself. Since everything that applies to Christ can be applied to those who believe on him (*LW* 27, 282), the following words also apply to the believer in Christ: "He renders satisfaction to all" (*LW* 27, 241). It is only in this fashion that by faith I am taken up into the humanity of Jesus Christ and justified thereby. "For those who trust in the name of the Lord all sins are forgiven and righteousness is imputed to them" (*LW* 27, 221).

[14] On Protestant soil this notion of infusion once more crept in after the Reformation. As I see it, however, the logical consequence of this change has not been drawn, namely, a doctrine of immortality which would be substantively parallel to, and in correspondence with, the altered doctrine of justification. On this point see Osiander's teaching of the transference and indwelling of Christ's essential righteousness which he propounded especially against Melanchthon's forensic portrayal of the doctrine of justification: *"Glacie frigidiora docent, nos tantum propterea remissionem peccatorum reputari justos, et non etiam propter justitiam Christi per fidem in nobis inhabitantis. Non enim tam iniquus deus est, ut eum pro justo habeat, in quo verae justitiae prorsus nil est."* See the *Disputatio de justificatione* of 1550, esp. theses 73-74, as well as the work *Concerning the Only Mediator Jesus Christ and Faith's Justification* of 1551. Concerning the whole "Osiandrian controversy" see R. Seeberg, *Lehrbuch der Dogmengeschichte,* vol. 4, 2nd and 3rd eds. (Leipzig, 1920), pp. 496 ff. A recent strongly Osiandrian position is to be found in A. Schlatter's commentary on the Epistle to the Romans, *Gottes Gerechtigkeit,* 3rd ed. (Stuttgart, 1959).

lished, nor will he let it be annulled by death. This is the certainty of my conquering death, founded not in me, but in God. "Where and with whomever God speaks, whether in anger or in grace, that person is surely immortal. The Person of God, who speaks, and the Word point out that we are the kind of creatures with whom God would want to speak eternally and in an immortal manner."[15]

At this point the reformers' biblical understanding of justification reaches, as it were, its high point. Just as I stand with empty hands before God and remain standing, just as I can only beseech God nevertheless to accept me, in just this fashion do I move into my death with empty hands and without any death-proof substance in my soul, but only with my gaze focused on God's hand and with the petition on my lips, "Hand that will last, hold thou me fast!"

In dying I come before God, who holds not only judgment but also life in his hands, and I come with the confidence that I have no need to trust in my good works nor my immortal soul. In fact I dare not even trust them (since the one really is not good and the other is not immortal) and yet I am confident that I am righteous and share in the resurrection by grace alone (2 Cor. 4:7; 5:1). I remain in fellowship with him who is Alpha and Omega, and with this knowledge I walk into the night of death, truly the darkest night; yet I know who awaits me in the morning.

From this it is clear how death undergoes transformation. Since the alien reality of Jesus Christ pulls me through, I may confess that it is no longer my own death that I die, a death conditioned by my Adamite existence, but rather that now I take the death of Jesus Christ and make it my own death. Everything that Jesus Christ has done I may now predicate of myself in the same way that Jesus Christ takes upon his shoulders everything that is my encumbrance. Luther writes, "Lord, Jesus, you are my righteousness, just as I am your sin. You have taken upon yourself what is mine and have given to me what is yours."[16] "Therefore a man can with confidence boast in Christ and say: 'mine are Christ's living, doing, and speak-

[15] *LW* 5, 76.
[16] *LW* 48, 12.

ing, his suffering and dying, mine as much as if I had lived, done, spoken, suffered, and died as he did.' "[17]

I live in fellowship with the Lord, and death cannot restrain him or his companions. This participation in Christ's dying expresses itself therefore quite concretely in the manner in which I carry out my death. It is the first trademark of this participating fellowship that I no longer endure death as a catastrophe to which I am simply exposed, but that I actually do "carry it out," that is, I willingly and affirmatively take hold of it. With the words "Yes, father!" I take hold of the reminiscence of my fall. I place myself under the judgment of God proclaimed therein. I face up to this judgment. In the process, however, I place myself under the cross of Christ and thereby once more into Christ's dying, which I appropriate and reproduce as my own in the sense of the Luther citations above. For Jesus Christ himself did not simply endure death, since he stood outside its sphere of power and beyond its lawful claim. He was not one striving to get out of bounds, for whom boundaries had to be set. Instead he carried out his death willingly. He affirmed the verdict rendered in death over mankind and let himself be struck by it. His dying was much more an act of his own than his enduring something that befell him.

When I in turn place myself into this action, my death is transformed into the death of Jesus Christ. It now carries the signature of the second Adam and no longer that of the first. I have factually exchanged the prototype which is the source of my existence. When I obediently affirm God as he speaks to me in the fate of death, I set myself loose from my addiction to the world and to my own self and surrender to the new destiny that awaits me in Christ. This is the inner transformation, highly factual and most concrete, which death undergoes by virtue of my participation in the death of Jesus Christ.[18] This is the ultimate victory over death which the Resurrected One mediates to his companions. He not only relegates it to being a biological mask, but he makes our death his own and his death our own.

[17] *LW* 31, 297. See also *LW* 26, 163; 27, 282.

[18] See Schmaus, *op. cit.*, 3II: 495-96.

Let us summarize our conclusions about how death is rendered impotent. They can be described in two directions. On the one hand, death being made impotent means that we are transplanted into the field of power represented by God's life and into fellowship with the Resurrected One. It means being transplanted into what John's Gospel calls *zōē.* On the other hand, death being made impotent also means that the boundary placed on my existence by death is removed and that, parabolically speaking, the cherub with the flaming sword no longer stands before the garden of God where life is to be found.

Therefore death for the Christian is only something that we have called a biological mask. That element which gave death its personal character and constituted its sting, namely, our being put back into bounds and the negative reaction of divine holiness manifesting itself therein, is removed.

To be sure, death is still there just as the *peccator in re*—the Christian remains *de facto* a sinner—is still there. But he too is only the same sort of mask. He has no power, no authority any longer, just as the snake whose fangs have been removed still remains a snake, but no longer possesses any power. The power of death consisted in its throwing us back behind an insurmountable boundary which we then took as the occasion (because of that very end) to make life an end in itself, to deify our goods, and in effect to say, "After us the deluge!" And what by contrast does it mean to be in the field of the Resurrected One's power, if we were to sketch out with a few more strokes the insight gained above?

To stand in the realm of the Resurrected One's power means to stand at the breakthrough point where Jesus has ruptured death's front line. It means to be enveloped by his life, wherein what we normally call our life is but a small segment. It is the pasture of the pilgrim wherein my life is enveloped in his life. His life is precisely my time line—what a transformation of thought!—during which I must believe and view the glory of God as in a glass darkly, yet someday I shall see him face to face and know him even as I now am known.

To stand in the realm of the Resurrected One's power means to be surrounded by his life, which gives enough comfort that for his sake we can die daily. If we live, we live unto the Lord, if we die, we die unto the Lord. Unto the Lord! We are in his living hand and only his hand is alive! Thus the only way we can die is to die into this hand. We can only fall into the hands of the living one. And in addition the disciple has the promise that he will actually gain his life if he loses it for his Lord's sake. For this Lord is alive and has indeed shattered the fetters of the prince of death. This world's time dies, but the Lord remains.

To stand in the realm of the Resurrected One's power means to have fellowship with God in Jesus and therefore to possess no fellowship with death. It means that I have one Lord and therefore am incapable of being dominated by death, or by the gods and goods of this life.[19]

I am, after all, a friend of Jesus. And where he is, there I too am to be. Is he not alive? Then I too am to live, and death shall not separate me from the love of God. "And when I am departing . . . ," at that time the prince of life will accompany me.

Now I will cling forever,
Christ's member, to my head;
My Lord will leave me never,
But leads me through the dread.
He rends death's iron chain,
He breaks through sin and pain,
He shatters hell's dark thrall,
I stay his friend through all.
—Paul Gerhardt

[19] See Appendix IV on "The Interim State."

Appendixes

Appendix I

The Notion of Palingenesis in Romanticism

A typical attempt to come to terms with death, an attempt farther removed from contemporary thinking although it proceeds along lines of thought similar to those we have described, is to be found in the notion of palingenesis in Herder, Novalis, and Kleist. Especially characteristic of this notion is the elimination of what we have called "uniqueness" and the "irreversibility of the time line." Here, for example, are some characteristic sentences of Herder.

"The old man in us ought to die so that a new youth may germinate. 'But how should that take place? Can a man return to his mother's womb and be born again?' In response to this doubt of old Nicodemus no other answer can be given than 'palingenesis'! Not revolution, but a fortunate evolution of the rejuvenating powers slumbering within us. What we call outliving ourselves, that is, death, is for better souls only slumber to a new awakening, a relaxing of the tension on the bow with a view to its being used again. Similarly the field lies fallow in order to bear richer harvest. The tree dies in winter in order to send out new blossoms and branches in the spring. Fate will not desert the good man as long as he does not desert himself, nor succumb to ignominious self-despair. The genius which seems to have departed from him returns again at the right moment and with it comes new activity, happiness, and joy."[1]

Thus this notion of palingenesis intends that the unique time of a man's life shall not come to an end but be repeated. In terms of the history of ideas, it amounts to an attempt "to make valid over

[1] *Herders Sämtliche Werke,* ed. B. Suphan (Berlin, 1877 —), 16:122.

against previous dualistic-transcendental answers the reconciliation achieved between monistic or pantheistic immanentalism (with its emphasis on '*Lebensgefühl* and '*Weltgedanke*') and the core content of historical Christianity, and to make it valid also in the area of the problem of immortality."[2]

[2] Rudolph Unger, "Herder, Novalis, und Kleist. Studien über die Entwicklung des Todesproblems im Denken und Dichten von Sturm und Drang zur Romantik," *Deutsche Forschungen,* ed. F. Panzer and I. Petersen, vol. 9 (Frankfurt a.M., 1922), p. 23. See also the related notion of reincarnation in Lessing's "Erziehung des Menschengeschlechts" in *Lessings Werke,* ed. Franz Bornmüller (Leipzig and Vienna: Bibliographisches Institut, n.d.), 5:612 ff. With reference to Lessing's concept of time, see my *Vernunft und Offenbarung. Eine Studie über die Religionsphilosophie Lessings* (Gütersloh, 1936). See also the characteristic developments of the notion of palingenesis in Kleist, e.g., in the letters to his bride Wilhelmine of 22 March 1801, to Caroline von Schlieben of 18 July 1801, and to Rühle of 31 August 1806. *Werke,* ed. Erich Schmidt (Leipzig: Bibliographisches Institut, n.d.), 5:200 ff., 232 ff., 325 ff.

Appendix II

Death in the Cosmos

One approaches the question in the wrong way if he treats the biological death of plants and animals as causally derivative from the sin of man, although it would even appear that there are some biblical grounds for this. For example, there is Romans 8:19, 22; 2 Thessalonians 2:6 and even the story of the flood, especially Genesis 6:7 as well as the report of the fall into sin.[1]

In response to this the following must be said: Biblically, the sin of man is viewed as a cosmic event, in the same way that redemption within eschatology is related to the first event and thus receives its cosmic character. Here we can only posit the fact of this doctrine without being able to reproduce that experience of existence which comes to expression in it. At least it is for this reason that I myself must refrain from dogmatic statements on the subject. Extraordinary attempts to make such statements nevertheless can be found in Edgar Dacqué's famous works, *Das verlorene Paradies* and *Natur und Erlösung*.

At the most the following statements seem to us to be valid:

1) Man is the crown of creation, as is already demonstrated by the depth of his fall. To the extent that nature is drawn into his sinful fate, the statement about nature is not an end in itself, but a means to the end of making man's royal position apparent. The light of man's existence is, as it were, made brighter in the shadow of the creaturely world. One notices this in the internal accents of

[1] See in this respect the material gathered esp. from late Jewish apocalyptic by Ethelbert Stauffer, *New Testament Theology* (New York: Macmillan, 1955), pp. 72 ff.

these statements about nature. It is especially apparent from the way the creation of the entire cosmos proceeds with a view to its culmination in man (see Gen. 1 and 2). In the same way, where announcement is made of the flood to come over all living things (Gen. 6:7), the animal realm stands, as it were, as a mere backdrop behind man. Again, those animals which participate in Noah's own escape in the ark do not appear, as it were, as independent participants in the fall and redemption, but as universal representatives of the living world whose head is the man Noah himself. Man's history casts its shadow into the cosmos, evidently not only in the sense of a direct relationship of man to the animal world ("The fear of you and the dread of you shall be upon every beast of the earth," Gen. 9:2), but in the sense of a certain common fate that encompasses the entire world. However, one dare not take a position about how this occurs. That is forbidden by the fact that all statements focus on *man* and *his* fall. The animal realm too lives in terms of guilt, since the world with its natural laws must remain intact in order to make possible the time of grace implicit in the covenant relationship, the "acceptable time" (Gen. 8:21-22; 9:11).

2) As part of the total picture comes the fact that the notion of vicarious representation permeating the entire Scriptures is applied in the positive sense only to Christ and to God's suffering servant. In the negative sense it occurs time and time again as responsibility for the other. For example, Adam vicariously carried out my sin and is, as it were, my representative in the sense of inclusive representation. In addition God visits the sins of the fathers upon the children, who thereby have been represented by their fathers. Similarly those who are born afterwards must suffer the consequence of the murder of Abel (Matt. 23:35). "The fathers have eaten sour grapes, and the children's teeth are set on edge" (Jer. 31:29). There is an influence which radiates outward from the individual existence, as the Old Testament citations listed below would seem to indicate. So also man as head of the cosmos is simultaneously its vicarious representative, and through his sinful act (which simply is no private matter but the act of a steward to whom creation was entrusted) he drags the cosmos which he represents along with him into the abyss.

3) With reference to the doctrine that death in the cosmos derives from man himself, we note that according to Genesis 3:17 ff., 5:29, and 8:22, the earth is cursed for the sake of man. In many passages of the law, the judgment executed upon a godless man includes his entire possessions, especially his animals. See, for example, Numbers 16:13 ff., Deuteronomy 13:12 ff., Joshua 7:15, 24 ff. According to Romans 1:18 ff., the wrath of God is revealed from heaven against all ungodliness. That is, heaven, the orderly character of the world, is itself an agent for the powers of destruction proceeding from the righteous God. According to Romans 8:20, the *ktisis,* that is, the nonhuman creation, is drawn by man into the bondage to decay and because of man is subjected to futility by God. There is no mention of a change in nature nor any demonstration of how this occurs. Precisely this fact is important to note in order to realize that here we have no biological speculation, we simply are not dealing with a causal relationship between personal guilt and biological effect. For if this were so, one would have to draw the connections between the kind of cause (personal guilt) and the kind of effect (depravity).

For myself I explain cosmic death as a consequence of sin in the following dogmatically cautious way. Within nature, conflict, competition, and death are natural law. Despite the exact parallel of all these events to the human world, magnified even more by man's own biological character, man experiences this reality, the conflict, competition, and death in a different way. As he looks back into the cosmos with his eyes now opened, he sees the events of nature in analogy to the human events. Is this a prejudicial incursion into nature or the airing of its ultimate mystery? Is it therefore the radial extension of human guilt? Who can seriously doubt the biblical perspective on things—as cautiously as he may dare to try to follow after them—when he looks into the eyes of a dog with the scriptural knowledge of guilt and redemption at his disposal. The cry for redemption goes through the cosmos. The destructive and deadly violence of the cosmos are related to the spell cast upon it, which Scripture represents in connection with human guilt. Who does not perceive the reality of this metarational connection? As Schlegel said, "There is a universal weeping as extensive as the stars do shine, coursing through the veins of nature. The creature strives and longs for transfiguration, languishing in anxious love to have this bestowed upon it."[2] The statements of Scripture appear to me much too cautious to allow much more to be said about this. About all they allow is that one may inquire in this general direction. Here a dogmatic statement surely cannot be made. Instead the problem can only be seriously addressed. We cannot and we would not wish to do any more. At least *we* do not, even though others may be able to do so, and a very few actually attempted to do so in earnest.

[2] Cited by F. W. Weber, *Gott in der Natur* (Berlin, 1936), p. 46.

Appendix III

The Biological and Personal Dimension of Sickness

It is most important in this respect to keep in mind that Luther views death as a personal event embedded in the medium of biological dying without making the attempt—and in no case allowing the validity of the attempt—to derive one from the other. We note with satisfaction that in contemporary medicine too there are tendencies to take seriously the problem of personhood and to come to a very similar anthropological view. Thus the neurologist Bovet in his extraordinarily penetrating and carefully prepared work *Die Ganzheit der Person in der ärtztlichen Praxis* (Zurich and Leipzig, n.d.) distinguishes in the phenomenon of pathological change the somatic and the psychic side. And he does this in such a fashion—which may be considered progress vis-à-vis the usual distinction of organic and psychogenic—that both sides are not simply maneuvered into causal dependence upon one another (as though organic phenomena were psychogenically conditioned and psychic phenomena organically conditioned, although in many individual diagnoses even this causal connection must be granted), but that the psychic side merely expresses itself via the medium of the organic. Thus a completely new connection between sin and sickness is discovered to the extent that within the pathological organism a disorder of the person makes itself manifest. These are, to be sure, rather imprecise comments about Bovet's work, which for all its solid philosophical foundations and considerable methodological promise is nonetheless an explicitly medical book. Herewith a few of the fundamental statements from the book with reference to our problem.

"What theologians as well as physicians have difficulty understanding is that there is a somatic and a psychic causal chain or motivation chain, both of which can be traced scientifically, and in reference to which something like sin or prayer-healing is never to be encountered. But right alongside this, from the perspective of a total person, one can just as well speak of sin and prayer as two decisive factors in the course of illness. One is always making the mistake either of placing sin and prayer in the same causal chain as streptococcus and tincture of iodine or, on the other hand, since one does not find them anywhere in that causal chain, of simply denying their existence and their functional reality. As a comparison—and it is only a comparison—one can adduce the relationship between body and soul. Here we know that we dare not mix the two phenomenal orders, that we dare not say someone's love of Gothic activated such and such a group of ganglion cells, or that a certain poem came into existence by virtue of a fortunate constellation in Goethe's *fissura sylvii.* And nevertheless there exists on the one side such a thing as Gothic and as poetry and on the other side ganglion cells and fissures. As physicians we may and we should continue unabashedly to operate causally and psychologically, but we must also know that behind this *sōma* and this *psuchē* there exists a person who sins and who prays."[1]

In this connection Bovet is able to speak of a "personal meaning of sickness" in which a psychic or somatic episode of illness can either confront one with the "God question" or conceal it. In any case it is able to shelter in its own medium a completely new and different event. This comes very close to our discussions about the background of human personhood for the event of death.[2]

[1] *Op. cit.,* p. 174.

[2] See also Tournier, *Krankheit und Lebensprobleme,* 6th ed. (Basel, 1955).

Appendix IV

The Interim State

Although the interim state between death and resurrection as an eschatological problem no longer belongs to our basic question, we may nevertheless make a few comments about the issue. As an element of eschatology, it really lies beyond a consideration of the reality of death, since the latter belongs in the field of anthropology.

If, nevertheless, we still want to take a look at the interim state between death and resurrection, we do so above all for the reason that from what we have said before there are certain consequences which seem to arise for this interim state and I would not like simply to delegate the task of deducing them to the reader without having expressed myself on them.

The consequences are conditioned above all by the fact of the totality of human personhood. If the separation of the I into body and soul is really not permissible and death consequently impinges upon the totality of the person, the reality of some interim state seems to fall by the wayside together with any immortality of the soul, and the conclusion seems to be a complete extinction of the somatic-psychic I in the nothingness of the night of death. Resurrection then would be a new creation *ex nihilo* on Judgment Day.

I myself am too strongly impressed by the airtight character of this notion in order not to sense at this point my basic distrust against all theological airtight arguments. Might it not be that this airtight argument simultaneously constricts the riches and overflowing fullness of biblical statements? Might it not be that an airtight case is only possible in the monologue of reflective thought and at the cost of constant preparedness to listen? We have occasion to be skeptical vis-à-vis all rationally drawn conclusions (even theologically rational ones), since reason doubtless is also implicated in man's fall and because it therefore isolates itself when it takes its object out of the context of faith like some scouting party animated by a hubris hungry for knowledge. It is a frequently manifested law of the history of theology that every illumination of any dogmatic locus (and perhaps our insight into the totality of human personhood at the moment of death is one such illumination) in certain other respects produces obscurity.

To be sure, Luther's doctrine of justification is a simple illumination of the soteriological event. But taken by itself and absolutized, it would obscure our view of many other biblical riches, such as eschatology, which are simply not deducible from the theses of justification. That Luther himself did not escape this law of obscurity constitutes an especially impressive example. Therefore extreme caution is in order.

More precisely the question is phrased as follows: Is it permissible to take our thesis of the totality of the human person which is extinguished in death and use it as a criterion against those statements of Scripture that speak of an interim state and thereby evaluate these as heterogenous (as remnants of Hellenism, etc.), or must we on the contrary let our thesis be criticized and loosened up by the richer fullness of biblical thought?

The New Testament assertions concerning an interim state that are usually brought up are the following: the parable of the rich man and Lazarus (Luke 16:19 ff.); Jesus' promise to the malefactor, "Today you will be with me in paradise" (Luke 23:43); Paul's words about a building in heaven after the earthly tent has been put away (2 Cor. 5); his desire to depart and be with Christ (Phil. 1:23); and last but not least the voices of the transfigured martyrs around the altar in Revelation 6:9. Significant also are the passages that speak of being at home with the Lord (e.g., Rom. 14:8) in several variations, while those which by contrast speak of distance and separation from God are, with the exception of Luke 16:19 ff., apparently intended in the sense of a cosmic eschatology (e.g., Matt. 13:42, 50; Matt. 5:26; Matt. 18:34-35).

All of these passages are unique in a double sense. In the first place, they all speak of a state after death but before the resurrection and renewal of the world. Secondly, these statements occur only indirectly and peripherally. It can easily be shown that all these passages involve something other than merely an assertion about the interim state after death. In the case of every single one of them the assertion about the interim state can be viewed as a helpful illustration having no independent force of its own.

Consequently one can draw the conclusion that as a matter of fact these almost dotted lines dare not be extended into any independent and thetical assertion about the interim state. One is probably justified in saying that the Bible would have taken pains to supply them if it had wanted to place such thetic statements at our disposal. Nevertheless the relatively frequent recurrence of these dotted lines is a sure warning that the reality here indicated cannot just be flatly denied. On this score there are certain experiences which I would simply have no right to dismiss as mere illusion.

In any case the sum of all the pertinent references seems to testify that there is something like a Being-at-home with Christ, and by contrast also a Being-far-away from him. But in no case is this state to be understood as a form of immortality based on some energy potential in the soul, nor a state analogous to the resurrection. One might more likely describe it with a Pauline picture of a state of divesting and waiting (2 Cor. 5:4 ff.). Expressed positively it is perhaps best characterized with the words "being with Christ" (Phil. 1:23).

From both perspectives one is able to arrive not at the notion of immortality, but at most at the notion of an indissoluble communion with Christ. That which is with Christ is not my soul or some particular piece of me, but it is "I," insofar as I am a participant in the fellowship with Jesus Christ: ". . . could the Head rise and leave its members dead?" In his promise to the dying malefactor, Jesus means his "Thou," not his soul, when he says, "Today, thou shalt be with me in paradise."

The emphasis here is not on some quality of mine that outlasts death, but on the quality of my Lord not to desert me. For this reason the phrase "with me" in Christ's word of promise to the malefactor takes on special significance. The form in which "I" am to be with him (somatic or psychic, interimistic or in eternal continuity) is no more a valid object for my questioning than is my authorization to analyze psychologically the state of the I which is the subject of faith. For faith does not live from the resources of the subjective qualifications of the I who does the believing, but from the resources of the alien righteousness of its Lord. Faith lives from the resources of its object. In the same way the interim state of one who has died in the faith is not characterized by his own qualifications but by Him who will not let the fellowship be broken off. And in the same way that Luther designated the subject of faith an unextended mathematical point, and frequently called progress in the faith *annihilatio* (literally, being reduced to nothing, with the corollary that God creates anew *ex nihilo*), so one can also understand existence after death with reference to the "how" or "what" of one's form of existence as an *annihilatio,* living from the resources of the greatness of the Lord who does not desert one in death. In this sense 2 Corinthians 4:7 may also be applied here: "We have this treasure in earthen vessels, to show that the transcendent power belongs to God and not to us."

When in this fashion we view not the subjective structure of continuing existence, but personal fellowship with Christ as determinative for the interim state, we can understand why the state of those who are separated from Christ is presented with even greater reservation. It consists simply in the absence of communion (in contrast to the hellish forced expulsion that occurs in judgment). The mysterious passage in 1 Peter 3:19 fits in here with its reference to preaching to the spirits in prison, whose situation is characterized by the fact that any connection with Christ is missing and must first be created.

It may well be an indication that the subjective structure after death is no valid area for questioning, that the conceptual terminology for the vehicle that has such continued existence is not definitively specified, but alternates between *psuchē* and *pneuma* (see Rev. 6:11 and 1 Pet. 3:19).

From all of this it is clear that we must respect the indirect character of all scriptural references about the interim situation of the person. These references, which surely accentuate not subjective qualifications but personal fellowship with Christ, fit very well into the context of total personhood which has been the subject of our theological examination. In any case such statements of Scripture by no means entail a doctrine of immortality or the presupposition of some division of the I. The assertions about the interim state confirm rather than contest biblical anthropology.

Indexes

Scripture References

Names and Subjects

Type, 11 on 13 and 10 on 12 Garamond
Display, Optima